Lab Manual for
CompTIA A+ Guide to Software: Managing, Maintaining, and Troubleshooting

Lab Manual for
CompTIA A+ Guide to Software: Managing, Maintaining, and Troubleshooting
NINTH EDITION

Jean Andrews, Ph.D.

Joy Dark

Jill West

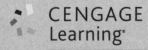

CENGAGE
Learning·

Australia • Canada • Mexico • Singapore • Spain • United Kingdom • United States

Lab Manual for CompTIA A+ Guide to Software: Managing, Maintaining, and Troubleshooting, Ninth Edition

Jean Andrews, Joy Dark, Jill West

SVP, GM Skills & Global Product Management: Dawn Gerrain

Product Director: Kathleen McMahon

Product Team Manager: Kristin McNary

Associate Product Manager: Amy Savino

Senior Director, Development: Marah Bellegarde

Product Development Manager: Leigh Hefferon

Senior Content Developer: Michelle Ruelos Cannistraci

Product Assistant: Abigail Pufpaff

Vice President, Marketing Services: Jennifer Ann Baker

Marketing Director: Michele McTighe

Senior Production Director: Wendy Troeger

Production Director: Patty Stephan

Senior Content Project Manager: Brooke Greenhouse

Managing Art Director: Jack Pendleton

Cover images:

©iStockphoto.com/traffic_analyzer

©iStockphoto.com/simon2579

For product information and technology assistance, contact us at
Cengage Learning Customer & Sales Support, 1-800-354-9706

For permission to use material from this text or product, submit all requests online at **www.cengage.com/permissions**
Further permissions questions can be e-mailed to
permissionrequest@cengage.com

Library of Congress Control Number: 2015957525

ISBN: 978-1-305-26656-8

Cengage Learning
20 Channel Center Street
Boston, MA 02210
USA

Cengage Learning is a leading provider of customized learning solutions with employees residing in nearly 40 different countries and sales in more than 125 countries around the world. Find your local representative at
www.cengage.com.

Cengage Learning products are represented in Canada by Nelson Education, Ltd.

To learn more about Cengage Learning, visit **www.cengage.com**

Purchase any of our products at your local college store or at our preferred online store **www.cengagebrain.com**

Notice to the Reader

Publisher does not warrant or guarantee any of the products described herein or perform any independent analysis in connection with any of the product information contained herein. Publisher does not assume, and expressly disclaims, any obligation to obtain and include information other than that provided to it by the manufacturer. The reader is expressly warned to consider and adopt all safety precautions that might be indicated by the activities described herein and to avoid all potential hazards. By following the instructions contained herein, the reader willingly assumes all risks in connection with such instructions. The publisher makes no representations or warranties of any kind, including but not limited to, the warranties of fitness for particular purpose or merchantability, nor are any such representations implied with respect to the material set forth herein, and the publisher takes no responsibility with respect to such material. The publisher shall not be liable for any special, consequential, or exemplary damages resulting, in whole or part, from the readers' use of, or reliance upon, this material.

Printed in the United States of America
Print Number: 01   Print Year: 2016

Table of Contents

Preface

This lab manual is designed to be the best tool on the market to help you get hands-on practical experience troubleshooting and repairing personal computers and operating systems. The manual contains more than 70 labs, each of which targets a practical problem you're likely to face when troubleshooting systems in the real world. Every attempt has been made to write labs that allow you to use generic hardware devices. A specific hardware configuration isn't necessary to complete the labs. In learning to install, support, and troubleshoot hardware devices and operating systems, the focus is on Windows 8 and Windows 7, with minor coverage of Windows Vista. Each chapter contains labs designed to provide the structure novices need, as well as labs that challenge experienced and inquisitive students.

This book helps prepare you for the new CompTIA A+ 220-902 Certification exam offered through the Computer Technology Industry Association (CompTIA). The A+ 220-902 exam focuses on operating systems, security, troubleshooting skills, and operational procedures.

Because this certification credential is quickly growing in popularity among employers, becoming certified increases your ability to gain employment, improve your salary, and enhance your career. To find more information about A+ Certification and its sponsoring organization, CompTIA, go to the CompTIA website at *comptia.org*.

Whether your goal is to become an A+ certified technician or a computer support technician, the *Lab Manual for CompTIA A+ Guide to Software*, Ninth Edition, along with Jean Andrews's textbooks, will take you there!

FEATURES

To ensure a successful experience for both instructors and students, this book includes the following pedagogical features:

- *Objectives*. Every lab opens with learning objectives that set the stage for students to absorb the lab's lessons.
- *Materials Required*. This feature outlines all the materials students need to successfully complete the lab.
- *Lab Preparation*. This feature alerts instructors and lab assistants to items to check or set up before the lab begins.
- *Activity Background*. A brief discussion at the beginning of each lab provides important background information.
- *Estimated Completion Time*. To help students plan their work, each lab includes an estimate of the total amount of time required to complete it.
- *Activity*. Detailed, numbered steps walk students through the lab. These steps are divided into manageable sections, with explanatory material between each section. Questions within each activity help students think through exactly what they are doing as they follow the steps.
- *Figures*. Where appropriate, photographs of hardware or screen shots of software are provided to increase student mastery of the lab topic.
- *Review Questions*. Questions at the end of each lab help students test their understanding of the lab material.
- *Website*. For updates to this book and information about other A+ and IT products, go to *login.cengage.com*.

WHAT'S NEW IN THE NINTH EDITION

◢ Steps are updated to focus on Microsoft Windows 8 and Windows 7. New projects cover Android and iOS.

◢ New projects are added to cover new technology and higher-level thinking skills, which reflect updates to CompTIA's A+ 220-902 exam.

◢ Enhanced coverage on supporting UEFI firmware is now included.

◢ Projects provide additional coverage of laptop parts.

◢ Enhanced coverage on supporting mobile devices is covered in the chapter, "Supporting Mobile Operating Systems."

ACKNOWLEDGMENTS

The authors would first like to thank Mary Pat Shaffer, the Developmental Editor, for keeping us on track and providing the occasional comic relief. Mary Pat, your meticulous work and encouraging attitude made the process more fun and made a significantly positive impact on the quality of the final product. Thank you to Michelle Ruelos Cannistraci, Kristin McNary, Amy Savino, Brooke Greenhouse, Danielle Shaw, and all the Cengage Learning staff for their instrumental roles in developing this lab manual. Michelle, Brooke, and Amy, we so appreciate all your hard work and impressive dedication to excellence. Many thanks to all the instructors who offered great suggestions for new labs and encouraged us to make other changes to the previous editions. Keep those suggestions coming!

This manual was written with the extraordinary help of awesome collaborators. We did it together, and we're grateful for your help:

Bill Jaber, Lee University, Cleveland, TN

Ronald E. Koci, Madison Area Technical College, Madison, WI

Isaias Leiva, San Francisco City College, San Francisco, CA

Terry Moberley, Unisys Corporation, Culpepper, VA

Robert Ray, Digital Communications & Display, LLC, Raleigh, NC

CLASSROOM SETUP

Lab activities have been designed to explore many different Windows and hardware setups and troubleshooting problems, while attempting to keep the requirements for specific hardware to a minimum. Most labs can be done alone, although a few ask you to work with a partner. If you prefer to work alone, simply do all the steps yourself. Lab activities that use an operating system have been designed to work in Windows 8 or Windows 7, although you can use Windows Vista for some labs. In some cases, Windows 8/7 Professional will be required.

Typical labs take 30 to 45 minutes; a few might take a little longer. For several of the labs, your classroom should be networked and provide access to the Internet. When access to Windows setup files is required, these files can be provided on the Windows installation DVD, a network drive made available to the computer, or some other type of removable storage media.

These are the minimum hardware requirements for Windows 8:

- 1 GHz or better Pentium-compatible computer
- 1 GB of RAM for 32-bit Windows 8 or 2 GB of RAM for 64-bit Windows 8
- 16 GB free hard drive space for 32-bit Windows 8 or 20 GB for 64-bit Windows 8
- DirectX 9 or higher video device
- A user account with administrator privileges

A few labs focus on special hardware. One lab requires a wireless card and router, and some labs require software that can be freely downloaded from the Internet.

LAB SETUP INSTRUCTIONS

CONFIGURATION TYPE AND OPERATING SYSTEMS

Each lab begins with a list of required materials. Before beginning a lab activity, each student workgroup or individual should verify access to these materials. Then, students should ensure the correct operating system is installed and in good health. Note that in some cases, installing an operating system isn't necessary. In some labs, device drivers are needed. Students can work more efficiently if these drivers are available before beginning the lab.

PROTECT DATA

In several labs, data on the hard drive might get lost or corrupted. For this reason, it's important that valuable data stored on the hard drive is backed up to another medium.

ACCESS TO THE INTERNET

Several labs require access to the Internet. If necessary, students can use one computer to search the Internet and download software or documentation and another computer for performing the lab procedures. If the lab doesn't have Internet access, students can download the required software or documentation before the lab and bring the files to the lab on some sort of storage medium or network share.

UTILITIES TO DOWNLOAD FROM THE WEB

The following table includes a list of software that can be downloaded free from the web. As new releases of software appear, the steps in the lab that use the software might need adjusting. It is suggested that instructors test each of these labs to make sure the software still works before students do the lab.

Lab	Software and URL
Lab 2.1: Use the Windows 8 Upgrade Assistant	Windows 8 Upgrade Assistant at *windows.microsoft.com/ en-us/windows-8/upgrade-assistant-download-online-faq*
Lab 2.6: Use Windows Virtual PC to Install Windows 7 in a Virtual Machine (VM)	Windows Virtual PC at *microsoft.com/en-us/download/details. aspx?id=3702*
Lab 4.7: Critical Thinking: Use Windows Utilities to Speed Up a System	Autoruns at *technet.microsoft.com/en-us/sysinternals/ bb963902*

(Continues)

Lab	Software and URL
Lab 5.8: Find a Driver for an Unknown Device	Hiren's BootCD at *hirensbootcd.org/download* Grub4Dos at *hirensbootcd.org/files/grub4dos.zip*
Lab 5.9: Research Data Recovery Software	Recuva at *piriform.com/recuva*
Lab 6.3: Create and Use a Custom Refresh Image	Chrome at *google.com/chrome* Firefox at *mozilla.org/firefox*
Lab 8.2: Research Android Apps and Use Dropbox	Dropbox at *dropbox.com*
Lab 8.3: Explore How Android Apps Are Developed and Tested	Java Platform (JDK) at *java.oracle.com* Android Studio for Windows at *developer.android.com*
Lab 10.4: Deal with a Rootkit	AVG Rescue CD (for USB stick) at *avg.com/us-en/download* EICAR virus test file at *eicar.org/85-0-download.html*
Lab 10.7: Download and Use Microsoft Security Essentials in Windows 7	Microsoft Security Essentials at *windows.microsoft.com/mse*
Lab 11.1: Use Oracle VirtualBox to Install and Explore Virtual Machines (VMs)	Oracle VirtualBox at *virtualbox.org*
Lab 11.3: Investigate Linux and Create a Bootable Ubuntu Flash Drive	Ubuntu at *ubuntu.com* Universal USB Installer at *pendrivelinux.com*
Lab 11.5: Use TeamViewer to Remotely Access Another Computer	TeamViewer at *teamviewer.com*
Lab 11.6: Set Up a VPN	Hotspot Shield at *hotspotshield.com*

ONLINE RESOURCES AND STUDY TOOLS

A few labs require students to download documents and optional content to use during the lab. For example, several labs use the Computer Inventory and Maintenance form made available online. To access the form, please go to *login.cengage.com*. After signing in or creating a new account, search for the ISBN of the title (from the back cover of the main textbook) using the search box at the top of the page to get to the product page where these free resources can be found.

CHAPTER 1

Survey of Windows Features and Support Tools

Labs included in this chapter:

LAB 1.1 RECORD YOUR WORK AND MAKE DELIVERABLES

OBJECTIVES

The goal of this lab is to use different methods to create a submission file for your instructor and to familiarize yourself with your version of the operating system. After completing this lab, you will be able to:

◢ Determine what type and version of operating system your computer is running

◢ Use the Snipping Tool to take a snapshot of your screen

◢ Create a submission file for your instructor in one of four formats

MATERIALS REQUIRED

This lab requires the following:

◢ Windows 8 or Windows 7 operating system

LAB PREPARATION

Before the lab begins, the instructor or lab assistant needs to do the following:

◢ Verify Windows starts with no errors

ACTIVITY BACKGROUND

The pages of this lab manual are perforated to allow students to tear off the pages and submit them to instructors for grading. However, your instructor might prefer you to submit your work using email or an online interface such as Moodle, Blackboard, or WebCT. This lab prepares you to submit your work using an electronic method.

ESTIMATED COMPLETION TIME: 20 MINUTES

 Activity

The Windows Snipping Tool lets you take screen shots or snips of the entire Windows desktop, a window, or any region of the desktop. Follow these steps to explore the Control Panel and System windows and take snips of your work on the desktop:

1. To open Control Panel, right-click **Start** and click **Control Panel**. (In Windows 7, click **Start**, type **Control Panel** in the Search programs and files box, and press **Enter**.)

2. Drill down into the links, icons, and options in the Control Panel window and familiarize yourself with all the icons and options in both Icons view (called Classic view in Vista and on the A+ exam) and in Category view. Figure 1-1 shows Control Panel in Large icons view in Windows 8. Explain in your own words the difference between Large icons view and Category view:

_____

_____

_____

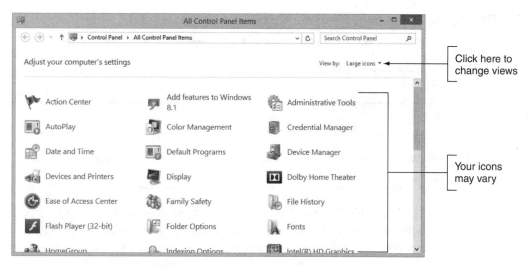

Figure 1-1 Windows 8 Large icons view

3. In Large icons view, click the **System** icon.

4. Examine the System window. What is the operating system and system type running on your computer? What processor is installed and how much installed memory (RAM) do you have on your computer?

_____

_____

5. If you're using a Windows 7 computer, what is the Windows Experience Index rating for your computer?

_____

6. Leave the System window open as your active window. Press **Win+S**, type **Snipping Tool** in the Search box, and then click **Snipping Tool**. (In Windows 7, click **Start**, and in the Search programs and files box, type **Snipping Tool**, and then press **Enter**.)

7. In the Snipping Tool dialog box, click the **New** drop-down arrow. What are the four types of snips you can take using the Snipping Tool?

_____

_____

_____

_____

8. Select **Free-form Snip** from the drop-down list. Click and hold the mouse button, drag your cursor around the edges of the System window, and then release the mouse button. The Snipping Tool window opens showing your snip.

9. On the menu bar, click **File, Save As**.

10. Save the file on your desktop using naming and file compression standards (usually in .jpg or .png format) as directed by your instructor.

11. Email the file to your instructor, or upload it to your online interface.

12. Close all windows.

REVIEW QUESTIONS

1. What are the eight categories in the Category view in Control Panel?

   _____

   _____

   _____

2. What are the four file types that can be used to save a snip using the Windows Snipping Tool?

   _____

3. The Windows Experience Index rates a computer's performance on a scale of 1.0 to 7.9. If you're using a Windows 7 system, what can you conclude about its performance based on the rating of your computer?

   _____

4. Search the web for information about the price of Windows 8. How much would it cost to buy your current edition (such as Home, Professional, etc.) of the Windows 8 operating system as an upgrade from Windows 7?

   _____

LAB 1.2 INSTALL A WINDOWS 8 APP AND MANAGE THE START SCREEN

OBJECTIVES

The goal of this lab is to become familiar with Windows 8. After completing this lab, you will be able to:

◢ Use the Windows 8 Start screen

◢ Find apps and settings

◢ Shut down Windows 8

MATERIALS REQUIRED

This lab requires the following:

◢ Windows 8 operating system

◢ Internet access

LAB PREPARATION

Before the lab begins, the instructor or lab assistant needs to do the following:

◢ Verify Windows starts with no errors

◢ Verify Internet access is available

ACTIVITY BACKGROUND

Windows 8 has a very different user interface than previous editions of Windows. It can feel a little awkward or clumsy at first, but with time and practice, you will become comfortable using the new user interface.

> **Notes** Windows 8 hides shortcuts and menus. You can access them by placing your pointer in the corners of the screen.

ESTIMATED COMPLETION TIME: 45 MINUTES

 Activity

Follow these steps to become familiar with the Start screen:

1. On the Start screen, find your user name in the upper-right corner of the screen. Click your **user name** icon.

2. Click **Lock** to password protect your screen. Click the **screen** to access the sign-in screen. Sign in to your account.

3. The Start screen has tiles used to open commonly used programs. Click the **Desktop** tile to access the Windows desktop. In Windows 8, the desktop is itself considered an app. To toggle between the Start screen and the desktop, use one of two methods:

   ◢ Click the **Start** (Windows logo) button in the taskbar. This button is hidden in this same corner when you're on the Start screen.

   ◢ Press the ▦ **Windows logo** key on your keyboard.

4. After you open the desktop, you can return to it from the Start screen using one of three methods:

   ◢ Click the **Desktop** tile on the Start screen.

   ◢ Move your mouse to the upper-left corner of the screen, and click the **desktop** thumbnail.

   ◢ Move your mouse to the lower-left corner of the screen, and click the ▦ Windows logo button that appears.

> **Notes** If more than one app is open, you can quickly view one of these apps by moving your mouse to the upper-left corner of the screen and then moving your mouse down the left side of the screen. Thumbnails of the open apps appear for you to choose the app you want to view.

5. The desktop is itself an app, and you close it as you would any app. To close an app, drag the top edge of the page to the bottom edge of the screen. Close the desktop, and return to the Start screen.

6. On the Start screen, move an app tile. To move a tile, click and drag the tile to a different location on the screen.

7. Not all the tiles are the same size. To change the size of a tile, right-click the tile, which opens the shortcut menu for the tile.

> **Notes** You can change the settings of multiple tiles at the same time if you hold down the Ctrl key while you right-click the tiles.

8. In the shortcut menu, click **Resize**. Choose a different size. Notice the size of the tile changes.

9. To open a program that does not have a tile on the Start screen, simply start typing the name of the program. To open the Paint program, on the Start screen, type **Paint**. The Search pane opens with a list of search results. Select the **Paint** program in the search results. The Paint program opens on the desktop.

10. Close the Paint program. Return to the **Start** screen.

11. You're looking for a cooking and recipes app, and a friend recommended Allrecipes. To search for and download a new app, click the **Store** tile. The Store app opens. In the Search box, type **Allrecipes**. In the results, click the **Allrecipes** icon.

12. Click **Install**, as shown in Figure 1-2. When Windows is done installing the Allrecipes app, a notification will appear on screen. Close the Store app by dragging the top edge of the page down to the bottom of the screen.

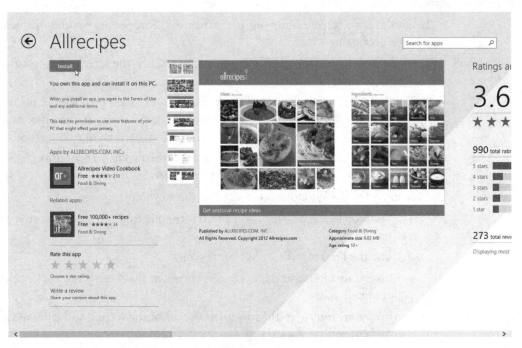

Figure 1-2 The Store is used to install the Allrecipes app
Source: Allrecipes.com

13. If you do not see the Allrecipes tile on the Start screen when you scroll to the right and left, type **Allrecipes**. In the search results, right-click the **Allrecipes** tile, and select **Pin to Start**. Click the **Start** screen to close the search results pane.

14. Scroll to the right until you see the Allrecipes tile. Open the **Allrecipes** app. Close the Allrecipes app.

15. To uninstall the Allrecipes app, right-click the **Allrecipes** tile. Click **Uninstall** in the status bar that appears at the bottom of the screen. Click **Uninstall** again.

16. Access the **charms** bar by moving your mouse to the upper-right or lower-right corner of the screen. You can access the charms bar from anywhere in Windows, but the items on the charms bar might change, depending on the situation. What are the items in the charms bar you see on the screen?

_____

17. On the charms bar, click the **Settings** charm (gear icon), and then click **Personalize**. Change the Start screen background picture or colors. Click the **Start** screen to close the Personalize pane.

18. On the Start screen, click the **down arrow** near the lower-left corner of the screen. The Apps screen appears, listing all apps installed on the computer. Click the **up arrow** to return to the Start screen.

19. There are two ways to shut down the system:

▲ Open the **charms** bar, and click the **Settings** charm. Click the **Power** button, and select **Shut down** to turn off your computer.

▲ Press ▦ **Windows logo + X**, select **Shut down or sign out**, and then click **Shut down**.

REVIEW QUESTIONS

1. How do you open the Windows desktop? How do you close the desktop?

_____

_____

2. How do you install an app that uses the Windows 8 interface? How do you uninstall a Windows 8 app?

_____

_____

3. How do you access the Apps screen?

_____

_____

4. How do you add a tile to the Start screen?

_____

_____

5. How do you sign out from the computer? How do you shut down the computer?

_____

_____

LAB 1.3 USE A MICROSOFT ACCOUNT AND ONEDRIVE

OBJECTIVES

The goal of this lab is to set up and use a Microsoft account. After completing this lab, you will be able to:

▲ Use a local account, a Microsoft account, and OneDrive

▲ Switch between a Microsoft account and a local account

MATERIALS REQUIRED

This lab requires the following:

▲ Windows 8 operating system

▲ Internet access

LAB PREPARATION

Before the lab begins, the instructor or lab assistant needs to do the following:

◢ Verify Windows starts with no errors

◢ Verify Internet access is available

ACTIVITY BACKGROUND

Windows 8 gives the user the option to log in with a Microsoft account. Using that account, the user can access his or her OneDrive without entering a password. In this lab, you learn how all this works.

> **ESTIMATED COMPLETION TIME: 45–60 MINUTES**

 Activity

1. What is the local account user name for your computer?

   _____

2. Do you have an existing Microsoft account using an Outlook.com, Hotmail.com, Live.com, or another email address? If so, what is the email address associated with your Microsoft account?

   _____

Windows requires that you sign in with a Microsoft account before you can use the OneDrive app. If you don't already have a Microsoft account, you'll have the opportunity to create one when you first attempt to open the app.

PART 1: USE A LOCAL ACCOUNT, A MICROSOFT ACCOUNT, AND ONEDRIVE

1. Sign in with a local account.

2. On the Start screen, click the **OneDrive** app. The OneDrive app opens, but because you are signed in using a local account, OneDrive cannot access your Microsoft account. Click **Go to PC settings**.

3. Click **Connect to a Microsoft account**. The "Switch to a Microsoft account on this PC" screen appears. Enter your local account password. Click **Next**.

4. If you already have a Microsoft account, enter your sign-in information now. If you do not have a Microsoft account, click **Create a new account**.

> **Notes**   If you already have a Microsoft account, sign in to OneDrive. When the OneDrive app opens, skip to Step 6.

5. A Microsoft account is associated with an email address. You can use an existing email address or create a new one. Windows 8 apps work best if your Microsoft account uses an Outlook.com, Hotmail.com, or Live.com email address. When you set up your Microsoft account, you can create an email address that has an Outlook.com or a Hotmail.com ending. What is your new Microsoft account email address? (You might also want to write down your password in a safe place so you won't forget it.)

   _____

6. Complete the steps to set up your new Microsoft account, including creating the email address and password, entering the security information, and finalizing the account.

7. You can skip the step to use the security code for now.

8. OneDrive is introduced. Click **Next**.

9. Click **Switch**. Your local account has now been switched to a Microsoft account on the computer. Now, when you sign in to your computer, you will use your Microsoft account information and *not* the local account sign-in information.

10. Close the OneDrive app, and reopen it to verify you are signed in.

To add a document to the OneDrive folder, you will first create one on the desktop. Follow these steps to upload a file to OneDrive:

1. Open the **desktop**.

2. Right-click the **desktop**, and select **New, Text Document**. Rename the document **OneDriveTest**.

3. Open the document, and type **This is my test document for OneDrive in Windows 8.** Save the file, and close Notepad. Return to the **OneDrive** app.

4. Right-click anywhere on the screen. Click the **Add items** icon in the status pane. A browsing screen opens.

5. With "This PC" showing, click the **Desktop** tile. (If "This PC" isn't showing, click the down arrow next to the title of the screen, and select "This PC".) Select the **OneDriveTest** file, and then click the **Copy to OneDrive** button. The file is added to your OneDrive account.

6. View your document from your OneDrive. Then return to the **Start** screen.

PART 2: SWITCH BETWEEN A MICROSOFT ACCOUNT AND A LOCAL ACCOUNT

Next, you'll disconnect the Microsoft account, and then reconnect it. Follow these steps to disconnect your Microsoft account from your local account:

1. From the Start screen, go to the **charms** bar, and click **Settings**. Click **Change PC settings**, and then click **Accounts** in the left pane.

2. On the Accounts screen, click **Disconnect** under your account name and email address, as shown in Figure 1-3. Confirm your current Microsoft password, and click **Next**.

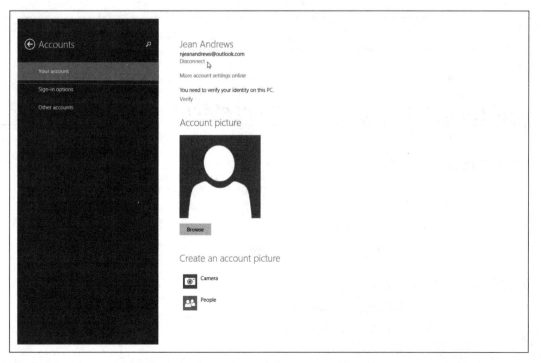

Figure 1-3   The Accounts page is used to connect or disconnect a Microsoft account to a local account

3. You cannot reuse your same local account user name; however, the user folders remain the same. Enter an alternate local account user name. Create the password and password hint. (You can reuse the local account password you used in the beginning of this lab.) Click **Next**.

4. You need to sign out, and then sign back in to complete the process. Click **Sign out and finish**.

5. Sign in to your new local account. Do you think you can now use the OneDrive app without entering your password again?

_____

6. Return to the **PC settings** screen, and reconnect to your Microsoft account.

7. Sign out, and then sign back in using your Microsoft account. Verify you can use the OneDrive app.

REVIEW QUESTIONS

1. Why can you not use the OneDrive app while signed in using a local account?

_____

2. What are the two domain name endings offered when creating a new Microsoft account?

_____

3. How do you access the menu to add a new document to your OneDrive?

_____

4. Why might you want to save files to OneDrive instead of just saving to your local hard drive?

_____

5. List the steps to disconnect your Windows 8 local account from a Microsoft user account:

_____

_____

_____

LAB 1.4 USE THE MAIL AND PEOPLE APPS

OBJECTIVES

The goal of this lab is to use your Microsoft account to learn about the Mail and People apps. After completing this lab, you will be able to:

◢ Use the Mail app

◢ Use the People app to connect to other social accounts

MATERIALS REQUIRED

This lab requires the following:

◢ Windows 8 operating system

◢ Internet access

LAB PREPARATION

Before the lab begins, the instructor or lab assistant needs to do the following:

◢ Verify Windows starts with no errors

◢ Verify Internet access is available

ACTIVITY BACKGROUND

After you have set up your Microsoft account, you can send and receive mail through the Mail app, and connect to other contacts—such as those in your Facebook and Twitter accounts—using the People app. In this lab, you learn how all this works.

ESTIMATED COMPLETION TIME: 45–60 MINUTES

 Activity

This activity is divided into two parts. In Part 1, you learn to use the Mail app. In Part 2, you learn to use the People app.

PART 1: USE THE MAIL APP

Follow these steps to check if your Mail app is syncing with your Microsoft account:

1. Sign in using the Microsoft account you set up in the previous lab.

2. Click the **Mail** tile. You don't need to add another account at this time.

3. Open the **charms** bar, and click **Settings**. In the Settings pane (see Figure 1-4), click **Accounts**. In the Account pane, verify the email address is correct. If no email address is listed or the address is wrong, click **Add an account**, and follow the on-screen instructions to set up your email using your Microsoft email. To close the Accounts pane, click somewhere else on the screen.

Figure 1-4 The Settings charm lists items specific to the Mail app

4. By default, the Inbox for your email account is selected in the left pane. The list of emails in your Inbox appears in the middle pane. When you click an email, its contents appear in the right pane.

5. Send an email to yourself (or exchange emails with a classmate) to test the Mail app. To send the test email, click the **New** button in the upper-right corner of the screen, and type a short message to yourself. Add a subject line, and click the **Send** button. The message quickly appears in your Inbox.

> **Notes** If you don't see the message, you might have typed the wrong email address. You can also try refreshing the sync with the mail server. Right-click somewhere in the Mail app. In the status bar, click **More**, then **Sync**.

6. There are a few ways to display the status bar, which includes options for handling your mail:

   ◢ Right-click in the Mail app.

   ◢ Place a check mark by the email to select it.

   ◢ Click the three dots in the lower-right corner of the screen.

   In the status bar that appears at the bottom of the screen, you can select an option to print the message or mark it as Junk mail, among other things.

7. By default, mail is downloaded as it arrives. To see other options, open the **Settings** charm, and click **Accounts**. Then click your **email** address in the Accounts pane. What are the options for how often email is downloaded?

   _____

   _____

8. Close the Mail app.

PART 2: USE THE PEOPLE APP

The People app is used to maintain all of your contacts, including those from Facebook, Outlook Mail, Google, and Twitter.

1. Return to the **Start** screen, and click the **People** app. Click **Connected to** in the lower-right corner to access the Accounts menu.

2. Click **Add an account**.

3. Choose **Facebook** from the list. Click **What else happens when I connect?**

4. Click **Connect**. A Facebook login screen appears.

5. Enter your Facebook email account and password, and then click **Log In**.

6. Microsoft asks to share your information, and then asks you a few other questions. Click **OK** for each question to complete the connection of the People app to Facebook.

REVIEW QUESTIONS

1. What are the steps to add a second email account to the Mail app?

   _____

   _____

   _____

   _____

2. By default, only email received in the last two weeks is downloaded to the Mail app. List the steps to have the Mail app download email from the last month:

_____

_____

_____

3. What are the steps to add an account in the People app?

_____

_____

_____

_____

_____

4. Using the People app, what can you do when connected to your Twitter account?

_____

_____

LAB 1.5 USE WINDOWS KEYBOARD SHORTCUTS

OBJECTIVES

The goal of this lab is to learn some keyboard shortcuts. After completing this lab, you will be able to use the keyboard to:

◢ Display the Start menu

◢ Launch Help and Support

◢ Switch between open applications

◢ Launch utilities with the Windows logo key

MATERIALS REQUIRED

This lab requires the following:

◢ Windows 8 or Windows 7 operating system

◢ A keyboard with the Windows logo key

LAB PREPARATION

Before the lab begins, the instructor or lab assistant needs to do the following:

◢ Verify Windows starts with no errors

ACTIVITY BACKGROUND

You can use certain keys or key combinations (called keyboard shortcuts) to perform repetitive tasks more efficiently. These shortcuts are also useful if your mouse is not working. In this lab, you learn to use some common keyboard shortcuts. You can find a full list of keyboard shortcuts by searching for "keyboard shortcuts" in the Windows Help and Support Center.

ESTIMATED COMPLETION TIME: 30 MINUTES

 Activity

The F1 key is the universal keyboard shortcut for launching Help. To learn more, follow these steps:

1. Click the desktop, and then press **F1**. Windows Help and Support opens.
2. Close Windows Help and Support.
3. Open File Explorer in Windows 8 or Windows Explorer in Windows 7.
4. With the File Explorer/Windows Explorer window as the active window, press **F1**.
5. Explore the Help options available for File Explorer/Windows Explorer.
6. Open Notepad.
7. With the Notepad window as the active window, press **F1**.
8. Explore the Help options available for Notepad.

    ◢ How are the Windows Help and Support options different when you press F1 when the desktop is active as opposed to when the File Explorer/Windows Explorer window or Notepad window is active?

    _____

    _____

    _____

9. Use Windows Help and Support to find a list of general keyboard shortcuts. What key can you press to activate the menu in an application window? Close all windows.

    _____

10. You can activate many shortcuts by pressing the Windows logo key in combination with other keys. An enhanced keyboard has two Windows logo keys, usually located between the Ctrl and Alt keys on either side of the Spacebar. Try the combinations listed in Table 1-1, and record the result of each key combination in the Result column. (Close each window you open before proceeding to the next key combination.)

To become more efficient and productive with your work by using shortcut keystrokes, follow these steps:

1. Press the Windows logo on your keyboard; the Start screen or menu opens. In Windows 8, type **notepad** and press **Enter**. In Windows 7, in the Search programs and files box, type **notepad** and press **Enter**. The Notepad opens.
2. Press the Windows logo on your keyboard; the Start screen or menu opens. In Windows 8, type **paint** and press **Enter**. In Windows 7, in the Search programs and files box, type **mspaint** and press **Enter**. Microsoft Paint opens.

Key or Key Combination	Result
▦ Windows logo	
▦ Windows logo + E	
▦ Windows logo + F	
▦ Windows logo + R	
▦ Windows logo + Pause	
▦ Windows logo + M	

Table 1-1 Key combinations using the Windows logo key

3. Press the Windows logo on your keyboard; the Start screen or menu opens. In Windows 8, type **calc** and **press** Enter. In Windows 7, in the Search programs and files box, type **calc** and press **Enter**. The Calculator opens.

4. With all those applications open, try the following key combinations:

    a. Press the **Alt + Tab** keys.

    b. Continue to hold down the **Alt** key, and repeatedly tap the **Tab** key.

    ◢ How can these key combinations assist you in being more efficient with your work?

    _____

    _____

CRITICAL THINKING (ADDITIONAL 15 MINUTES)

Using the keyboard skills you have learned in this lab, complete the following steps without using the mouse, and answer the respective questions:

1. Where online can you find a more complete list of keyboard shortcuts for Windows operating systems? Record the URL for this list:

    _____

    _____

2. Using the Windows Help and Support utility, what key combination can be used for printing a document?

    _____

3. Using the Windows Help and Support utility, what key combination can be used to save your work in a document in progress?

    _____

4. What key combination can you use with Internet Explorer that may help you when browsing?

    _____

REVIEW QUESTIONS

1. What key is universally used to launch help?

_____

2. How many Windows logo keys are usually included on an enhanced keyboard?

_____

3. What keyboard shortcut combinations can be used to copy and paste a block of text?

_____

4. Which key can you press to open the Start menu?

_____

5. What is the result of pressing the ▦ Windows logo + P key combination? Describe a situation in which a user might find this menu helpful:

_____

_____

LAB 1.6 GATHER AND RECORD SYSTEM INFORMATION

OBJECTIVES

The goal of this lab is to document a system configuration. In this lab, you use the operating system to determine how the system is configured. You also observe the condition of the system using a health report. After completing this lab, you will be able to:

◢ Gather system information using Windows tools

◢ Use available Windows tools to evaluate the condition of a system

MATERIALS REQUIRED

This lab requires the following:

◢ Windows 8 operating system

◢ Network connection

LAB PREPARATION

Before the lab begins, the instructor or lab assistant needs to do the following:

◢ Verify Windows starts with no errors

◢ Verify each computer is connected to the network

ACTIVITY BACKGROUND

This lab is completed in two parts. In Part 1, you identify the Windows configuration by using Windows tools. In Part 2, you learn an interesting shortcut to help you find several different ways to customize settings in Windows 8.

Activity

PART 1: EXPLORE THE SYSTEM USING WINDOWS TOOLS

The System Information window provides information about your system. Follow these steps to gather information about your system using the System Information window:

1. Open the Windows desktop. Right-click the **Start** button in the taskbar, and select **System**, or simply press the ■ **Windows logo + Pause** keys. The System window opens.

2. If necessary, expand this window so you can see all the information, and then record the following information:

   ◢ OS edition: _____

   ◢ Processor: _____

   ◢ Processor speed: _____

   ◢ Installed memory (RAM): _____

   ◢ System type: _____

   ◢ Computer name: _____

   ◢ Workgroup: _____

3. Close the System window.

The System Information utility provides additional information about hardware components and configuration of your system. Do the following to gather this information:

1. *System manufacturer and model:* To open the System Information utility, right-click the **Start** button, click **Run**, type **msinfo32.exe** in the Run box, and then press **Enter**. The System Information window opens. On the System Summary page, find your system's manufacturer and model number and record them here:

   System manufacturer: _____

   System model: _____

2. *Drives:* Click the **+** sign next to the Components node on the navigation tree in the left pane. Next, click the **+** sign next to the Storage node, and then click **Drives**. Record the following information:

Drive #1		Drive #2		Drive #3	
#1 Drive letter		#2 Drive letter		#3 Drive letter	
#1 Description		#2 Description		#3 Description	
#1 Size		#2 Size		#3 Size	
#1 Vol. name		#2 Vol. name		#3 Vol. name	
#1 Serial no.		#2 Serial no.		#3 Serial no.	

3. *Disks:* Click **Disks** in the navigation tree, and record the following information:

Disk #1		Disk #2	
#1 Manufacturer		#2 Manufacturer	
#1 Model		#2 Model	
#1 Partitions		#2 Partitions	
#1 Size		#2 Size	

4. Close the System Information window.

The Network screen offers information about your network connections. Follow these steps to gather information about your network connection:

1. On the charms bar, click the **Settings** charm, and then click **Change PC settings**.

2. Click **Network** in the left pane. Click to open your network connection. Record the following information:

   IP address: _____

   Physical address: _____

3. Close the Network Properties page.

PART 2: TRY A COOL SHORTCUT FOR WINDOWS 8

Windows 8 offers all kinds of settings to customize the Windows experience. The problem is that these settings can sometimes be hard to find. Follow these steps to create a shortcut to many settings, all to one easy-to-locate icon.

1. On the desktop, create a new folder.

2. Rename this folder using this text (no spaces):
   Settings.{ED7BA470-8E54-465E-825C-99712043E01C}

3. The icon changes appearance and is now named Settings. Double-click the new icon on your desktop, and explore the settings that are included in this new Settings window. The first category of settings is the Action Center, which has 17 items (see Figure 1-5). How many categories of settings do you see in your Settings window?

_____

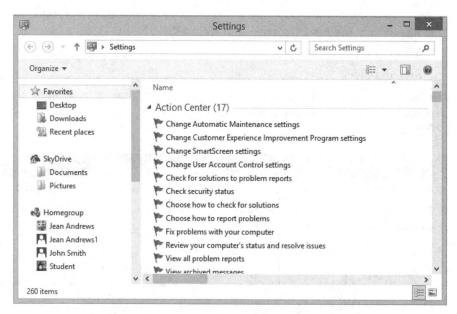

Figure 1-5 The desktop shortcut provides a Settings window

REVIEW QUESTIONS

1. What are two ways to access the System window?

_____

_____

2. Using the charms bar, what are the steps to set the network security so that your computer does not automatically connect to devices, such as on a public network?

_____

_____

3. Based on the system information you gathered, what component of your computer would you upgrade first? Why?

_____

_____

4. Why is it beneficial to keep a written record of your system's configuration?

_____

_____

LAB 1.7 MANAGE WINDOWS 7 LIBRARIES

OBJECTIVES

The goal of this lab is to learn to use Windows 7 libraries to help manage user folders. After completing this lab, you will be able to:

◢ Understand the structure of the Documents library

◢ Create a library and add three folders to it

MATERIALS REQUIRED

This lab requires the following:

◢ Windows 7 operating system, any edition

LAB PREPARATION

Before the lab begins, the instructor or the lab assistant needs to do the following:

◢ Verify Windows starts with no errors

ACTIVITY BACKGROUND

A Windows 7 library works like a folder that can contain files and other folders. These files and other folders can be located in any storage media on the local computer or on the network. Users might keep their data files in many locations on the local computer or on the network. A library is a good way to collect all these folders in a central, easy-to-access location. One good reason to set up a library is to make it easier for a technician to back up data. When a technician uses the Windows Backup and Restore utility to schedule a backup of a library, all the individual folders in that library are backed up. In this lab, you learn to examine the structure of a library, set up a library, and add folders to it.

ESTIMATED COMPLETION TIME: 30 MINUTES

Activity

Windows 7 creates four libraries by default (Documents, Music, Pictures, and Videos), and you can create additional libraries. Three libraries (Documents, Pictures, and Music) are pinned to the right side of the Start menu by default (see Figure 1-6), and you can access these pinned libraries by clicking them.

Figure 1-6 Windows 7 creates four libraries by default, three of which have links on the Start menu

You can use Windows Explorer to manage libraries. Follow these steps to see how the default Documents library is constructed:

1. To open the Documents library, click **Start,** and then click **Documents.** The Documents library opens in Windows Explorer. See Figure 1-7.

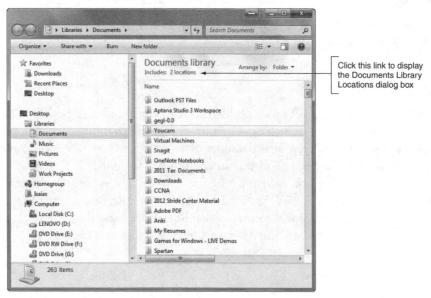

Figure 1-7 Contents of the Documents library

2. In Windows Explorer, above the Documents library, click **2 locations**. The Documents Library Locations dialog box appears (see Figure 1-8). Close the dialog box.

Figure 1-8 The Documents library gathers files from two locations by default

To learn more about the Documents library, follow these steps:

1. In the left pane of Windows Explorer, right-click the **Documents** library, and select **Properties** from the shortcut menu. The Documents Properties dialog box opens. Notice the check mark beside the My Documents folder.

2. Select the **Public Documents** folder, and then click **Set save location**. Notice the check mark is now beside the Public Documents folder. Files placed in the Documents library will now be stored in the Public Documents folder.

3. Select the **My Documents** folder, and click **Set save location**. Files placed in the Documents library will now be stored in the My Documents folder.

4. Click **OK** to close the Documents Properties window.

To create a library with three folders, follow these steps:

1. You can use Windows Explorer to create a folder in the root directory of drive C: To do so, click **Local Disk(C:)** to select it. The contents of drive C: appear in the right pane of Windows Explorer.

> **Notes** If drive C: has been assigned a volume name on your computer, you might see the volume name beside C: in Windows Explorer rather than Local Disk.

2. In the menu bar of Windows Explorer, click **New folder**.

3. To name the folder, type **Project One** in the highlighted area, and then press **Enter**.

4. Repeat Steps 2 and 3 to create two more folders in the root directory of drive C: Name the folders **Project Two** and **Project Three**.

You should see the three folders listed together in Windows Explorer as subfolders of Local Disk (C:).

To create a new library, follow these steps:

1. Click **Libraries** in the left pane of Windows Explorer to select it. The libraries appear in the right pane of Windows Explorer.

2. In the menu bar of Windows Explorer, click **New library**. A new library is created and its name is highlighted.

3. In the highlighted area, type **Work Projects**, and then press **Enter**. The new library is created, as shown in Figure 1-9.

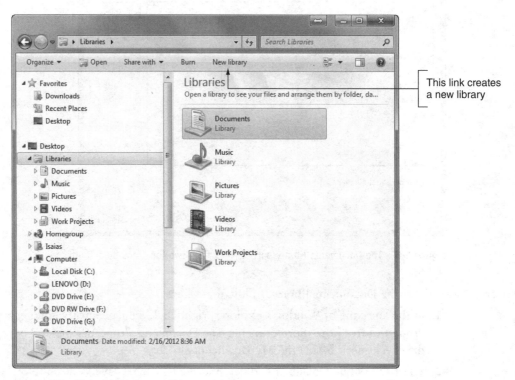

Figure 1-9   List of Libraries on this computer

To add folders to the newly created Work Projects library, follow these steps:

1. Double-click **Work Projects** in the right pane of Windows Explorer. The Work Projects library should be empty.

2. Click **Include a folder**.

3. Browse to the Project One folder you just created, and add that folder to the library.

4. If necessary, click **Work Projects** in the left pane of Windows Explorer. The contents of the Work Projects appear in the right pane.

5. At the top of the right pane, click **1 location**. The Work Projects Library Locations dialog box opens (see Figure 1-10).

6. To add additional folders to the library, click **Add**. In the Include Folder in Work Projects dialog box, navigate to the Project Two folder, and click **Include folder**.

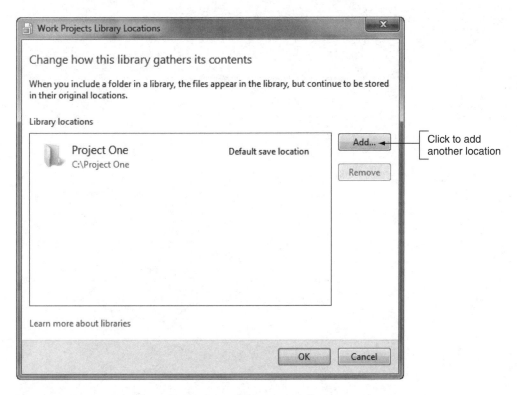

Figure 1-10 New folders can be added to a newly created library

7. Repeat Step 6 to add the Project Three folder to the Work Projects library. The library now has three folders.

8. Click **OK** to close the Work Projects Library Locations dialog box.

9. Close all windows.

REVIEW QUESTIONS

1. What four libraries does Windows 7 create by default?

   _____

   _____

2. What two folders are included in the Documents library by default?

   _____

3. What dialog box is used to change the save location of a library?

   _____

4. What are the steps to create a new library?

   _____

   _____

   _____

5. Research online, and decide if and how libraries can be used in Windows 8:

   _____

   _____

Installing Windows

Labs included in this chapter:

- **Lab 2.1:** Use the Windows 8 Upgrade Assistant
- **Lab 2.2:** Perform a Clean Installation of Windows 8.1
- **Lab 2.3:** Upgrade to Windows 8
- **Lab 2.4:** Update to Windows 8.1 Using Windows Store
- **Lab 2.5:** Use Client Hyper-V to Manage a Virtual Machine (VM)
- **Lab 2.6:** Use Windows Virtual PC to Install Windows 7 in a Virtual Machine (VM)

> **Notes** The instructions in these labs assume that you are using a mouse and a keyboard. If you're using a touch screen, simply tap instead of click, press and hold instead of right-click, double-tap instead of double-click, and swipe to scroll the screen to the right or left.

LAB 2.1 USE THE WINDOWS 8 UPGRADE ASSISTANT

OBJECTIVES

The goal of this lab is to decide if you should upgrade your computer to Windows 8. After completing this lab, you will be able to:

◢ Verify the compatibility of your computer, apps, and connected devices with Windows 8

MATERIALS REQUIRED

This lab requires the following:

◢ Windows 7 operating system

◢ Internet access

LAB PREPARATION

Before the lab begins, the instructor or lab assistant needs to do the following:

◢ Verify Windows starts with no errors

◢ Verify Internet access is available

ACTIVITY BACKGROUND

There are many reasons to upgrade your computer from Windows 7 to Windows 8. Maybe Windows 8 is a requirement for your job, or maybe you just want to see what all the fuss is about. No matter the reason, you need to make sure your computer is compatible with the new OS before you perform the upgrade. Microsoft offers the Windows 8 Upgrade Assistant to scan your hardware, apps, and connected devices for compatibility for an upgrade. Before installing Windows 8, run the Upgrade Assistant from the Microsoft website.

ESTIMATED COMPLETION TIME: 30 MINUTES

 Activity

To download and run the Windows 8 Upgrade Assistant, follow these steps:

1. Open **Internet Explorer**, and browse to **windows.microsoft.com/en-us/windows-8/ upgrade-assistant-download-online-faq**. Review the information given about the Windows 8 Upgrade Assistant.

> **Notes** Websites change often. If you can't find the Upgrade Assistant at the link provided, try this search string using Google.com: **Windows 8 Upgrade Assistant site:microsoft.com**.

2. Click **Download Windows 8 Upgrade Assistant**.

3. Internet Explorer pops up a notification asking if you want to run or save the file Windows8-UpgradeAssistant.exe. Select **Save**, and Internet Explorer automatically saves the file to the Downloads folder for the current user. When the download is complete, click **View downloads**.

4. In the View Downloads window, click **Downloads** beside the file name you just downloaded. What is the path and file name (including file extension) of the downloaded file? What is the size of the file?

---

5. Close Internet Explorer and the View Downloads window.

6. To use the Upgrade Assistant, double-click the file you just downloaded to your Downloads folder. In the warning dialog box, click **Run**.

7. When the scan is complete, click **See compatibility details** to review the items scanned. Write down all the items you need to review and all actions you take to resolve the compatibility issues:

_____

_____

_____

_____

_____

_____

_____

_____

_____

8. To save the report, click **Save**. What is the path and file name (including file extension) of the downloaded file? What is the size of the file?

_____

9. Email the file to your instructor, or upload it to your online interface.

10. In the Windows 8 Upgrade Assistant, click **Next**.

11. With Windows settings, personal files, and apps selected, click **Next**.

12. The Windows 8 Upgrade Assistant displays the Windows 8 options for your computer. Which version or versions of Windows 8 can you upgrade to?

_____

13. Click **Close**.

REVIEW QUESTIONS

1. Why is it a good idea to run the Windows 8 Upgrade Assistant before upgrading to Windows 8?

_____

2. What is the URL for the Windows 8 Upgrade Assistant?

_____

3. When preparing for an upgrade, is it more important to make sure you have Windows 8 drivers for your network adapter or your sound card? Explain your answer:

_____

_____

4. Describe the difficulty level of preparing your computer for an upgrade to Windows 8 and the problems you might encounter as you work:

_____

_____

_____

LAB 2.2 PERFORM A CLEAN INSTALLATION OF WINDOWS 8.1

OBJECTIVES

The goal of this lab is to install Windows 8.1 without already having an OS installed on your computer. After completing this lab, you will be able to:

◢ Perform a clean installation of Windows 8.1

MATERIALS REQUIRED

This lab requires the following:

◢ Windows 8.1 setup DVD or installation files on another medium, such as a USB flash drive; any edition of Windows 8 will work in this lab.

◢ Product key from Windows 8.1 package or downloaded from the web

> **Notes** This lab gives steps for performing a clean installation of Windows 8.1. If you are using Windows 8, your steps might differ slightly.

LAB PREPARATION

Before the lab begins, the instructor or lab assistant needs to do the following:

◢ Verify the computer powers up properly

◢ Provide each student with access to the Windows 8.1 installation files and product key

◢ Verify any necessary Windows 8.1 drivers are available

ACTIVITY BACKGROUND

When deciding whether to do a clean installation or an upgrade to Windows 8.1, you need to consider the condition of your current system. If the Windows 7 system is giving trouble, performing a clean installation is a good idea so that current problems don't follow you into the new installation. Also, you might do a clean installation if your computer does not already have an OS installed, such as on a new virtual machine.

ESTIMATED COMPLETION TIME: 60 MINUTES

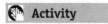 **Activity**

Follow these steps to perform a clean installation using a Windows 8.1 installation DVD:

1. Start up your computer, and access UEFI/BIOS setup. Change the boot sequence so the DVD-ROM is the first boot device.

> 📝 **Notes** If the installation files are on a USB flash drive, change UEFI/BIOS to first boot to USB.

2. Insert the Windows 8.1 DVD into the optical drive.

3. Shut down your computer, and start it up again.

4. You might be asked to press any key on your keyboard to boot from the DVD. The computer should boot the DVD and begin the installation process.

5. A Windows Setup dialog box appears asking you to select your language, time and currency format, and keyboard input method. Make the appropriate selections. Click **Next**.

6. In the next Windows Setup dialog box, click **Install now**.

7. A Windows Setup dialog box asks for the product key that is used to activate Windows. Enter the product key for Windows 8.1, and click **Next**.

8. The License terms dialog box appears. Check **I accept the license terms**, and click **Next**.

9. When prompted for the type of installation, select **Custom: Install Windows only (advanced)**.

10. In the next dialog box, select a drive and volume, and then click **Next**. (If you need clarification at this point in the installation, ask your instructor for assistance.) The installation process, which can take several minutes, begins. What is the size of the partition that will hold Windows 8.1?

_____

11. The computer might restart by itself several times as part of the installation process. If prompted to press any key to boot the DVD, *ignore the message* because pressing any key will start the installation again from scratch.

12. The Personalize screen asks you to choose a screen color and type the PC name. Enter the PC name as assigned by your instructor. Click **Next**.

13. In the Settings window, click **Use express settings**.

14. You will set up a local account to sign in to Windows. In the "Sign in to your Microsoft account" window, click **Create a new account** from the options at the bottom of the screen, as shown in Figure 2-1. Click **Sign in without a Microsoft account** to create a local account. Type the user name, the password (in both boxes), and the password hint. Click **Finish**. So you do not forget your password, write your user name and password here:

_____

15. The computer takes a few minutes while Windows 8.1 finalizes settings, and then the Start screen appears. You are finished performing a clean installation of Windows 8.1.

16. Open **File Explorer** or the **Computer** window. How much space on the hard drive did the Windows 8.1 installation use?

_____

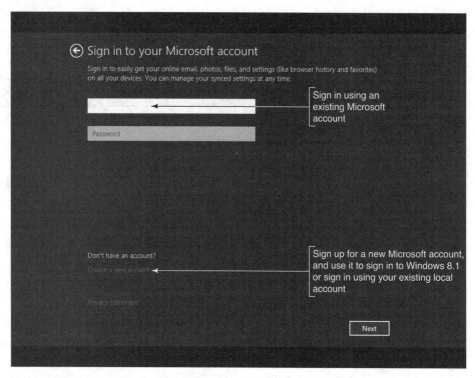

Figure 2-1 Decide which account you will use to sign in to Windows 8.1

REVIEW QUESTIONS

1. Was the Windows 8.1 installation a success? If so, what did you find most challenging about the installation process?

   _____

   _____

2. When is a clean installation preferred over an upgrade to Windows 8.1?

   _____

   _____

   _____

   _____

3. In this lab, you created a local account to sign in to Windows. Was it necessary to be connected to the Internet to create the account? If you had created a Microsoft account to sign in to Windows, would it be necessary to be connected to the Internet to create the account?

   _____

4. Why do you need to access UEFI/BIOS setup before the installation process?

   _____

   _____

5. Did Windows automatically activate during the installation? How can you find out if Windows is activated?

_____

_____

LAB 2.3 UPGRADE TO WINDOWS 8

OBJECTIVES

The goal of this lab is to upgrade to Windows 8. After completing this lab, you will be able to:

◢ Upgrade to Windows 8

MATERIALS REQUIRED

This lab requires the following:

◢ Windows 7 operating system

◢ Windows 8 setup DVD or installation files on another medium, such as a USB flash drive; the Windows 7 edition must qualify for the upgrade license for the Windows 8 edition. Windows 7 Starter, Home Basic, and Home Premium can upgrade to Windows 8 or Windows 8 Pro. Windows 7 Professional and Ultimate can upgrade to Windows 8 Pro.

◢ Product key from Windows 8 package or available on the web

> **Notes** If you are performing an upgrade to Windows 8.1, your steps might differ slightly.

LAB PREPARATION

Before the lab begins, the instructor or lab assistant needs to do the following:

◢ Verify Windows starts with no errors

◢ Provide each student with access to the Windows 8 installation files and product key

◢ Verify any necessary Windows 8 drivers are available

ACTIVITY BACKGROUND

Performing an upgrade to Windows 8 takes less time than performing a clean installation of Windows 8. It also has the advantages that user preferences and settings are not lost and applications are left in working condition. If there isn't a reason for a clean install, an upgrade is recommended.

ESTIMATED COMPLETION TIME: 45 MINUTES

 Activity

The following steps are representative of a typical upgrade. Don't be alarmed if your experience differs slightly. Use your knowledge to solve any problems on your own, and ask your instructor for help if you get stuck. You might want to record any differences between these steps and your own experience. Also, record any decisions you make and any information you enter during the installation process.

Follow these steps to perform an in-place upgrade to Windows 8 when you're working with a Windows 8 setup DVD:

1. As with any upgrade installation, before you start the upgrade, do the following:

   a. Scan the system for malware using an updated version of anti-malware software. When you're done, be sure to close the anti-malware application so it's not running in the background.

   > **Notes** If you need help running anti-malware software, refer to the lab "Protect Against Malware in Windows 8" in the chapter, "Security Strategies."

   b. Uninstall any applications or device drivers you don't intend to use in the new installation.

   c. Make sure your backups of important data are up to date, and then close any backup software running in the background.

2. Insert the Windows 8 setup DVD. If the setup program doesn't start automatically, open Windows Explorer, and double-click the setup program in the root of the DVD. (If you're not using a DVD to perform the upgrade, launch the setup program from wherever it is stored.)

3. Respond to any UAC dialog boxes.

4. The setup program loads files, examines the system, and reports any problems it finds. If it finds the system meets minimum hardware requirements, setup asks permission to go online for updates. Make your selection, and click **Next**.

5. The next window requests the product key. Enter the product key, and click **Next**.

6. The product key is verified, and then the License terms window appears. Check **I accept the license terms**, and click **Accept**.

7. On the "Choose what to keep" screen, with **Keep Windows settings, personal files, and apps** selected, click **Next**.

8. On the next screen, verify the choices listed, and click **Install** to begin the installation.

9. During the installation, setup might restart the system several times. If prompted to press any key to boot into the DVD, *ignore the message* because pressing any key will start the installation again from scratch.

10. The Personalize window asks you to choose a screen color. Click **Next**.

11. On the Settings window, click **Use express settings**.

12. On the next screen, enter the password for your local user account.

13. On the next screen, you are given the opportunity to enter a Microsoft account. To skip this step, click **Skip**. You can set up a Microsoft account later. The computer takes a few minutes while Windows 8 finalizes settings, then the Start screen appears. You are finished performing an upgrade installation of Windows 8.

REVIEW QUESTIONS

1. Was the Windows 8 installation a success? If so, what did you find most challenging about the upgrade process?

2. Using File Explorer, find out how much free space is on drive C: Also, how large is the Windows folder?

_____

_____

3. What is the size of the Windows.old folder? What is the purpose of this folder?

_____

_____

4. When performing a clean install of Windows, setup gives you the opportunity to create a user account and password during the installation process. Why do you think setup skipped this step in an upgrade installation?

_____

LAB 2.4 UPDATE TO WINDOWS 8.1 USING WINDOWS STORE

OBJECTIVES

The goal of this lab is to update to Windows 8.1. After completing this lab, you will be able to:

◢ Update to Windows 8.1 using the Windows Store

MATERIALS REQUIRED

This lab requires the following:

◢ Windows 8 operating system that does not have the Windows 8.1 update

◢ Internet access

LAB PREPARATION

Before the lab begins, the instructor or lab assistant needs to do the following:

◢ Verify Windows starts with no errors

◢ Verify Internet access is available

◢ Verify any necessary Windows 8.1 drivers are available

ACTIVITY BACKGROUND

Windows 8.1 is offered as a free upgrade if you already have Windows 8 installed on your computer. The Windows 8.1 release works for any edition of Windows 8. To make sure you have the latest features of Windows 8, always install new releases of Windows 8 as they become available.

ESTIMATED COMPLETION TIME: 30 MINUTES

 Activity

Follow these steps to update to Windows 8.1:

1. As with any update, before you start the update, do the following:

   a. In Windows 8, use the **System** window to check for updates and verify all important updates are installed. If the KB2871389 updated is not installed, the Windows 8.1 update will not appear in the Windows Store.

   b. Scan the system for malware using an updated version of anti-malware software. When you're done, be sure to close the anti-malware application so it's not running in the background.

> **Notes** If you need help running anti-malware software, refer to the lab "Protect Against Malware in Windows 8" in the chapter, "Security Strategies."

   c. Uninstall any applications or device drivers you don't intend to use after the update.

   d. Make sure your backups of important data are up to date, and then close any backup software running in the background.

2. To view which release of Windows is installed, press **Win+X**, and click **System**. The System window reports the release. Which release is installed? Is the installation a 32-bit or 64-bit installation?

   _____

3. Go to the **Start** screen, and open the **Store** app. Find and download the Windows 8.1 release. The process of installing Windows 8.1 is similar to installing Windows as an upgrade.

4. You must restart Windows, accept the license agreement, decide how settings are handled, and set up a user account or use an existing account. Sign in using a local account. To use a local account, when asked to sign in to your Microsoft account, click **Create a new account**. Then click **Sign in without a Microsoft account**.

REVIEW QUESTIONS

1. Was the Windows 8.1 update a success? If so, what did you find most challenging about the update process?

   _____

   _____

2. Why is it a good idea to scan your system for malware before performing an update?

   _____

   _____

3. Why do you not need the Windows 8 setup DVD or installation files to update to Windows 8.1?

   _____

   _____

4. Where do you find the Windows 8.1 update?

   _____

LAB 2.5 USE CLIENT HYPER-V TO MANAGE A VIRTUAL MACHINE (VM)

OBJECTIVES

The goal of this lab is to install and use virtual machines with Client Hyper-V in Windows 8 Pro. After completing this lab, you will be able to:

◢ Turn on Hyper-V in Windows 8 Pro

◢ Set up Hyper-V to allow a VM to connect to the network

◢ Create a VM using Hyper-V

◢ Use the VM in Hyper-V

MATERIALS REQUIRED

This lab requires the following:

◢ Windows 8 Professional 64-bit operating system

◢ Windows 8 setup DVD or installation files on another medium, such as a flash drive

> **Notes** The steps in this lab use Windows 8.1 Professional. If you are using a different edition of Windows 8, your screens and steps may differ slightly from those presented here.

LAB PREPARATION

Before the lab begins, the instructor or lab assistant needs to do the following:

◢ Verify Windows starts with no errors

◢ Provide each student with access to the Windows 8 installation files and product key

ACTIVITY BACKGROUND

If you need quick and easy access to more than one operating system or to different configurations of the same operating system, a virtual machine is a handy tool to have. The virtual machine creates a computer within a computer, almost as if you are remotely controlling a computer in a different location from a window on your desktop. Virtual machines are heavily used by IT support to replicate and resolve issues, test software, and learn about new operating systems.

> **Notes** Hyper-V will not work in Windows 8 Pro that is installed in a virtual machine. In other words, you can't use Hyper-V to create a VM within a VM. You must have the 64-bit version of Windows 8 Pro installed to use Hyper-V. Also, Hyper-V does not play well with other virtual machine management software, so be mindful if you try to install another virtual machine management software when you are already using Hyper-V.

ESTIMATED COMPLETION TIME: 45 MINUTES

 Activity

The steps to set up a VM using Windows 8 Pro are presented in three parts in this lab. In Part 1, you prepare Hyper-V to create a VM, and then you create the VM in Part 2. In Part 3, you manage and use the VM.

PART 1: PREPARE HYPER-V USING WINDOWS 8 PRO

To configure Hyper-V in Windows 8 Pro, follow these steps:

1. For Hyper-V to work, hardware-assisted virtualization (HAV) must be enabled in UEFI/ BIOS setup. If you are not sure it is enabled, power down your computer, turn it back on, go into UEFI/BIOS setup, and make sure hardware-assisted virtualization is enabled. Also make sure that all subcategory items under HAV are enabled. Save your changes, exit UEFI/BIOS setup, and allow the system to restart to Windows 8.

> **Notes** HAV might have a different name in the UEFI/BIOS setup screens for your motherboard. Intel UEFI/BIOS calls HAV Intel Virtualization Technology. AMD calls it AMD-V.

2. Open the **System** window. Which edition and version of Windows 8 is installed? If 64-bit Windows 8 Pro is not installed, don't continue with this lab.

3. Hyper-V is disabled in Windows 8 Pro by default. To turn it on, press **Win+X**. In the Quick Launch menu that appears, click **Programs and Features**.

4. Click **Turn Windows features on or off**. Place a check mark next to Hyper-V, as shown in Figure 2-2, and click **OK**.

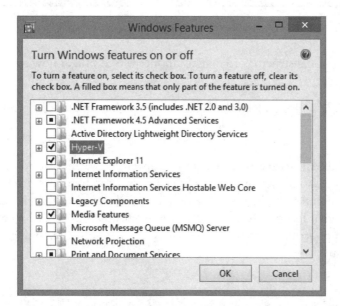

Figure 2-2   Turn on or off a Windows feature

5. Windows applies the changes. Click **Restart now**, and sign in to the computer after it has restarted a couple of times.

6. To launch the Hyper-V Manager, go to the Start screen, start typing **Hyper-V**, and then click the **Hyper-V Manager** tile. The Hyper-V Manager window appears on the desktop.

7. In the left pane of the Hyper-V Manager, select the host computer.

8. To make sure your VMs have access to the network or the Internet, you need to first install a virtual switch in Hyper-V. To create a virtual switch, in the Actions pane on the right, click **Virtual Switch Manager**.

9. The Virtual Switch Manager dialog box appears. In the left pane, make sure **New virtual network switch** is selected. To bind the virtual switch to the physical network adapter so the VMs can access the physical network, select **External** in the left pane, and click **Create Virtual Switch**.

10. In the Virtual Switch Properties pane that appears, make sure **Allow management operating system to share this network adapter** is checked, and then click **Apply**. Click **Yes**, and the virtual switch is created. Click **OK** to close the Virtual Switch Manager.

PART 2: CREATE A VM USING HYPER-V

To create a VM, follow these steps:

1. In the Actions pane of the Hyper-V Manager window, click **New**, and then click **Virtual Machine**. The New Virtual Machine Wizard launches. Click **Next**.

2. In the next dialog box, assign a name to the VM. Click **Next**. What is the name you assigned the VM?

_____

3. In the Specify Generation dialog box, Generation 1 is selected. Click **Next**.

4. In the next dialog box, set the amount of RAM for the VM at **4096 MB**. Check **Use Dynamic Memory for this virtual machine**. Click **Next** to continue.

5. In the Configure Networking dialog box, in the drop-down options, select the new virtual switch you created earlier, and click **Next**.

6. In the Connect Virtual Hard Disk dialog box, with **Create a virtual hard disk** selected, leave the default settings. Click **Next**.

7. Your instructor will provide access to operating system installation files. In the Installation Options dialog box, decide how you will install an OS in the VM, and click **Next**. How are you planning to install an OS in the VM?

_____

8. The last dialog box shows a summary of your selections. Click **Finish** to create the VM. The new VM is listed in the Virtual Machines pane in the Hyper-V Manager window.

PART 3: MANAGE AND USE THE VM

Follow these steps to configure and use the VM:

1. To manage the VM's virtual hardware, select the VM, and click **Settings** near the bottom of the Actions pane. The Settings dialog box for the VM appears.

2. Explore the hardware listed in the left pane, and apply your settings in the right pane. Using the right pane, you can mount a physical CD or DVD to the drive or you can mount an ISO file.

3. To install an OS in the VM, you can boot the VM to the DVD drive, which is mounted either to a physical setup DVD or to a bootable ISO file. To boot to the DVD drive, use the Settings dialog box to verify UEFI/BIOS for the VM has the correct boot priority order. To view and change this setting, click **BIOS** in the left pane.

4. Click **OK** to close the Settings dialog box. To start the VM, select it, and click **Start** in the Actions pane. The VM boots up, and you can then install an OS. Which OS are you installing?

_____

5. A thumbnail of the VM appears in the bottom-middle pane of the Hyper-V Manager window. To see the VM in its own window, double-click the thumbnail, as shown in Figure 2-3.

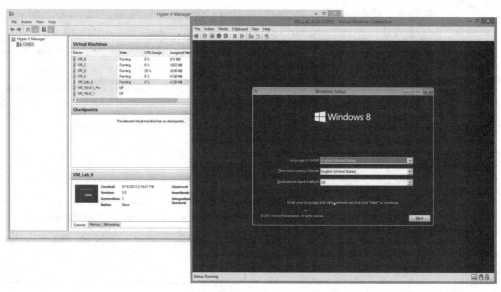

Figure 2-3   Windows 8 setup is running in the VM

6. Install the OS, and start the operating system in the VM.

7. In the VM, open **Internet Explorer** to confirm the VM has a good Internet connection.

8. Hyper-V allows you to close the application without shutting down virtual machines that are running in it. Close the VM window. Notice the state of the VM is listed as Running. How much memory is currently assigned to the VM?

_____

9. Close the Hyper-V Manager window and any other open Windows. Restart **Windows 8**.

10. After Windows restarts, sign in to Windows. On the Start screen, launch the **Hyper-V Manager**. What is the state of the VM you created? How much memory is currently assigned to the VM?

_____

11. Open the VM window, and use the VM to surf the web. Finally, using the toolbar in the Virtual Machine Connection window, under "Action," select **Shut Down**. Confirm your action by clicking **Shut Down** again. Now what is the state of the VM?

_____

12. Close all open windows.

REVIEW QUESTIONS

1. Were you able to successfully install the virtual machine using Hyper-V? If so, what did you find most challenging about the process?

_____

_____

2. Which edition and version of Windows 8 did you use during this lab, and why?

_____

3. Why did you create a virtual switch?

_____

_____

_____

_____

4. Why would you use dynamic memory with a virtual machine?

_____

5. When you close the Hyper-V application and have VMs running in it, what happens to the states of the VMs? What happens to the VM states when you open Hyper-V?

_____

_____

LAB 2.6 USE WINDOWS VIRTUAL PC TO INSTALL WINDOWS 7 IN A VIRTUAL MACHINE (VM)

OBJECTIVES

The goal of this lab is to install Windows 7 in a virtual machine. After completing this lab, you will be able to:

◢ Install Windows Virtual PC and use it to set up a new VM

◢ Install Windows 7 in the VM

> **Notes** You will use Virtual PC and the VM with Windows 7 installed in it in future labs in this lab manual.

MATERIALS REQUIRED

This lab requires the following:

◢ A computer running Windows 7, any edition and any version (32-bit or 64-bit)

◢ A minimum of 2.0-GHz CPU power is advised

◢ A minimum of 4 GB of RAM is advised

◢ A minimum of 20 GB of available hard disk drive space

◢ Internet access

> **Notes** Virtual machine software and virtual machines tend to require heavy system resources. Don't forget that whatever memory you assign to a VM will not be available to the host operating system while the VM is open.

LAB PREPARATION

Before the lab begins, the instructor or lab assistant needs to do the following:

- ◢ Verify Windows 7 starts with no errors
- ◢ Verify Internet access is available
- ◢ Create or download an ISO file of a Windows 7 operating system, and make this file available to students. The OS can be any edition of Windows 7, but needs to be a 32-bit version.

ACTIVITY BACKGROUND

Virtual machines borrow hardware power from the host operating system to run operating systems in a virtual or simulated computer environment. In this lab, you install Virtual PC and use it to install Windows 7 in a virtual machine.

Your instructor has created an ISO image file that you will use to install Windows 7 in the virtual machine. Ask your instructor for the following information:

- ◢ What is the name and path to this ISO file?

- ◢ What is the edition of Windows 7 in the ISO image?

- ◢ What is the product key for the Windows installation?

ESTIMATED COMPLETION TIME: 60-120 MINUTES

 Activity

PART 1: INSTALL WINDOWS VIRTUAL PC

Follow these steps to download and install Windows Virtual PC:

1. Click **Start**, right-click **Computer**, and then select **Properties**. The System window opens.
   - ◢ What edition of Windows 7 are you using?

   - ◢ Are you using a 32-bit version or 64-bit version of the OS?

   ---

2. Go to the Windows Virtual PC home page at **microsoft.com/en-us/download/details. aspx?id=3702**.
3. In the drop-down list of languages, select **English**.
4. Click **Download**. Choose the file you want to download, depending on whether you are using a 32-bit OS or a 64-bit OS. Click **Next**.

Notes The x86 file is for 32-bit operating systems. The x64 file is for 64-bit operating systems.

5. Follow the on-screen directions to **Save** (not Run) the program file.

◢ What folder was used to receive the download?

_____

◢ What is the name of the downloaded file?

_____

6. Double-click the downloaded file. A dialog box appears asking if you want to install a Windows update. Click **Yes**. (Virtual PC is part of this update.)

7. A License terms box opens. Click **I Accept**. When you are asked permission to restart the computer, click **Restart Now**. After the restart, log back on to Windows. Virtual PC is now installed on your system.

PART 2: CREATE A NEW VM AND INSTALL WINDOWS 7 IN IT

Follow these steps to create a new VM and install Windows 7:

1. Click **Start**, **All Programs**, and then **Windows Virtual PC**. Click **Windows Virtual PC** again. The Virtual Machines folder opens in Windows Explorer. In the menu bar, click **Create virtual machine**.

2. The "Create a virtual machine" dialog box opens (see Figure 2-4). Enter the name of the virtual machine. A good practice is to name the VM by the OS you plan to install, such as **Windows 7 Home Premium** or **Windows 7 Professional**. By default, the VM is stored in a folder in your user profile. What name did you assign to your VM?

_____

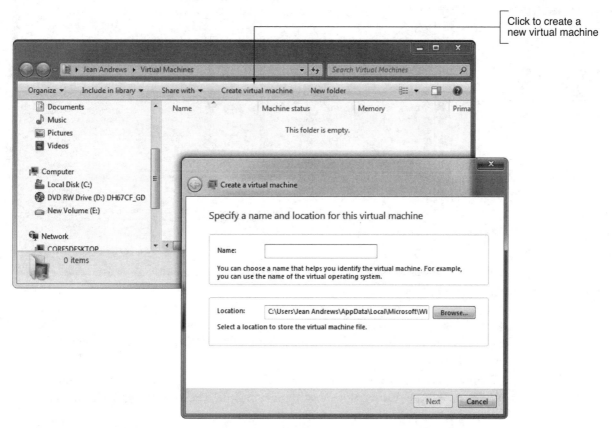

Figure 2-4 Virtual PC steps you through the process of creating a new virtual machine

3. If you want to change the location of the virtual machine file, click **Browse**, navigate to a new location, and click **OK**. What is the drive and folder where your VM will be stored?

_____

4. Click **Next**. In the "Specify memory and networking options" box, enter **2024** for the amount of RAM. Verify **Use computer network connections** is checked. Click **Next**.

5. In the "Add a virtual hard disk" dialog box, leave the selection at **Create a dynamically expanding virtual hard disk**. Click **Create**. The VM is created.

You are now ready to mount the ISO file that holds the Windows 7 installation files to the virtual DVD drive. Follow these steps:

1. In Windows Explorer, in the Virtual Machines folder, click your VM to select it. Click **Settings** in the menu bar. The Settings dialog box opens.

2. In the left pane of the Settings dialog box, click **DVD Drive**. In the right pane of the Settings dialog box, select **Open an ISO image**. See Figure 2-5.

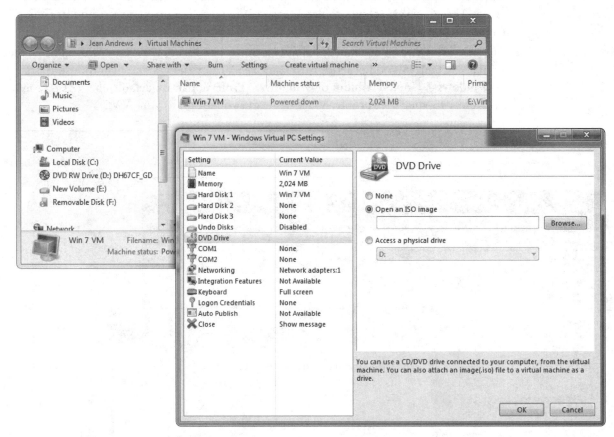

Figure 2-5   Mount the ISO image file to the DVD drive in the VM

3. Click **Browse**, and navigate to the location of the ISO file provided by your instructor. If necessary, double-click the ISO file to select it. Click **OK** to close the Settings dialog box for your VM.

4. When you boot up your VM, it will find the Windows 7 virtual DVD and launch Windows 7 setup. To start the VM, double-click it. The VM boots, Windows loads setup files, and the Windows installation begins.

5. Complete the installation of Windows 7.

◢ What is the user account you created during the Windows 7 installation?

_____

◢ What is the password to this user account?

_____

6. After you click inside the VM window, your keyboard and mouse are captured by the VM until you release them. To release the keyboard and mouse to your host Windows desktop, press the **Alt + Tab** keys. To return to the VM, click inside the VM window.

7. After Windows is installed in the VM, shut down the VM using the **Start** menu on the VM Windows desktop.

You will use this virtual machine installation of Windows 7 in future labs in this lab manual.

REVIEW QUESTIONS

1. How much memory or RAM does Virtual PC allot to a VM by default?

_____

2. By default, where does Virtual PC store the files for a virtual machine?

_____

3. After you installed Windows 7 in the VM, what is the size of the Virtual Machine Hard Drive Image file?

_____

4. How would you configure your virtual machine if you wanted to install Windows 7 from a DVD rather than an ISO image?

_____

5. What keystroke combination can you use to release your keyboard and mouse from a VM window in Virtual PC?

_____

_____

CHAPTER 3

Maintaining Windows

Labs included in this chapter:

- **Lab 3.1:** Perform Hard Drive Routine Maintenance
- **Lab 3.2:** Back Up and Restore Files in Windows 7
- **Lab 3.3:** Set Up a Virtual Hard Drive in Windows
- **Lab 3.4:** Manage Hard Drive Partitions Using a Virtual Machine (VM)
- **Lab 3.5:** Learn to Work from the Command Line
- **Lab 3.6:** Use the Xcopy and Robocopy Commands

LAB 3.1 PERFORM HARD DRIVE ROUTINE MAINTENANCE

OBJECTIVES

The goal of this lab is to perform routine maintenance on a hard drive. After completing this lab, you will be able to:

▲ Delete unneeded files on a hard drive

▲ Verify defragment settings on a hard drive

▲ Scan a hard drive for errors

MATERIALS REQUIRED

This lab requires the following:

▲ Windows 8 operating system

LAB PREPARATION

Before the lab begins, the instructor or lab assistant needs to do the following:

▲ Verify Windows starts with no errors

ACTIVITY BACKGROUND

To ensure that your hard drive operates in peak condition, you should perform some routine maintenance tasks regularly. For starters, you need to ensure that your hard drive has enough unused space (which it requires to operate efficiently). In other words, you should remove unnecessary files from the drive.

In addition, files on a hard drive sometimes become fragmented over time; defragmenting the drive can improve performance because files can be read sequentially without jumping around on the drive. Other routine maintenance tasks include scanning the hard drive for errors and repairing those errors. In this lab, you learn about three tools you can use for important disk maintenance tasks. You should use these tools on a scheduled basis to keep your hard drive error free and performing well.

ESTIMATED COMPLETION TIME: 30–45 MINUTES

 Activity

PART 1: USE THE DISK CLEANUP TOOL

Follow these steps to delete unnecessary files on your hard drive:

1. Close all open applications.

2. Open **Control Panel**. Open Administrative Tools, and then open **Disk Cleanup**.

3. If the Disk Cleanup Drive Selection dialog box opens, select the drive you want to clean up in the drop-down list, and click **OK** to close the Disk Cleanup Drive Selection dialog box.

4. The Disk Cleanup dialog box opens, listing the various types of files you can clean up. To include more items in the list, click **Clean up system files**. If a UAC dialog box appears, respond to it. If the Disk Cleanup Drive Selection dialog box appears, select the drive you want to clean up, and click **OK** to close the dialog box.

5. You need to select the types of files you want Disk Cleanup to delete. Select all the file types in the list you want to delete. Depending on your system, these options might include Downloaded Program Files, Recycle Bin, Temporary files, and Temporary Internet Files.

   ◢ How much disk space does each group of files take up?

   _____

   _____

   _____

   _____

   ◢ Click on the name of a file group you might want to delete to read a description of the files included in that group. Based on information in the Disk Cleanup dialog box, what is the purpose of each group of files listed in the Disk Cleanup dialog box? Record that information here:

Downloaded Program Files	
Temporary Internet Files	
Offline Webpages	
Game Statistics Files	
Recycle Bin	
Setup Log Files	
Temporary Files	
Thumbnails	
Per User Archived Windows Error Reporting	
System Archived Windows Error Reporting	

   ◢ What is the total amount of disk space you would gain by deleting all of these files?

   _____

   ◢ What types of files might you not want to delete during Disk Cleanup? Why?

   _____

   _____

6. Click **OK** to delete the selected groups of files.

7. When asked to confirm the deletion, click **Delete Files**. The Disk Cleanup dialog box closes, and a progress indicator appears while the cleanup is under way. The progress indicator closes when the cleanup is finished, returning you to the desktop.

PART 2: USE THE CHKDSK TOOL

The next step in routine maintenance is to use Windows Chkdsk to examine the hard drive and repair errors. Follow these steps:

1. Close any open applications so they aren't trying to write to the hard drive while it's being repaired.

2. On the Start screen, type **cmd** in the Start Search box. Right-click **Command Prompt** in the Search pane, and click **Run as administrator**. Respond to the UAC dialog box. The command prompt window opens.

3. Several switches (options) are associated with the Chkdsk utility. To show all available switches, type **chkdsk /?** at the command prompt, and press **Enter**. Answer the following:

   ◢ What are two switches used to fix errors that Chkdsk finds?

   _____

   ◢ Why do the /I and /C switches in Chkdsk reduce the amount of time needed to run the scan?

   _____

4. To use the Chkdsk utility to scan the C: hard drive for errors and repair them, type **chkdsk C: /R** and press **Enter**. (Note: You may have to substitute a different drive letter depending on your computer's configuration.) A message appears saying that Chkdsk cannot run because the volume is in use by another process. Type **Y** and then press **Enter** to run Chkdsk the next time the system is restarted. Close the command prompt window, and restart your computer.

5. After Chkdsk runs, log back on to Windows.

PART 3: USE THE DEFRAGMENT AND OPTIMIZE DRIVES TOOL

The last step in routine hard drive maintenance is to use the Optimize Drives tool to locate fragmented files and rewrite them to the hard drive in contiguous segments. You should do the defragmentation last because other actions, such as cleaning up files, can further fragment the files on the disk. Follow these steps:

1. Close all open applications.

2. From the desktop, right-click the Windows logo, and select **Control Panel**. Open Administrative Tools, and then open **Defragment and Optimize Drives**.

3. Confirm that your primary hard drive is included in the system's list of drives to be optimized. Why would a solid-state drive not appear in the list of drives in the Optimize Drives window?

   _____

4. Confirm that scheduled optimization is turned on. If it's not on, or if you want to adjust the schedule, click **Change settings**. Figure 3-1 shows the schedule box for Optimize Drives.

5. To analyze the drive's degree of fragmentation before defragmenting, highlight the primary hard drive and click **Analyze**. If the disk is less than 10% fragmented, there's no need to defragment now.

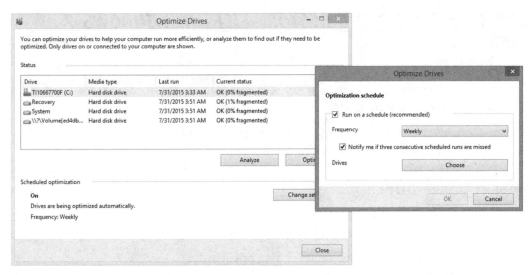

Figure 3-1 Confirm that optimization is scheduled

6. If the disk is at least 10% fragmented, click **Optimize**. If prompted, select the drive you want to defragment. The Optimize Drives tool begins defragmenting the drive.

> **Notes** Fully defragmenting your hard drive can take a few hours, depending on how fragmented it is. If you don't have time to wait, you can stop the process by clicking **Stop**.

7. When defragmentation is completed, close the Optimize Drives window.

REVIEW QUESTIONS

1. Why should you run Disk Cleanup before running the Optimize Drives tool?

   _____

   _____

2. How does defragmentation improve performance?

   _____

   _____

3. When you ran the Chkdsk command in this lab, it had to run during the startup process. Why was this necessary? What form of the Chkdsk command can you use in a command prompt window that does not require a restart to run?

   _____

   _____

4. Based on what you learned in this lab along with your other experiences with Disk Cleanup, which type of files removed by Disk Cleanup took up the most space?

   _____

   _____

LAB 3.2 BACK UP AND RESTORE FILES IN WINDOWS 7

OBJECTIVES

The goal of this lab is to use Windows Backup and Restore to back up and recover lost files. After completing this lab, you will be able to:

- Set up a Windows backup, and back up files
- Restore deleted or modified files

MATERIALS REQUIRED

This lab requires the following:

- Windows 7 operating system
- An account with administrator privileges

LAB PREPARATION

Before the lab begins, the instructor or lab assistant needs to do the following:

- Verify Windows starts with no errors
- Verify each student has access to a user account with administrator privileges
- Decide which backup media will be used, for example, an external hard drive, a CD/DVD/BRD drive, or a USB flash drive

ACTIVITY BACKGROUND

Windows provides the File History tool in Windows 8 and the Backup and Restore tool in Windows 7 to help you safeguard data and Windows system files. Using this tool, you can back up one or more folders, or even an entire drive. You should back up your files to a different storage device than your hard drive, such as a CD, DVD, or Blu-ray disc; an external hard drive; or a USB flash drive. Windows 8 and Windows 7 Professional and Ultimate also allow you to back up files to a network server. In this lab, you back up and restore your Documents library using Windows Backup and Restore.

ESTIMATED COMPLETION TIME: 45 MINUTES

 Activity

Follow these steps to create some files in the Documents library and then back up the Documents library:

1. Start Windows and log on using an administrator account. Connect or plug in your backup media (USB flash drive or other storage device) to the computer.

2. To make sure your storage device is large enough to hold all the files and folders in your Documents library, open the Computer window or Windows Explorer, and use it to answer these questions:

   - What backup storage device are you using? (For example, are you using a USB flash drive or an external hard drive?) What is the drive letter assigned to this device?

   - What is the storage capacity of your backup storage device? How much free space is on the device?

◢ What is the size of your Documents library?

_____

◢ Does your storage device have enough free space to hold the backup of the Documents library?

_____

3. Using Notepad, create a text file in your Documents library named **File1.txt**. Enter into the text file your name and address and the name of your favorite movie. Close the file.

4. Using Notepad, create a second text file in your Documents library named **File2.txt**. Enter into this file your email address. Close the file.

5. Open **Control Panel,** and click **Back up your computer** in the System and Security group. The Backup and Restore window opens. What options are shown at the top of the left pane of the Backup and Restore window?

_____

_____

_____

6. If a backup schedule has never been configured on this system, the _Set up backup_ link appears in the upper-right area of the window. If a backup schedule has previously been configured, you will see the backup schedule information and the link _Change settings._

◢ Does your computer already have a backup schedule in place?

_____

7. If you are creating the first backup schedule for this system, click **Set up backup**. If a backup schedule is already in place, click **Change settings**. Follow the steps in the Backup Wizard to decide where to save the backup. What is the drive letter and name of the device that will receive your backup?

_____

8. When asked "What do you want to back up?", click **Let me choose,** and then click **Next**. Uncheck all items designated for backup. Be sure you uncheck **Include a system image of drives: System Reserved, (C:)**. In this lab, you are not backing up the system image.

9. Drill down to the **Documents Library** and check it. In this backup, the only item that will be backed up is the Documents library. The backup will include all files and folders in the library.

10. Follow the wizard to review your backup information, and verify you are only backing up the Documents library. What is the day and time the backup is scheduled to run? Save your changes, and run the backup now.

_____

11. The Backup and Restore window shows the progress of the backup. After the backup completes, close the **Backup and Restore** window.

12. Now you will make some changes to the files you backed up. Open the **Documents** library, delete **File1.txt**, and then empty the Recycle Bin. Open **File2.txt,** and add another email address. Save and close the document. What steps did you use to empty the Recycle Bin?

_____

Follow these steps to restore the deleted file from backup:

1. Open the Backup and Restore window, and click **Restore my files**. The Restore Files dialog box appears.

2. Click **Browse for files**, and drill down to the **File1** text file. What is the path to the file?

_____

3. Click on the file to select it, and then click **Add files**. File1 is listed in the Restore Files box. Click **Next**.

4. In the next box, decide where you want to restore the file. The default setting is the original location, but you can also change that to a new location. For this lab, restore the file to the original location. Click **Restore**. Click **Finish**. (If the file already existed at this location, you would have had to choose whether to Copy and Replace, Don't Copy, or Copy, but keep both files.)

5. Open the Documents library, and verify File1 is restored. Open File1. Are the file contents as you created them?

_____

Sometimes a file gets corrupted or you make changes to a file that you wish you could undo. If your file is backed up, you can restore it to that previous version. Follow these steps to find out how:

1. Open the Backup and Restore window to run a backup. In the window, click **Back up now**.

2. Open **File2** in your Documents library, and add a third email address. Close the file.

3. Use the Backup and Restore window to run the backup. You should now have three backups of File2.

4. To see the different backups of File2 from which you can choose, open Windows Explorer and locate File2. Right-click **File2** and click **Properties**. The Properties dialog box for the file appears. Click the **Previous Versions** tab. See Figure 3-2.

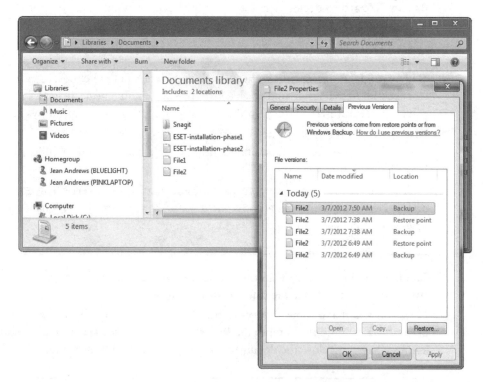

Figure 3-2 Use the Previous Versions tab to restore a file from backup

5. To restore a file, first select it, and then click **Restore**. A box appears giving you the options to Copy and Replace, Don't Copy, or Copy, but keep both files. Choose the last option, **Copy, but keep both files,** and then click **Finish**.

6. Keep restoring previous versions of File2 until you have one copy of File2 that has one email address in it, another copy of File2 with two email addresses in it, and a third copy of File2 with three email addresses in it.

   ◢ What is the name of the file that contains one email address? Two email addresses? Three email addresses?

   _____

   _____

   ◢ The Previous Versions tab indicates that some backups of File2 are stored at the backup location and others are stored in a restore point. Where does Windows store a restore point? Why would a backup of a file in a restore point not be available if the hard drive crashes?

   _____

CRITICAL THINKING (ADDITIONAL 10 MINUTES)

Windows 8 offers the File History utility to replace the Windows 7 Backup and Restore Center for backing up personal data files and folders, and for creating system images. List two methods for accessing the File History utility:

_____

_____

_____

_____

REVIEW QUESTIONS

1. Is it more important to back up Windows system files or data files? Why?

   _____

   _____

2. By default, how often does Windows back up?

   _____

3. In the lab, you saw two ways to restore files: use the Backup and Restore window or use the Previous Versions tab. Which method is best to use when you want to restore a corrupted file? Three deleted folders? When you want to recover a folder from a backup made over three weeks ago?

   _____

4. What is a system image, and how do you create one?

   _____

5. If you decide to restore a corrupted file from a restore point, what should you do first so you don't overwrite the corrupted file? Why?

_____

6. In the lab, File2 appears in the Documents library. What is the actual folder that File2 is stored in?

_____

7. Based on the information you see in Figure 3-2, what action triggers Windows to create a restore point?

_____

LAB 3.3 SET UP A VIRTUAL HARD DRIVE IN WINDOWS

OBJECTIVES

The goal of this lab is to learn how to create a virtual hard drive in your Windows system. After completing this lab, you will be able to:

◢ Create a virtual hard drive (VHD)

◢ Use File Explorer or Windows Explorer to explore the VHD

MATERIALS REQUIRED

This lab requires the following:

◢ Windows 8 or Windows 7 operating system

◢ A USB flash drive or other storage media; if the device is not already formatted using the NTFS file system, all data on the device will be lost.

LAB PREPARATION

Before the lab begins, the instructor or lab assistant needs to do the following:

◢ Verify Windows starts with no errors

ACTIVITY BACKGROUND

A virtual hard drive (VHD) is a file that acts like a hard drive. You can create a VHD and access it through File Explorer in Windows 8 or Windows Explorer in Windows 7. You can also attach an existing VHD to your Windows installation. In Windows 8 and Windows 7, a system image is stored in a VHD. A VHD is sometimes used to hold a deployment image when that image is deployed to computers over the network. Using Windows 8 or Windows 7, it is possible to boot a computer to Windows installed on a VHD. A VHD is used as a hard drive in a virtual machine. In this lab, you create a VHD in your regular Windows installation, and then explore the VHD using File Explorer or Windows Explorer.

Activity

Follow these steps to create a new VHD:

1. Plug in your USB flash drive. In Windows 8, right-click the **Windows logo**, and select **Disk Management**. In Windows 7, click **Start**, type **diskmgmt.msc** in the Search box, and then press **Enter**. How many disks are installed in your system? List the Disk number and size of each disk:

   _____

   _____

2. For best results, a VHD should be installed on a device using the NTFS file system. What file system is used for the USB flash drive? If the file system is not NTFS, format it for NTFS. To format for NTFS, right-click the drive, click **Format**, select **NTFS** for the File system, and click **OK**. A warning message displays. Click **OK** again. The drive is formatted, and all data on the drive is lost.

3. To create the VHD, on the menu bar, click **Action**, and then click **Create VHD**. In the Create and Attach Virtual Hard Disk window, click **Browse**, and then browse to the location where you want to store the VHD. In the Browse Virtual Disk files box, navigate to your USB flash drive or other storage device. Enter the name of your VHD as **VHD001**. Click **Save**.

4. Enter **5000** for the virtual hard disk size in MB. Under Virtual hard disk format, select **Dynamically expanding**. Click **OK** to create the VHD.

   ◢ What is the number assigned to the disk by Disk Management? What is the status of your VHD in the Disk Management window?

   _____

   ◢ What is the reported size of the disk?

   _____

5. To initialize the disk, right-click in the Disk area, and select **Initialize Disk** in the shortcut menu. In the Initialize Disk box, if necessary, select the **GPT partitioning system**, and then click **OK**.

6. The next step to prepare the disk for use is to create and format a volume on the disk. To start the process, right-click in unallocated space on the disk, and select **New Simple Volume** in the shortcut menu. The New Simple Volume Wizard starts. Step through the wizard to assign all unallocated space to the volume and format the volume using the NTFS file system. What drive letter did Windows assign to the volume?

   _____

7. Close Disk Management and open File Explorer/Windows Explorer. What capacity does it report for the new volume? How much free space is available?

   _____

8. Drill down into your USB flash drive and locate the VHD001 file.

◢ What is the file size? What is the file name, including the file extension?

◢ What happens when you double-click or otherwise attempt to open the VHD001 file?

REVIEW QUESTIONS

1. How does Windows 8/7 use a VHD when creating a backup of the Windows volume?

2. How is a VHD sometimes used when deploying Windows 8/7 in an enterprise?

3. Why can you not use an array of VHDs to create a striped volume in a Windows system?

4. List the steps you would take to attach (or install) the VHD001 virtual disk on another computer:

LAB 3.4 MANAGE HARD DRIVE PARTITIONS USING A VIRTUAL MACHINE (VM)

OBJECTIVES

The goal of this lab is to explore the different features of the Disk Management utility using a virtual machine. After completing this lab, you will be able to:

◢ Create a virtual hard disk drive in a virtual machine

◢ Format a partition using the Disk Management utility

◢ Assign a drive letter to a partition using the Disk Management utility

◢ Split a partition using the Disk Management utility

MATERIALS REQUIRED

This lab requires the following:

◢ Oracle VirtualBox or Windows Virtual PC installed on a Windows 8 or Windows 7 system

◢ Installation of Windows 7 in a virtual machine

LAB PREPARATION

Before the lab begins, the instructor or lab assistant needs to do the following:

◢ Verify Windows starts with no errors

◢ Verify Windows 7 is installed in a virtual machine in your local host machine

◢ Verify Windows 7 starts in the virtual machine (VM) with no errors

ACTIVITY BACKGROUND

Disk Management is a Windows utility that can be used to perform disk-related tasks, such as creating and formatting partitions and volumes, and assigning drive letters. Additionally, Disk Management can be used to extend, shrink, or split partitions, and to manage unallocated space. In most cases, you can perform Disk Management tasks without having to restart the system or interrupt users. Most configuration changes take effect immediately.

A virtual machine (VM) is a great tool to use when learning to use Disk Management, because you can install a new hard drive in a virtual machine without having to physically install a hard drive in a computer case. In this lab, you use a VM with Windows 7 installed in it. You can use Windows 7 installed in either Oracle VirtualBox or in Windows Virtual PC.

ESTIMATED COMPLETION TIME: 30 MINUTES

 Activity

In the field, you might be required by your client to install a second hard drive—either physically or virtually—to increase the storage capacity of a system. In this lab, you'll gain some experience installing a second hard drive in a VM and preparing it for first use.

PART 1: EXAMINE THE DRIVES IN YOUR VM

In addition to the powerful features of Disk Management, in its most basic form the utility displays installed disks' configurations, which can be useful if you need to document current information before making a decision on disk-related tasks. To learn more, first start your virtual machine that has Windows 7 installed in it.

If you are using Oracle VirtualBox, follow these steps:

1. Start Oracle VirtualBox Manager. The Oracle VM VirtualBox Manager window opens (see Figure 3-3). The left pane lists the VMs installed in VirtualBox.

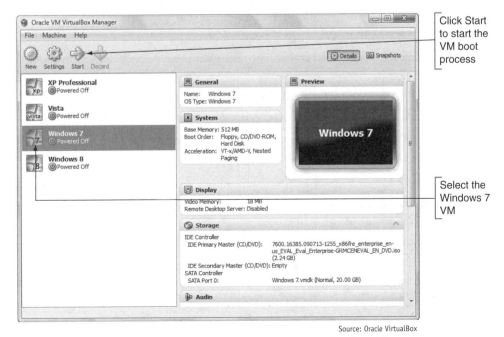

Source: Oracle VirtualBox

Figure 3-3 Oracle VM VirtualBox Manager displaying available virtual machines

2. In the list of virtual machines in the left pane, click the Windows 7 virtual machine. The name of your VM might be different than the one shown in Figure 3-3.

3. In the toolbar, click **Start**. The Windows 7 virtual machine starts. Close any information or warning boxes that appear in the VM. Log on to Windows, and wait for the Windows 7 desktop to display.

If you are using Windows Virtual PC, follow these steps:

1. Start Windows Virtual PC, and view the Virtual Machines folder in File Explorer/ Windows Explorer.

2. To start the Window 7 VM, double-click it. The VM opens. Log on to Windows, and wait for the Windows 7 desktop to display.

To examine the drives in your VM, do the following:

1. To open the Computer Management console in the VM, click **Start**, right-click **Computer**, and select **Manage** in the shortcut menu. The Computer Management console opens.

2. In the left pane of the console, under the heading Storage, click the subheading **Disk Management**. Use the current disk configuration to answer the following questions:

   ◢ How many hard drives does your VM currently have? What is the size of each drive?

   _____

   ◢ How many volumes are currently configured on the system?

   _____

   ◢ What drive letter is assigned to each volume?

   _____

   ◢ What is the size of the primary partition for drive C:?

   _____

3. Close the Computer Management console, and shut down Windows 7 in the virtual machine. The virtual machine window closes.

If you are using Oracle VirtualBox, continue to Part 2 to install a second hard drive in the VM. If you are using Windows Virtual PC, proceed to Part 3 to install a second hard drive in the VM.

PART 2: USE ORACLE VIRTUALBOX TO INSTALL A SECOND HARD DRIVE IN A VM

To install a virtual hard disk drive in the VM using Oracle VirtualBox, follow these steps:

1. If necessary, start the Oracle VirtualBox Manager.

2. Click the Windows 7 virtual machine to select it.

3. On the toolbar, click **Settings**. The Windows 7 Settings dialog box displays.

4. In the left pane of the dialog box, click **Storage**. The Storage Tree options are displayed in the center of the dialog box.

5. In the Storage Tree options, right-click **SATA Controller**. In the shortcut menu, click **Add Hard Disk**.

6. A dialog box displays with options for creating a new virtual hard disk. Click **Create new disk**. The Create New Virtual Disk Wizard appears.

7. Select **VHD (Virtual Hard Disk)**, and click **Next**.

8. In the Virtual disk storage details box, click **Dynamically allocated,** and then click **Next**.

9. The options for Virtual disk file location and size display. Under Location, type **NewHardDisk5**.

10. Using the drag ruler, select a size of around 10 GB, and then click **Next**. The Summary dialog box displays.

11. After inspecting the information in the Summary dialog box, click **Create**.

12. When the system is finished creating the virtual disk, it displays the Storage Tree options with the newly created virtual hard disk, as shown in Figure 3-4. Click **OK** to close the dialog box.

Proceed to Part 4 to use the new virtual hard drive installed in your VM.

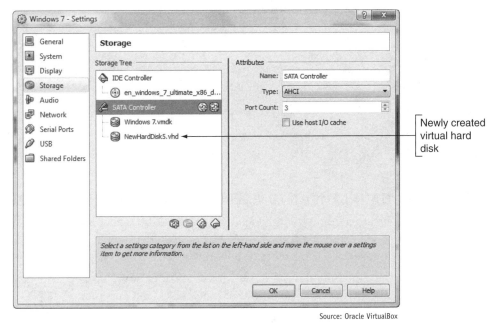

Source: Oracle VirtualBox

Figure 3-4 Oracle VirtualBox VM settings displaying the Storage Tree with newly created virtual hard drive

PART 3: USE WINDOWS VIRTUAL PC TO INSTALL A SECOND HARD DRIVE IN A VM

To install a virtual hard disk drive in the VM using Windows Virtual PC, follow these steps:

1. If the Virtual Machines folder in Windows Explorer is not already open, open it.

2. Click on the Windows 7 VM to select it. (Do not open the VM.)

3. Click **Settings** in the toolbar. The Settings dialog box for this VM opens.

4. Click **Hard Disk 2**. In the right pane, click **Virtual hard disk file** (see Figure 3-5).

5. Click **Create**. In the box that appears, click **Dynamically expanding**. For the name of the hard disk, enter **HDD2**, and click **Next**.

6. For the size of the disk, enter **10000 MB**, and then click **Create**.

7. The new hard disk is added to the VM. Click **OK** to close the Settings dialog box.

Continue to Part 4 to use the new virtual hard disk installed in your VM.

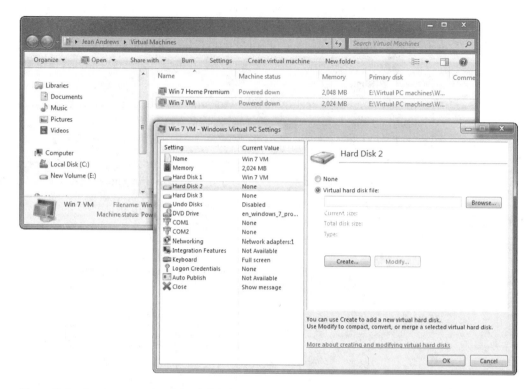

Figure 3-5 Create a new virtual hard disk for the VM

PART 4: USE DISK MANAGEMENT TO PREPARE A NEW HARD DRIVE FOR FIRST USE

You have created a new virtual hard disk and added it to the system. Further configuration is required to allow the operating system to acknowledge the drive's existence so that you can begin taking advantage of the newly acquired storage space. To learn more, follow these steps:

1. Start your VM. Windows 7 in the virtual machine starts up and displays the logon screen. Log on to the system. The Windows desktop appears.

2. To open the Computer window, click **Start**, and then click **Computer**. Answer the following questions:

   ◢ How many drives does Windows Explorer display?

   _____

   ◢ Which drive letters have been assigned to the displayed drives, including optical drives?

   _____

3. Close all windows.

When a new hard drive is first installed, neither the Computer window nor Windows Explorer is able to see it. You need to use Disk Management to initialize, partition, and format the drive. Follow these steps:

1. Open the Computer Management console. Click **Disk Management**.

2. The Initialize Disk dialog box displays automatically because the system has detected the presence of a new storage device. In the Initialize Disk dialog box, select **MBR (Master Boot Record)**, and click **OK**. The newly installed 10 GB disk is displayed as a Basic disk with unallocated space.

3. Right-click in the unallocated space, and click **New Simple Volume** in the shortcut menu. The New Simple Volume Wizard displays. Click **Next**.

4. In the Specify Volume Size dialog box, leave the size of the volume at the maximum size, and click **Next**.

5. In the Assign Drive Letter or Path dialog box, to the right of *Assign the following drive letter*, select **F** in the drop-down list. (This letter is the default value.) Click **Next**.

6. In the Format Partition dialog box, select **Format this volume with the following settings:** and select **NTFS** for the File system. Select **Default** for the Allocation unit size. Enter your name as the Volume label.

7. If necessary, check the box for **Perform a quick format**, and click **Next**.

8. To close the wizard, click **Finish**. The newly created partition is displayed, as shown in Figure 3-6.

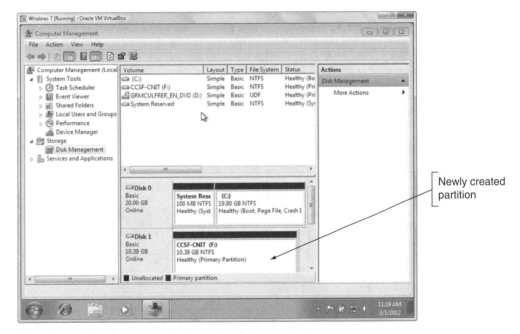

Figure 3-6 Disk Management displays all partitions and volumes

9. Right-click in the New Volume (F:) area. A shortcut menu displays, listing eleven items. List each item in the shortcut menu, and write a brief description of its purpose:

_____

_____

_____

_____

_____

_____

_____

_____

_____

_____

_____

10. Close all windows.

11. Open the **Computer** window. How many drives do you see? List the drive letter and size of each drive:

_____

_____

CRITICAL THINKING (ADDITIONAL 20 MINUTES)

In this lab, you installed a 10 GB virtual hard disk and formatted it with the NTFS file system using a single partition (or volume) that used all available space on the disk. Using Disk Management, split the new partition you have just created on the new virtual hard disk. Do the following:

1. Use File Explorer/Windows Explorer or a command prompt window to copy all the files in the \Program Files\Internet Explorer folder to a new folder on the new hard drive named \Copytest. How large is the \Copytest folder?

_____

2. Without erasing the \Copytest folder, use Disk Management to split the partition on the new hard drive into two partitions. Make one partition 6 GB and the other partition 4 GB. Each partition should use the NTFS file system. List the steps you took to split the partition:

_____

_____

_____

_____

REVIEW QUESTIONS

1. What are two reasons to add a second hard disk to a computer?

_____

2. Why is it better to practice installing a second hard disk by using a VM rather than a physical computer?

_____

3. When installing a new virtual hard disk in a VirtualBox VM or a Virtual PC VM, why is it better to use a dynamically expanding virtual hard disk rather than a fixed-size virtual hard disk?

_____

4. What is the purpose of formatting a drive using Disk Management?

5. What must you do in Disk Management so that Windows Explorer can recognize and use a new hard disk?

6. Other than using the Computer Management console, what is another way to access Disk Management?

LAB 3.5 LEARN TO WORK FROM THE COMMAND LINE

OBJECTIVES

The goal of this lab is to explore some commands used when working from the command line. In this lab, you change and examine directories and drives, and then perform a copy operation. You also learn how to use the command-line Help feature and how to read Help information. After completing this lab, you will be able to:

⬩ Create a file and folder with Notepad and Computer

⬩ Examine directories

⬩ Switch drives and directories

⬩ Use various commands at the command prompt

MATERIALS REQUIRED

This lab requires the following:

⬩ Windows 8 or Windows 7 operating system

⬩ A USB flash drive

LAB PREPARATION

Before the lab begins, the instructor or lab assistant needs to do the following:

⬩ Verify Windows starts with no errors

ACTIVITY BACKGROUND

Experienced technicians use the command line for tasks that just can't be done in a graphical interface, especially when troubleshooting a system. For most tasks, however, you'll rely on a graphical interface, such as File Explorer. In this lab, you use File Explorer in Windows 8 or Windows Explorer in Windows 7 to create a new folder and a new file. Then you use the command line to delete that file. In this lab, it's assumed that Windows is installed on the C: drive. If your installation is on a different drive, substitute that drive letter in the following steps.

Activity

To create a new folder and text file using File Explorer or Windows Explorer, follow these steps:

1. Open File Explorer or Windows Explorer, and double-click **drive C** in the left pane. The contents of the drive C: root appear in the right pane.

2. Right-click anywhere in the blank area of the right pane, point to **New** in the shortcut menu, and then click **Folder**. A new folder icon appears with "New folder" highlighted as the default name, ready for you to rename it.

3. To rename the folder, type **Tools**, and press **Enter**.

4. To create a file in the Tools folder, double-click the **Tools** folder icon, and then right-click anywhere in the blank area of the Tools pane. Point to **New**, and then click **Text Document**. A new file icon appears in the Tools pane with "New Text Document" highlighted, indicating it's ready for renaming.

5. Double-click the **New Text Document.txt** icon to open the file in Notepad.

6. On the Notepad menu, click **File**, and then click **Save As**.

7. In the Save As dialog box, name the file **Deleteme**, and make sure the selection in the Save as type drop-down list is **Text Documents**. Click the **Save** button.

8. Close Notepad.

9. In the Computer window, right-click **New Text Document.txt**, and then click **Delete** in the shortcut menu. Click **Yes** to confirm the deletion.

10. Close all open windows.

To practice using the command-line environment, follow these steps:

1. Open the command prompt window, and notice that the cursor is flashing at the command prompt.

2. The title bar of the command prompt window varies with different versions of Windows, and depends on the user name of the person currently logged in, for example:

   C:\Users\James Clark>

   The command prompt indicates the working drive (drive C:) and the working directory (for example, the \Users\James Clark directory). Commands issued from this prompt apply to this folder unless you indicate otherwise.

3. Type **DIR** and press **Enter**. Remember that DIR is the command used to list a directory's contents. If the list of files and directories that DIR displays is too large to fit on one screen, you see only the last few entries. Entries with the <DIR> label indicate that they are directories (folders), which can contain files or other directories. Also listed for each directory and file are the time and date it was created, and the number of bytes a file contains. (This information is displayed differently depending on which version of Windows you're using.) The last two lines in the list summarize the number of files and directories in the current directory, the space they consume, and the free space available on the drive.

As you'll see in the next set of steps, there are two ways to view any files that aren't displayed because of the length of the list and the window size. To learn more about displaying lists of files in the command-line environment, perform the following steps:

1. First, you'll go to a particularly large directory so you have more files to experiment with. Type **CD C:\Windows** and press **Enter**. The new command prompt should look like this: C:\Windows>.

2. Maximize the command prompt window.

3. Type **DIR /?** and press **Enter** to display Help information for the directory command. You can view Help information for any command by entering the command followed by the /? parameter (also called a "switch").

4. Type **DIR /W** and press **Enter**. What happened?

_____

_____

5. Type **DIR /P** and press **Enter**. What happened?

_____

_____

6. Type **DIR /OS** and press **Enter**. What happened?

_____

_____

7. Type **DIR /O-S** and press **Enter**. What happened? What do you think the hyphen between O and S accomplishes?

_____

_____

8. Insert a USB flash drive in a USB port.

9. Open File Explorer/Windows Explorer, and find out what drive letter Windows assigned to the flash drive. (The drive will be listed in the left pane with the assigned drive letter in parentheses.) What is that drive letter? The following steps assume that the drive letter is H:, but your drive letter might be different.

_____

10. Close File Explorer/Windows Explorer. In the command prompt window, type **H:** and press **Enter**. The resulting prompt should look like this: H:\>. What does the H: indicate?

_____

11. What do you think you would see if you issued the DIR command at this prompt?

_____

_____

12. Type **DIR** and press **Enter**. Did you see what you were expecting?

_____

13. Change back to the C: drive by typing **C:** and then pressing **Enter**.

14. Type **DIR C:\Tools** and press **Enter**. This command tells the computer to list the contents of a specific directory without actually changing to that directory. In the resulting file list, you should see the file you created earlier, Deleteme.txt.

File attributes are managed by using the Attrib command. Follow these steps to learn how to view and manage file attributes:

1. To make C:\Tools the default directory, type **CD C:\Tools** and press **Enter**.
2. To view the attributes of the Deleteme.txt file, type **Attrib Deleteme.txt** and press **Enter**.
3. To change the file to a hidden file, type **Attrib +H Deleteme.txt** and press **Enter**.
4. View the attributes of the Deleteme.txt file again.

   ◢ What command did you use?

   _____

   ◢ How have the attributes changed?

   _____

5. To view the contents of the C:\Tools directory, type **DIR** and press **Enter**. Why doesn't the Deleteme.txt file show in the directory list?

   _____

6. To change the attributes so that the file is a system file, type **Attrib +S Deleteme.txt** and press **Enter**. What error message did you get?

   _____

7. Because you can't change the attributes of a hidden file, first remove the hidden attribute by typing **Attrib -H Deleteme.txt** and then pressing **Enter**.
8. Now try to make the file a system file. What command did you use?

   _____

9. Use the DIR command to list the contents of the C:\Tools directory. Are system files listed?

   _____

10. To remove the file's system attribute, type **Attrib -S Deleteme.txt** and press **Enter**.
11. To move to the root directory, type **CD C:** and press **Enter**.

To learn how to delete a file from the command prompt, follow these steps:

1. Type **DEL Deleteme.txt** and press **Enter** to instruct the computer to delete that file. You'll see a message stating that the file couldn't be found because the system assumes that commands refer to the working directory unless a specific path is given. What command could you use to delete the file without changing to that directory?

   _____

2. The current prompt should be C:\>. The \ in the command you typed indicates the root directory.
3. Type **CD Tools** and press **Enter**. The prompt now ends with "Tools>" (indicating that Tools is the current working directory).
4. Now type **DEL Deleteme.txt /p** and press **Enter**. You're prompted to type **Y** for Yes or **N** for No to confirm the deletion. If you don't enter the /p switch (which means "prompt for verification"), the file is deleted automatically without a confirmation message. It's a good practice to use this /p switch, especially when deleting multiple files with wildcard characters. Also, when you delete a file from the command line, the file doesn't go to the Recycle Bin, as it would if you deleted it in File Explorer/Windows

Explorer or the Computer window. Because deletion from the command line bypasses the Recycle Bin, recovering accidentally deleted files is more difficult.

5. Type **Y** and press **Enter** to delete the Deleteme.txt file. You're returned to the Tools directory.

To display certain files in a directory, you can use an asterisk (*) or a question mark (?) as wildcard characters. Wildcard characters are placeholders that represent other unspecified characters. The asterisk can represent one or more characters, and the question mark represents any single character. The asterisk is the most useful wildcard, so it's the one you'll encounter most often. To learn more, follow these steps:

1. Return to the root directory. What command did you use?

_____

2. Type **DIR *.*** and press **Enter**. How many files are displayed? How many directories are displayed?

_____

3. Type **DIR U*.*** and press **Enter**. How many files are displayed? How many directories are displayed?

_____

4. Explain why the results differed in the previous two commands:

_____

_____

CRITICAL THINKING (ADDITIONAL 30 MINUTES)

Follow these steps to practice using additional commands at the command prompt:

1. Copy the program file Notepad.exe from the \Windows to the \Tools directory. What command did you use?

_____

2. Rename the file in the \Tools directory as **Newfile.exe**. What command did you use?

_____

3. Change the attributes of Newfile.exe to make it a hidden file. What command did you use?

_____

4. Type **DIR** and press **Enter**. Is the Newfile.exe file displayed?

_____

5. Unhide **Newfile.exe**. What command did you use?

_____

6. List all files in the \Windows directory that have an .exe file extension. What command did you use?

_____

_____

7. Create a new directory named \New in the root directory of drive C:, and then copy Newfile.exe to the \New directory. What commands did you use?

_____

_____

8. Using the /p switch to prompt for verification, delete the \New directory. What commands did you use?

_____

_____

9. Open Windows Help and Support. Use the Search text box or the Internet to answer the following questions:

◢ What is the purpose of the Recover command?

_____

_____

◢ What is the purpose of the Assoc command?

_____

_____

REVIEW QUESTIONS

1. What command/switch do you use to view Help information for the DIR command?

_____

2. What do you add to the DIR command to list the contents of a directory that's not the current working directory?

_____

3. What command do you use to change directories?

_____

4. What command do you use to delete a file?

_____

5. What command do you use to switch from drive A: to drive C:?

_____

LAB 3.6 USE THE XCOPY AND ROBOCOPY COMMANDS

OBJECTIVES

The goal of this lab is to observe differences in the Xcopy and Robocopy commands. After completing this lab, you will be able to:

◢ Copy files and folders with the Xcopy or Robocopy command

MATERIALS REQUIRED

This lab requires the following:

◢ Windows 8 or Windows 7 operating system

◢ A USB flash drive or another form of removable media

LAB PREPARATION

Before the lab begins, the instructor or lab assistant needs to do the following:

◢ Verify Windows starts with no errors

ACTIVITY BACKGROUND

The Copy command allows you to copy files from one folder to another folder. Using a single Xcopy command, you can copy files from multiple folders, duplicating an entire file structure in another location. The Robocopy command is basically a new version of Xcopy, with a few more features, including the ability to schedule copying to run automatically and the ability to delete the source files when the copying is finished. In this lab, you learn to copy files using either of these commands.

ESTIMATED COMPLETION TIME: 30 MINUTES

 Activity

Before you begin using the Xcopy and Robocopy commands, you need to create a test directory to use when copying files. Follow these steps:

1. Open a command prompt window, and make the root of drive C: the current directory. The quickest way to change to the root of a drive is to type **T:** (where T is the drive letter), and then press **Enter**.

2. Make a directory in the drive C: root called **copytest**.

Now you can begin experimenting with the Xcopy command. Follow these steps:

1. Type **Xcopy /?** and press **Enter**. Xcopy Help information is displayed. Notice all the switches you can use to modify the Xcopy command. In particular, you can use the /e switch to instruct Xcopy to copy all files and subdirectories in a directory, including any empty subdirectories, to a new location.

2. Type **Robocopy /?** and press **Enter**. What are some new features unique to Robocopy?

_____

_____

_____

_____

3. Type **Xcopy "C:\program files\internet explorer" C:\copytest /e** and then press **Enter**. (You must use quotation marks in the command line to surround a path, file name, or folder name containing spaces.) You'll see a list of files scroll by as they are copied from the C:\program files\internet explorer folder to the C:\copytest folder.

4. When the copy operation is finished, check the copytest folder to see that the files have been copied and the subdirectories created.

5. Enter a DIR command with switches that will give you the total size of the copytest directory, including all the files in the directory and its subdirectories.

   ◢ What command did you use?

   _____

   ◢ What is the total size of the copytest directory in bytes, including all files in the directory and its subdirectories?

   _____

   ◢ What is the total size in MB? In GB?

   _____

6. Insert a USB flash drive or attach an equivalent removable device. To find the capacity of your USB flash drive, enter the command DIR H:. (You might have to substitute the drive letter assigned to your storage device for H:) Add the bytes of used space and free space to determine the capacity of the drive.

   ◢ What is the drive capacity of your USB flash drive in MB? In GB?

   _____

   ◢ What is the free space on your USB flash drive?

   _____

   ◢ Will all the files in the C:\copytest directory fit on your flash drive?

   _____

7. Type **MD H:\copytest**, and then press **Enter**. This command creates a directory named copytest on the H: drive. (Remember to use the letter for the drive assigned to your media device.)

8. To copy all files in the copytest directory on the hard drive to the copytest directory on drive H:, type **Xcopy C:\copytest H:\copytest** and then press **Enter**.

9. The system begins copying files. If the flash drive does not have enough free space to hold the entire C:\copytest directory, the system displays a message stating that the device is out of space and asking you to insert another device. Did you get this error message? If so, what is the exact error message?

   _____

   _____

10. If you don't have enough free space, stop the copying process. To do that, press **Ctrl+Pause/Break**. You're returned to the command prompt.

REVIEW QUESTIONS

1. Can a single Copy command copy files from more than one directory?

   _____

2. What switch do you use with Xcopy or Robocopy to copy subdirectories?

   _____

3. Why might you want to schedule a Robocopy command to occur at a later time?

   _____

   _____

4. Which Xcopy switch suppresses overwrite confirmation?

   _____

3

Optimizing Windows

Labs included in this chapter:

- **Lab 4.1:** Use the Microsoft Management Console
- **Lab 4.2:** Analyze a System with Event Viewer
- **Lab 4.3:** Use Task Manager
- **Lab 4.4:** Edit the Registry with Regedit
- **Lab 4.5:** Identify a Hard Drive Bottleneck by Using Performance Tools
- **Lab 4.6:** Use the System Configuration Utility
- **Lab 4.7:** Critical Thinking: Use Windows Utilities to Speed Up a System

LAB 4.1 USE THE MICROSOFT MANAGEMENT CONSOLE

OBJECTIVES

The goal of this lab is to add snap-ins and save settings using the Microsoft Management Console (MMC) to create a customized console. After completing this lab, you will be able to:

▲ Use the MMC to add snap-ins

▲ Save a customized console

▲ Identify how to launch a console from the Start menu

MATERIALS REQUIRED

This lab requires the following:

▲ Windows 8 or Windows 7 operating system, Professional edition or higher

▲ An account with administrator privileges

> **Notes** This lab works great in a Windows 8 or Windows 7 virtual machine.

LAB PREPARATION

Before the lab begins, the instructor or lab assistant needs to do the following:

▲ Verify Windows starts with no errors

▲ Verify each student has access to a user account with administrator privileges

ACTIVITY BACKGROUND

The Microsoft Management Console (MMC) is a standard management tool you can use to create a customized console by adding administrative tools called snap-ins. You can use snap-ins provided by Microsoft as well as those from other vendors. Many of the administrative tools you have already used (such as Device Manager) can be added to a console as a snap-in. The console itself serves as a convenient interface that helps you organize and manage the administrative tools you use most often. In this lab, you use the MMC to create a customized console.

> **ESTIMATED COMPLETION TIME: 30 MINUTES**

 Activity

Follow these steps to build a customized console:

1. Log on to Windows as an administrator.

2. In the Run box, type **mmc**, and then press **Enter**. If Windows needs your permission to continue, click **Yes**. An MMC window for Console1 opens. The left pane displays the list of snap-ins in the console. Currently, nothing appears in this list because no snap-ins have been added to Console1 yet.

3. On the Console1 menu bar, click **File**, and then click **Add/Remove Snap-in**. The Add or Remove Snap-ins dialog box opens. Available snap-ins are listed on the left side of this dialog box (see Figure 4-1). Note that this list includes some administrative tools you have already used, such as Device Manager and Event Viewer. To add Device Manager as a snap-in, click **Device Manager**, and then click **Add**.

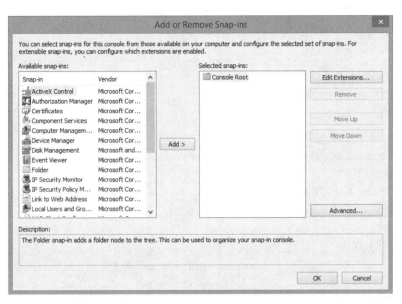

Figure 4-1 Adding snap-ins to the Microsoft Management Console

4. The Device Manager dialog box opens, and you can specify here which computer you want this Device Manager snap-in to manage. You want it to manage the computer you're currently working on, so verify the **Local computer** button is selected, and then click **Finish**.

5. Next, you add Event Viewer as a snap-in. Click **Event Viewer** in the Available snap-ins list, and then click **Add**. The Select Computer dialog box opens.

6. Verify the **Local computer** button is selected, and then click **OK**.

7. Click **OK** to close the Add or Remove Snap-ins dialog box. The two new snap-ins are listed in the left and middle panes of the Console1 window.

You have finished adding snap-ins for the local computer to your console. Next, you add another Event Viewer snap-in to be used on a network computer. If your computer isn't connected to a network, you can read the following set of steps, but you won't be able to perform them because Windows won't be able to find any networked computers. If your computer is connected to a network, follow these steps:

1. Add another Event Viewer snap-in, and then click the **Another computer** button in the Select Computer dialog box. Now you need to specify the name of the computer to which you want this Event Viewer snap-in to apply. You could type the name of the computer, but it's easier to select the computer by using the Browse button.

2. Click the **Browse** button. A different Select Computer dialog box opens. Click **Advanced** to open a third Select Computer dialog box. Click **Find Now** to begin searching the network for eligible computers. Eventually, a list of eligible computers is displayed.

3. Click the name of the computer to which you want to apply this Event Viewer snap-in, and then click **OK**. The third Select Computer dialog box closes, and you return to the second Select Computer dialog box.

4. Click **OK** twice to close the two remaining Select Computer dialog boxes. Close the Add or Remove Snap-ins box. A second Event Viewer snap-in is added below the first. The new Event Viewer listing is followed by the name of the remote computer in parentheses. Note: If the second Event Viewer snap-in does not show up and you get an error message

instead, write the error message here and continue with the rest of the lab. The remote computer might not be configured to allow event logging on the network.

_____

_____

You're finished adding snap-ins and are ready to save your new, customized console so you can use it whenever you need it. Follow these steps:

1. Verify the left pane of the Console Root folder now contains the following items: Device Manager on local computer, Event Viewer (Local), and, if you were able to complete the network portion, Event Viewer (*remote computer name*).

2. On the Console1 window menu bar, click **File**, and then click **Save As**. The Save As dialog box opens. Unless the location was previously changed, the default location is set to the Administrative Tools folder in your user profile. In Windows 7, if you save your customized console in this location, Administrative Tools is added to your Start menu. Instead, in Windows 8, choose **Desktop** for the Save in location, and in Windows 7, in the Save in drop-down list, choose the **Start Menu** folder in your user profile. This folder is two levels up from the default Administrative Tools folder.

3. Name the console **Custom.msc**, and then click **Save**. The Save As dialog box closes. What is the exact path and file name to the console?

_____

4. Close the Console window.

Follow these steps to open and use your customized console:

1. In Windows 8, open the Custom console from the Desktop. In Windows 7, click **Start**, point to **All Programs**, and then click **Custom**. If the UAC dialog box opens, click **Yes**. Your customized console opens in a window named Custom - [Console Root].

2. Maximize the console window, if necessary.

3. In the left pane, click **Device Manager on local computer**, and observe the options in the middle pane.

4. In the left pane, click the arrow next to Event Viewer (Local). Subcategories are displayed below Event Viewer (Local). List the subcategories you see:

_____

_____

_____

5. Click **Event Viewer** (*remote computer name*), and observe that the events displayed are events occurring on the remote computer.

6. On the Custom - [Console Root] menu bar, click **File**, and then click **Exit**. A message box opens, asking if you want to save the current settings.

7. Click **Yes**. The console closes.

8. Launch the customized console again, and record the items listed in the middle pane when the console opens:

_____

REVIEW QUESTIONS

1. What term is used to refer to the specialized tools you can add to a console with the MMC? What are they used for?

   _____

   _____

2. Suppose you haven't created a customized MMC yet. How would you start the MMC?

   _____

   _____

3. How can a customized console be used to manage many computers from a single machine?

   _____

   _____

4. Why might you want the ability to manage a remote computer through a network?

   _____

   _____

5. In Windows 7, in what folder do you put a console so that it appears in the Start menu when you log on to your user account?

   _____

6. In Windows 7, in what folder do you put a console so that it appears in the Start menu for all users?

   _____

LAB 4.2 ANALYZE A SYSTEM WITH EVENT VIEWER

OBJECTIVES

The goal of this lab is to learn to work with Windows Event Viewer. After completing this lab, you will be able to use Event Viewer to:

- View Windows events
- Save events
- View event logs
- Compare recent events with logged events

MATERIALS REQUIRED

This lab requires the following:

- Windows 8 or Windows 7 operating system
- Network access
- An account with administrator privileges

LAB PREPARATION

Before the lab begins, the instructor or lab assistant needs to do the following:

◢ Verify Windows starts with no errors

◢ Verify each student has access to a user account with administrator privileges

ACTIVITY BACKGROUND

Most of what your computer does while running Windows 8 or Windows 7 is recorded in a log. In this lab, you will take another look at the Event Viewer tool, which provides information on various operations and tasks (known as events) in Windows. Event Viewer notes the occurrence of various events, lists them chronologically, and gives you the option of saving the list so you can view it later or compare it with a future list. You can use Event Viewer to find out how healthy your system is and to diagnose nonfatal startup problems that still allow Windows to start. (Fatal startup problems that prevent a successful startup don't allow you into Windows far enough to use Event Viewer.)

ESTIMATED COMPLETION TIME: 30 MINUTES

 Activity

Follow these steps to begin using Event Viewer:

1. Log on as an administrator.

2. Open the Control Panel window.

3. Click **Administrative Tools**. The Administrative Tools window opens.

4. Double-click **Event Viewer** to open the Event Viewer window. The console tree is shown in the left pane, with Event Viewer (Local) listed at the top. If necessary, click **Event Viewer (Local)** to select it. The Overview and Summary section is in the center pane, with available Actions in the right pane (see Figure 4-2). Maximize the Event Viewer window to see more information in the middle pane.

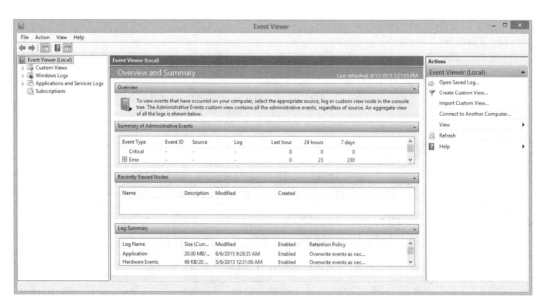

Figure 4-2 Event Viewer tracks failed and successful events

5. You can drag the lines separating the panes to widen or narrow each pane. Widen the center pane because it contains the most useful information.

6. In the console tree, expand **Windows Logs**, and then click **System** in the Windows Logs group. The System log appears in the center pane. In the center pane, if necessary, you can drag the bar between the boxes down so you can see more of the list of events in the top box. The symbols to the left of each event indicate important information about the event. For example, a lowercase "i" in a white circle indicates an event providing information about the system, and an exclamation mark in a yellow triangle indicates a warning event, such as a disk being near its capacity. An exclamation mark in a red circle is an error, and an X in a red circle is a critical event. Each event entry includes the time and date it occurred. Click on several events to see what information changes in various parts of the Event Viewer window when selecting different events.

For each of the four most recent events, list the source (what triggered the event), the time, and the date:

_____

_____

_____

_____

7. Double-click the top (most recent) event. The Event Properties dialog box opens. What additional information does this dialog box provide?

_____

_____

_____

8. Close the Event Properties dialog box.

Because Event Viewer provides so much information, it can be difficult to find what you need; however, events can be sorted by clicking the column headings. Do the following to find the most important events:

1. To sort by Level, click **Level**. Events are listed in the following order: Critical, Error, Warning, and Information.

2. To sort events by Date and Time, click **Date and Time**.

3. To see a list of only Critical, Error, and Warning events, expand **Custom Views** in the console tree, and then select **Administrative Events**. How many Critical, Error, and Warning events are recorded on your system?

_____

You can save the list of events shown in Event Viewer to a log file. When naming a log file, it's helpful to use the following format: *Typelog*EV*mm-dd-yy*.evtx (*mm* = month, *dd* = day, and *yy* = year). For example, you would name a log file of System events saved on January 27, 2016 as SystemEV01-27-16.evtx. After you create a log file, you can delete the current list of events from Event Viewer, allowing the utility to begin creating an entirely new list of events. A short log and resulting log file is easier to view and easier to send to other support technicians when you need help.

Follow these steps to save the currently displayed events as a log file, and then clear the current events:

1. Open File Explorer/Windows Explorer, and create a folder called **Logs** in the root directory of drive C:.

2. Leaving File Explorer/Windows Explorer open, return to Event Viewer, and then click **System** in the console tree in the left pane. The System log is selected but no particular event is selected. How many events are there in this log?

_____

3. To save the System log to a log file, on the menu bar, click **Action**, and then click **Save All Events As**.

4. Navigate to the **Logs** folder created in Step 1. Name the file **SystemEV***mm-dd-yy* (remember to replace the italicized portion with today's date), click **Save**, and then click **OK**. What is the name of your log file, including the file extension?

_____

5. Now you're ready to clear the current list of events from Event Viewer. With the System log still selected, click **Action**, and then click **Clear Log**.

6. When asked if you want to save the System log, click **Clear**. The Event Viewer window now displays only one event. What is this event?

_____

7. Close Event Viewer.

It can be useful to save a log that shows the events of a successful, clean boot, so you can use it as a reference when you have a problem with a boot. You can compare the two logs to help you identify a problem. To save a log of a boot, follow these steps:

1. With your System events log recently cleared, reboot your computer.

2. Return to Event Viewer. How many events are now recorded in your System log?

_____

3. Does this list of events include any Warning or Error events? If so, describe these events here:

_____

4. Save a new file of System events to your Logs folder, and name the file **SystemBootEV***mm-dd-yy*. What is the name of the log file, including the file extension?

_____

5. Now, with the System log still selected, clear the System log.

6. Close Event Viewer.

Next, you create an intentional problem by disconnecting the network cable from your computer. Then, you observe how the resulting errors are recorded in Event Viewer. Do the following:

1. Carefully disconnect the network cable from the network port on the back of your computer.

2. Open Internet Explorer, and try to surf the web.

3. Close Internet Explorer, and then open Event Viewer. How many new events are displayed?

_____

4. List the source, date, and time for any Error or Warning events you see:

_____

5. Click each error or warning event, and read the details. How does Event Viewer describe what happened when you unplugged the network cable?

_____

To restore the network connection and verify the connection is working, follow these steps:

1. Reconnect the network cable to the network port on the back of your computer. Open Internet Explorer. Can you surf the web?

_____

2. In the center pane of the Event Viewer window, the System log reports that new events are available. To see these events, on the menu bar, click **Action**, and then click **Refresh**. How many events are now listed?

_____

When troubleshooting a system, comparing current events with a list of events you previously stored in a log file is often helpful because you can spot the time when a particular problem occurred. Follow these steps to compare the current list of events with the log you saved earlier:

1. Use Windows Explorer to locate the System log files in the C:\Logs folder you created earlier in this lab. Double-click one of these log files. A second instance of Event Viewer opens displaying this log file. Notice in this new window the saved log file is listed in the console tree under Saved Logs.

◢ List all the saved logs that are displayed:

_____

◢ What happens when you click on a saved log?

_____

2. To compare two logs, you can position the two Event Viewer windows side by side. Snap one Event Viewer window to the right of your screen by dragging the window to the right edge of the screen, and then snap the other Event Viewer window to the left of your screen.

3. Widen or narrow the panes in each window so you can see the events listed in each window. In a troubleshooting situation, you would look for differences in the two logs to help you find the source of a problem.

4. Close both Event Viewer windows.

REVIEW QUESTIONS

1. Judging by its location in Control Panel, what type of tool is Event Viewer?

_____

2. What is the file extension that Event Viewer assigns to its log files?

_____

3. How can you examine events after you have cleared them from Event Viewer?

_____

_____

4. Explain how to compare a log file with the current set of listed events:

_____

_____

5. Why might you like to keep a log file of events that occurred when your computer started correctly? List the steps to create a log of a successful startup:

_____

_____

_____

_____

_____

LAB 4.3 USE TASK MANAGER

OBJECTIVES

The goal of this lab is to use Task Manager to examine your system. After completing this lab, you will be able to:

◢ Identify applications that are currently running

◢ Launch an application

◢ Display general system performance and process information in Task Manager

MATERIALS REQUIRED

This lab requires the following:

◢ Windows 8 or Windows 7 operating system, Professional edition or higher

◢ Installed CD/DVD drive, installed/onboard sound card, and an audio CD

◢ An account with administrator privileges

LAB PREPARATION

Before the lab begins, the instructor or lab assistant needs to do the following:

◢ Verify Windows starts with no errors

◢ Verify a CD drive and sound card have been installed on all student computers

◢ Verify each student has access to a user account with administrator privileges

ACTIVITY BACKGROUND

Task Manager is a useful tool that allows you to switch between tasks, end tasks, and observe system use and performance. In this lab, you use Task Manager to manage applications and observe system performance.

ESTIMATED COMPLETION TIME: 30 MINUTES

 Activity

Follow these steps to use Task Manager:

1. Log on to Windows as an administrator.

2. Press **Ctrl+Alt+Del**, and then click **Task Manager** in Windows 8 or **Start Task Manager** in Windows 7. Alternatively, you can right-click any blank area on the taskbar, and then click **Task Manager** in Windows 8 or **Start Task Manager** in Windows 7 in the shortcut menu. The Task Manager window opens, with tabs you can use to find information about applications, processes, and programs running on the computer and information on system performance.

3. If necessary, click the **Processes** tab in Windows 8 or the **Applications** tab in Windows 7. What groups of processes or applications are currently listed in the Task list box?

_____

_____

_____

4. Open Windows Help and Support, and then observe the change to the list of processes or applications. What change occurred in the list?

_____

_____

5. In Windows 8, click **File** on the menu bar, and then click **Run new task**. In Windows 7, click the **New Task** button in the lower-right corner of the window. The Create new task dialog box opens, showing the last command entered.

6. Replace whatever command is in the Open text box with **cmd**, and then lick **OK**. A command prompt window opens. Examine the applications listed in Task Manager, and note that C:\Windows\system32\cmd.exe now appears in the list. In Windows 8, expand the Windows Command Processor to view the process listed.

7. Click the title bar of the command prompt window, and drag the command prompt window so it overlaps the Task Manager window. The command prompt window is the active window and appears on top of Task Manager.

You can customize Task Manager to suit your preferences. Among other things, you can change the setting that determines whether Task Manager is displayed on top of all other open windows, and you can change the way information is displayed. To learn more about changing Task Manager settings, make sure the command prompt window is still open and is on top of the Task Manager window. Follow these steps:

1. In Task Manager, click **Options** on the menu bar. A menu with a list of options opens. Note that the check marks indicate which options are currently applied. Check **Always On Top**, which keeps the Task Manager window on top of all other open windows. List other options in the Options menu here:

_____

_____

_____

2. Click the command prompt window in the taskbar. What happens?

_____

_____

_____

3. On the Task Manager menu bar, click **View**. You can use the options on the Update Speed submenu to change how quickly the information is updated. List the available and current settings:

_____

_____

_____

Follow these steps in Task Manager to end a task and observe system use information:

1. Notice the information listed in columns in Windows 8, and in the bar at the bottom of Task Manager in Windows 7. What information do you see, and what are their values?

_____

_____

_____

2. While observing these values, move your mouse around the screen for several seconds and then stop. Did any of the values change?

_____

3. Next, move your mouse to drag an open window around the screen for several seconds, and then stop. How did this affect the values?

_____

4. End the Help and Support process using Task Manager. *Caution*: Be careful about ending processes; ending a potentially essential process (which is one that other processes depend on) could have serious consequences. Because Help and Support is not critical to core Windows functions, it's safe to end this process. In the list of applications, click **Microsoft Help and Support** or **Windows Help and Support**, and then click the **End Task** button.

5. Compare the current number of processes, CPU usage, and commit charge (memory usage) with the information recorded in Step 1. How much memory was Windows Help and Support using?

_____

Follow these steps in Task Manager to observe performance information:

1. Click the **Performance** tab, which displays CPU usage and memory usage in bar graphs. What other categories of information are displayed on the Performance tab?

_____

_____

2. Insert and play an audio CD. Observe the CPU and page file or memory usage values, and record them here:

_____

_____

3. Stop the CD from playing, and again observe the CPU usage and page file or memory usage. Compare these values with the values from Step 2. Which value changed the most?

_____

4. When you're finished, close all open windows.

REVIEW QUESTIONS

1. Record the steps for one way to launch Task Manager:

_____

2. Which Task Manager tab do you use to switch between applications and end a task?

_____

3. Why could it be dangerous to end a process with Task Manager?

_____

_____

4. How can you tell whether the processor had recently completed a period of intensive use but is now idle?

_____

5. Did the playback of an audio CD use more system resources than moving the mouse? Explain:

_____

_____

LAB 4.4 EDIT THE REGISTRY WITH REGEDIT

OBJECTIVES

The goal of this lab is to learn how to save, modify, and restore the Windows registry. After completing this lab, you will be able to:

◢ Back up and modify the registry

◢ Observe the effects of a modified registry

◢ Restore the registry

MATERIALS REQUIRED

This lab requires the following:

◢ Windows 8 or Windows 7 operating system

Notes This lab works great in a Windows 8 or Windows 7 virtual machine.

LAB PREPARATION

Before the lab begins, the instructor or lab assistant needs to do the following:

◢ Verify Windows starts with no errors

ACTIVITY BACKGROUND

The registry is a database of configuration information stored in files called hives. Each time Windows boots, it rebuilds the registry from the configuration files and stores it in RAM. When you need to modify the behavior of Windows, you should consider editing the registry only as a last resort. Errors in the registry can make your system inoperable, and there's no way for Windows to inform you that you have made a mistake. For this reason, many people are hesitant to edit the registry. If you follow the rule of backing up the system before you make any change, however, you can feel confident that even if you make a mistake, you can restore the system to its original condition. In this lab, you back up, change, and restore the registry.

ESTIMATED COMPLETION TIME: 45 MINUTES

 Activity

Windows allows you to create a restore point so that you can restore Windows to a time before any changes were made. Follow these directions to back up the system (including the registry):

1. In Control Panel, open the System window. In the System window, click **System protection**. The System Properties dialog box opens.

2. Select drive **C**.

3. Click **Create,** and then type a name for your restore point. The current time and date will be added automatically. Click **Create** again to create the restore point.

4. When the restore point is completed, close all open windows and dialog boxes.

5. Open the System Properties dialog box again, and then click **System Restore** on the System Protection tab. In the System Restore Wizard, click **Next,** and check the **Show more restore points** check box. Make sure the name and description of the backup you just created are listed by checking the date and time the file was created. Record the name, date, and time of this file:

_____

6. Click **Cancel** to close the System Restore Wizard, and then click **Cancel** again to exit from System Properties.

7. Close any open windows.

As you know, you can use Windows tools such as Control Panel to modify many Windows settings, ranging from the color of the background to power-saving features. Control Panel provides a safe, user-friendly graphical interface that modifies the registry in the background. Sometimes, however, the only way to edit the registry is to do it yourself. These modifications are sometimes referred to as registry tweaks or hacks. In these steps, you will make a relatively small change to the registry by editing the name of the Recycle Bin. To open the registry using the registry editor, do the following:

1. In the Run box, type **regedit,** and then press **Enter.**

2. If Windows presents a UAC dialog box, click **Yes.** The Registry Editor opens, displaying the system's registry hierarchy in the left pane along with any entries for the selected registry item in the right pane.

The registry is large, and searching through it requires a little bit of practice. The section of the registry that governs the naming of the Recycle Bin is HKEY_CURRENT_USER\Software\Microsoft\Windows\ CurrentVersion\Explorer\CLSID\{645FF040-5081-101B-9F08-00AA002F954E}. See Figure 4-3.

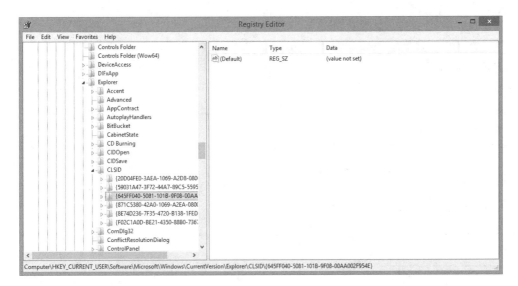

Figure 4-3 The status bar at the bottom of the Registry Editor window shows the currently selected key

To navigate to this section and rename the Recycle Bin, follow these steps:

1. Click the arrow on the left side of the **HKEY_CURRENT_USER** hive.

2. Click the arrows next to **Software**, and then **Microsoft**. Scroll down the list, and then click the arrows next to **Windows, CurrentVersion, Explorer**, and, finally, **CLSID**.

3. Click **{645FF040-5081-101B-9F08-00AA002F954E}** to select it.

4. In the right pane, double-click **Default**, and the Edit String dialog box displays.

5. To rename the Recycle Bin as Trash Bin, in the Value data box, type **Trash Bin,** and then click **OK**.

6. Notice that Trash Bin now displays under the Data column.

7. To close the Registry Editor, on the menu bar, click **File**, and then click **Exit**. You weren't prompted to save your changes to the registry because they were saved the instant you made them. This is why editing the registry is so unforgiving: There are no safeguards. You can't undo your work by choosing to exit without saving changes, as you can, for instance, in Microsoft Word.

8. Right-click the desktop, and click **Refresh** in the shortcut menu. Note that the Recycle Bin icon is now named Trash Bin.

Finally, you need to undo your changes to the Recycle Bin. Follow these steps to use System Restore to restore the registry's previous version:

1. Open the System Properties dialog box again, and then click **System Restore** on the System Protection tab. In the System Restore Wizard, click **Next**. Check the **Show more restore points** check box.

2. Choose the restore point you created earlier, and then click **Next**.

3. When you're asked to confirm your restore point, click **Finish**. Click **Yes** when the system warns you that a system restore cannot be undone.

4. After the system restore, the computer will have to reboot.

5. After the boot is completed, notice that the name of the Recycle Bin has been restored.

Use Windows Help and Support or the Internet to answer the following questions about the registry:

◢ How often does Windows save the registry automatically?

_____

◢ Where are registry backups usually stored?

_____

◢ What files constitute the Windows 8/7 registry? What type of file are they saved as during backup?

_____

_____

REVIEW QUESTIONS

1. Why does Windows automatically save the registry?

_____

_____

2. Where is the registry stored while Windows is running?

_____

3. What type of safeguards does the Registry Editor have to keep you from making mistakes?

_____

4. What are the files that make up a system registry called?

_____

5. In this lab, how did you check to make sure your registry was restored?

_____

LAB 4.5 IDENTIFY A HARD DRIVE BOTTLENECK BY USING PERFORMANCE TOOLS

OBJECTIVES

The goal of this lab is to learn to use the performance monitoring tools in Windows to identify bottlenecks in the system caused by the hard drive or the applications using it. After completing this lab, you will be able to:

◢ Use the Windows 7 Experience Index

◢ Use the Windows Performance Monitor

◢ Identify a hard drive performance bottleneck

MATERIALS REQUIRED

This lab requires the following:

⊿ Windows 7 operating system

⊿ Internet access

⊿ An account with administrator privileges

LAB PREPARATION

Before the lab begins, the instructor or lab assistant needs to do the following:

⊿ Verify Windows starts with no errors

⊿ Verify Internet access is available

⊿ Verify each student has access to a user account with administrator privileges

ACTIVITY BACKGROUND

A problem with slow Windows performance can be caused by hardware or software. Key hardware components that can cause a bottleneck include the processor, memory, and the hard drive. Several factors can affect hard drive performance: the speed of the drive, the amount of free space on the drive, file fragmentation on the drive, hard drive thrashing, and applications that make excessive demands on the drive. In this lab, you determine if the hard drive is a bottleneck to your system by examining all these factors.

Performance Monitor offers hundreds of counters used to examine various aspects of the system related to performance. Two hard drive counters you will use in this lab are the % Disk Time counter and the Avg. Disk Queue Length counter. The % Disk Time counter represents the percentage of time the hard drive is in use. The Avg. Disk Queue Length counter represents the average number of processes waiting to use the hard drive. If the Avg. Disk Queue Length is above two and the % Disk Time is more than 80%, you can conclude that the hard drive is working excessively hard and processes are slowed down waiting on the drive. Anytime a process must wait to access the hard drive, you are likely to see degradation in overall system performance.

ESTIMATED COMPLETION TIME: 45 MINUTES

 Activity

The Windows Experience Index can give you a quick overview of any bottleneck that might be affecting system performance. To view the Windows Experience Index, follow these steps:

1. Log on to the Windows 7 system using a user account with administrative privileges.

2. In the taskbar, click the **Action Center flag**. In the small box that opens, click **Open Action Center**.

3. In the left pane of the Action Center, click **View performance information**. Answer these questions:

⊿ What is the Base score of the Windows Experience Index?

_____

⊿ What component yielded this base score?

_____

4. Click **View and print detailed performance and system information**. A second Performance Information and Tools window opens. Answer these questions:

◢ What is the total amount of system memory?

_____

◢ What is the number of processor cores?

_____

◢ Will this processor support 64-bit computing?

_____

◢ Is the currently installed operating system a 32-bit or 64-bit system?

_____

◢ What is the total size of the hard drive?

_____

◢ What is the amount of free space on the hard drive?

_____

◢ What is the total available graphics memory? Dedicated graphics memory?

_____

◢ Based on the information you have just recorded, what one recommendation do you have to improve system performance?

_____

5. Close the Performance Information and Tools window that was opened in Step 4.

Performance Monitor, which can be configured to measure how well the hard drive is performing, works by displaying counters related to hardware and software components. Follow these steps to use the Performance Monitor to display two counters related to the hard drive:

1. In the left pane of the Performance Information and Tools window, click **Advanced tools**. On the Advanced Tools window, click **Open Performance Monitor**. The Performance Monitor window opens. (Note that you can also open the window by typing *perfmon.exe* in the Search programs and files box.)

> **Notes** Performance Monitor is also available in Windows 8.

2. If necessary, click the triangle to the left of Monitoring Tools to expand this category. Under Monitoring Tools, click **Performance Monitor**.

3. By default, current activity of the processor information object displays in a line graph and the line is red (see Figure 4-4). The list of counters currently selected for display appears at the bottom of the window. In the figure, the one counter selected is % Processor Time. You need to delete any counters you do not need so that you will not unnecessarily use system resources to monitor these counters. To delete the % Processor Time counter, click somewhere in the row to select it. Next, click the **red X** above the graph to delete the counter from the graph. The graph is now empty.

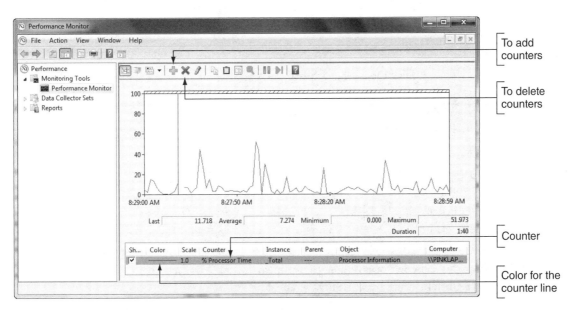

Figure 4-4 Performance Monitor displays current activity of the processor information object

4. To add a new object and counter to the graph, click the **green plus sign** above the graph. The Add Counters box opens.

5. To add a counter for hard drive activity, under *Available counters*, scroll to and click the down arrow to the right of the **PhysicalDisk** object. The counters under the PhysicalDisk object appear, and all these counters are selected. In the list of counters, click **% Disk Time**. This action causes all the other counters to be deselected and this one counter to be selected. Click **Add**. The % Disk Time counter appears in the Added counters area.

6. In the list of counters, click **Avg. Disk Queue Length,** and then click **Add**. The Avg. Disk Queue Length counter appears in the Added counters area. To close the box, click **OK**.

7. The two hard drive counters now appear in the Performance Monitor line graph. Answer these questions:

   ◢ What is the color of the line for the % Disk Time counter?

   _____

   ◢ What is the color of the line for the Avg. Disk Queue Length counter?

   _____

8. Keep the Performance Monitor window open as you perform other activities on your computer. In a real-life situation, you would open the applications a user normally uses and work as the user would normally work to attempt to produce a typical working environment needed to monitor performance. In this lab, try playing a game or surfing the web, keeping both the game and the browser open at the same time. As you work, watch the Performance Monitor window as it shows peaks in both counters.

9. Reading the counters by watching peaks is not as accurate as reading the actual data. To read actual values of the counters, mouse over the line and read the counter value that appears in a bubble window.

10. Performance Monitor also records the average, minimum, and maximum counter values under the graph. In the list of counters at the bottom of the Performance Monitor window, select the **% Disk Time** counter and answer these questions:

◢ What is the maximum value for the % Disk Time counter?

_____

◢ Select the **Avg. Disk Queue Length** counter. What is the maximum value for this counter?

_____

11. Close the Performance Monitor window and the Advanced Tools window.

Follow these steps to use Task Manager to identify a process that might be hogging hard drive resources:

1. To open Task Manager, right-click the **taskbar**, and then select **Start Task Manager** in the shortcut menu. The Windows Task Manager window opens.

2. Click the **Processes** tab. Task Manager does not normally monitor disk usage, but you can configure it to do so. Click **View** on the menu bar, and then click **Select Columns**. The Select Process Page Columns dialog box opens.

3. Scroll through the list of columns that appear on the Task Manager Processes tab. Deselect all items that are currently selected.

4. In the list, select three items: **I/O Read Bytes**, **I/O Write Bytes**, and **Description**. Click **OK** to close the dialog box.

5. Any process listed in Task Manager that shows either the I/O Read Bytes column or the I/O Write Bytes column constantly changing indicates this process is hogging hard drive resources. Search the Task Manager processes for constantly changing values and answer these questions:

◢ List the processes that show constantly changing values, and include in your list the description of the process:

_____

_____

_____

_____

◢ Of the processes you listed, which processes belong to Windows?

_____

◢ Of the processes you listed, which processes do not belong to Windows?

_____

_____

6. Close the Windows Task Manager window.

If processes that belong to Windows are constantly changing, most likely the problem is caused by hard drive thrashing. Hard drive thrashing happens when the system is short on memory and must, therefore, constantly swap data from memory to the page file and back to memory. This situation can best be corrected by installing more memory.

If a particular process that belongs to an application is hogging resources, consider upgrading or replacing the application with a more efficient version or product.

If you suspect the hard drive is a performance bottleneck, you should investigate whether the drive has enough free space and whether files on the drive are fragmented. Follow these steps to check these two possibilities:

1. A hard drive needs a minimum of 15% free space on the drive. Looking back at the hard drive information you gathered earlier in this lab, answer these questions:

   ◢ What is the total size of the hard drive?

   _____

   ◢ What is the free space on the hard drive?

   _____

   ◢ What is the percentage of free space on the hard drive?

   _____

2. Examine the hard drive and answer these questions:

   ◢ How much space can be cleared up on the drive by performing a complete disk cleanup?

   _____

   ◢ Describe how you found your answer:

   _____

   _____

3. Fragmented files can also slow down hard drive performance. If the default setting has not been changed, Windows 7 automatically defrags the hard drive weekly. Answer these questions:

   ◢ Is Windows 7 configured to defragment the drive weekly?

   _____

   ◢ What day of the week and time of day is defragmentation scheduled?

   _____

   ◢ Describe how you found your answers:

   _____

   _____

After eliminating processes hogging hard drive resources and determining that you have adequate free space on the hard drive, if you still suspect the hard drive is a performance bottleneck, you might consider upgrading the hard drive to a faster or larger drive. Follow these steps to determine the speed of your drive:

1. Open **Device Manager**. In the Device Manager window, expand the **Disk drives** category. Answer this question:

   ◢ What is the brand and model of your hard drive?

   _____

2. Open your browser and go to **google.com**. In the Google search box, enter the brand and model number of your drive exactly as it appears in the Device Manager window.

Click links to find the website of the hard drive manufacturer or other sites where you can find specifications for your drive. Answer these questions:

◢ Is the drive a solid-state drive or a magnetic drive?

_____

◢ If the drive is a magnetic drive, what is the RPM rating for the drive?

_____

◢ Standard RPM ratings for a hard drive for personal computers are 5400, 7200, and 10,000 RPM. Do you consider your drive a slow, moderate, or fast drive?

_____

3. Close all open windows.

Challenge Activity (Additional 15 Minutes)

The Windows Experience Index is often thought to have disappeared with Windows 8; however, it is still there, you just have to know how to find it. To access the Windows Experience Index scores in Windows 8, complete the following steps:

1. Open a command prompt with administrator privileges. Enter **winsat prepop** and then press **Enter**. This command runs a benchmark utility and stores the results in an XML file.

2. Next, open Windows PowerShell, enter **Get-WmiObject -Class Win32_WinSAT** and then press **Enter**. This command analyzes the results of the benchmark utility and then displays the results as scores, similar to the Windows Experience Index seen in Windows 7.

◢ After performing these steps on a Windows 8 system, what is the system's base score?

_____

◢ What are the scores for each category?

◢ Processor score: _____

◢ 3D graphics capabilities score: _____

◢ Hard disk score: _____

◢ Graphics score: _____

◢ Memory score: _____

REVIEW QUESTIONS

1. If you determine that the hard drive is experiencing excessive use, but the Windows Experience Index says that memory is the system bottleneck, which component do you upgrade first, memory or the hard drive? Why?

_____

_____

_____

_____

2. What values for the % Disk Time and Avg. Disk Queue Length counters of Performance Monitor collectively indicate the hard drive is a performance bottleneck?

_____

_____

3. Based on the maximum values for both hard drive counters you measured using Performance Monitor in this lab and the criteria for the two counters given in the Activity Background section of this lab, is the hard drive a performance bottleneck in your system? Why or why not?

_____

_____

_____

4. What can you conclude if a Windows process is constantly reading and writing to the hard drive?

_____

_____

5. How much free space does a hard drive need to prevent a performance slowdown?

_____

_____

LAB 4.6 USE THE SYSTEM CONFIGURATION UTILITY

OBJECTIVES

The goal of this lab is to learn to diagnose problems using the System Configuration utility. After completing this lab, you will be able to:

◢ Use options in System Configuration that can later help you troubleshoot Windows startup problems

◢ Explore the startup functions of Windows

MATERIALS REQUIRED

This lab requires the following:

◢ Windows 8 or Windows 7 operating system

◢ For Windows 7, two or more applications installed that appear in the Start, All Programs menu (for example, Adobe Reader, Microsoft Security Essentials, or other freeware)

◢ An account with administrator privileges

LAB PREPARATION

Before the lab begins, the instructor or lab assistant needs to do the following:

◢ Verify Windows starts with no errors

◢ For Windows 7, verify two or more applications are installed that appear in the Start, All Programs menu

◢ Verify each student has access to a user account with administrator privileges

ACTIVITY BACKGROUND

Windows offers many wizards and utilities that technicians use to troubleshoot a malfunctioning computer. One of these utilities, the System Configuration utility (also called Msconfig), is used to troubleshoot Windows startup problems. This utility allows you to make changes to boot files and startup parameters, which can help you determine which boot file, startup parameter, or startup program is causing a problem.

In this lab, you work with the features included in System Configuration to learn how to detect problems that might occur when a Windows service, application service, or application fails to load at Windows startup.

ESTIMATED COMPLETION TIME: 30 MINUTES

 Activity

Follow these steps to learn about two methods to start the System Configuration utility:

1. Log on to Windows using an administrator account. An administrator account is required to use all the features of System Configuration.

2. To launch System Configuration, in the Run box type **msconfig.exe** and then press **Enter**. The System Configuration dialog box opens (see Figure 4-5).

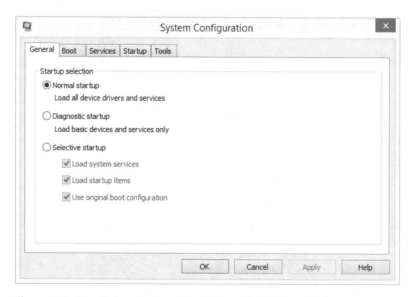

Figure 4-5 The System Configuration utility with the General tab open

3. A technician needs to know more than one method to reach utilities and tools in an operating system. To see an alternate way to open the System Configuration utility, close the System Configuration dialog box, and then open **Control Panel**.

4. In Control Panel, click **Administrative Tools**, and then double-click **System Configuration**. The System Configuration dialog box opens. Answer the following questions:

◢ Of the three startup selections listed on the General tab, which one loads all device drivers and services set to load when Windows starts?

◢ Which startup selection loads only basic devices and services?

◢ Which startup selection allows you to load only system services and no startup applications?

◢ Which startup selection is currently selected?

4

Diagnostic startup allows you to start the computer with only the most basic devices and services that are needed for the computer to run. This clean environment can help with Windows troubleshooting. Do the following to find out more:

1. To perform a diagnostic startup, click **Diagnostic startup** on the General tab, and then click **Apply**. The wait icon appears while Windows processes this change. If it encounters a problem, it rejects Diagnostic startup and reverts to Selective startup. Which startup selections are chosen when the wait icon disappears?

---

2. If Diagnostic startup is not still selected, select **Diagnostic startup**. Click **OK** to close the System Configuration dialog box. A new System Configuration dialog box appears saying that your computer must be restarted to apply this change. Click **Restart**.

3. As Windows restarts, log back on to Windows as an administrator, and watch carefully for error messages.

    ◢ Record any problems or error messages you see during the restart:

    ◢ What changes do you notice to your Windows desktop, video, and taskbar?

    ◢ If the system gives an error message using this bare-bones startup method, how might that be helpful when troubleshooting the system?

    ---

4. Open the System Configuration utility. Record any differences you noted when starting the utility compared with how it started earlier in the lab:

Now let's explore the Selective startup option, which can be used to limit Windows startup only to services, but not other programs. Doing so can help you eliminate startup programs that are not services from the types of programs that might be causing a Windows startup problem. Follow these steps to find out more:

1. Click **Selective startup**. Check the **Load system services** check box. Uncheck **Load startup items**. Click **OK**. In the new dialog box that appears, click **Restart**.

2. Windows restarts. Log back on to the system as an administrator. Record any problems or error messages you see during the restart, and record any differences in the video, desktop, and taskbar compared with a normal startup:

_____

_____

3. Open the System Configuration utility again. Record any differences you noted when starting the utility compared with how it started at the beginning of this lab:

_____

Now let's explore the Services tab of System Configuration. The Services tab can help you troubleshoot problems related to system and application services that load at startup. Follow these steps:

1. To reset startup settings, on the General tab, click **Normal startup**.

2. Click the **Services** tab. On this tab, check the **Hide all Microsoft services** check box. List the non-Microsoft services installed on this machine and the status of each:

_____

_____

_____

_____

_____

3. To disable all the non-Microsoft services, click **Disable all**. To restart the system using this setting, click **OK**. In the next dialog box, click **Restart**.

4. Windows restarts. Log on again as an administrator. What do you notice about the system that is different from a normal startup?

_____

In a real troubleshooting situation, you would not need to disable all Microsoft services except in the most extreme situations. In many cases, you might choose to disable all non-Microsoft services and only disable a particular system service that you suspect is causing a problem. To practice disabling system services, follow these steps to disable all non-Microsoft and system services:

1. Open the System Configuration utility again. Go to the **Services** tab, and uncheck the **Hide all Microsoft services** check box. Click **Disable all**, and then click **OK**. In the dialog box that appears, click **Restart**.

2. Windows restarts. Log on as administrator. Carefully watch what happens as the Windows desktop loads. Record any error messages and differences in the video, desktop, or taskbar compared with a normal startup:

_____

3. Because many system services are not running, Windows functions differently than it does during a normal startup. To see some of these differences, open **Control Panel** and the **Network and Sharing Center**. Describe any differences you notice in these tools compared with a normal startup:

_____

_____

4. Open the System Configuration utility, and return startup to a Normal startup with all services enabled. Click **OK** and restart the system. Windows restarts normally. Log on to the system as an administrator.

5. Open the System Configuration utility, and select the **Boot** tab. List each operating system installed and the drive and folder where it is installed:

_____

Here is an explanation of each option on the Boot tab:

Safe boot: Minimal. Boots to Safe Mode with networking disabled.

Safe boot: Alternate shell. Boots to a Windows command prompt in Safe Mode; networking is disabled.

Safe boot: Active Directory repair. Boots to Safe Mode; used to repair Active Directory on a domain.

Safe boot: Network. Boots to Safe Mode with Networking.

No GUI boot. No Windows splash screen is displayed when booting.

Boot log. Boot logging is stored in *%SystemRoot%*Ntbtlog.txt.

Base video. Boots to minimal VGA mode.

OS boot information. Displays driver names as the drivers are loaded during the boot.

Make all boot settings permanent. Changes you have made in System Configuration are permanent; you cannot roll back your changes by selecting Normal startup on the General tab.

The Startup tab lists applications launched at startup, including how they are launched from a startup folder or registry key. This information can be really useful when you are investigating how a program is launched at startup. For example, malware that launches at startup might not be found by anti-malware software. You can use this tab to find the folder or registry key where a program is launched so that you can delete the entry. Follow these steps to find out more:

1. Select the **Startup** tab. In Windows 8, you need to click the link to view Startup items in Task Manager. In Windows 7, it might be necessary to select the first item in the list to view the Command column. Record the following for the first item in the list:

   ◢ Startup item:

   _____

   ◢ Publisher/manufacturer:

   _____

The Tools tab provides a convenient list of diagnostic tools and other advanced tools that you can run from System Configuration. Follow these steps to find out more:

1. Click the **Tools** tab, and then click **Action Center**. What is the path and program name of the Action Center?

   _____

2. Click the **Launch** button. What was the result of your action?

   _____

3. Close all windows and the System Configuration utility.

REVIEW QUESTIONS

1. Which tab in System Configuration can you use to find out if the computer is using a dual-boot configuration? What information on this tab tells you that two operating systems are installed?

   _____

2. How can enabling and disabling items listed on the Startup tab be useful when you are troubleshooting a problem boot?

   _____

   _____

3. Which tab in System Configuration can be used to restart the system in Safe Mode?

   _____

4. Which tab in System Configuration can you use to find out if a service is currently running?

   _____

5. How can the Tools tab in System Configuration be useful to a technician?

   _____

LAB 4.7 CRITICAL THINKING: USE WINDOWS UTILITIES TO SPEED UP A SYSTEM

OBJECTIVES

The goal of this lab is to learn how to clean up processes that might slow Windows performance. After completing this lab, you will be able to:

- Use Windows tools to clean up startup
- Investigate processes that are slowing down Windows
- Configure the system to keep it clean and free of malware

MATERIALS REQUIRED

This lab requires the following:

- Windows 8 or Windows 7 operating system
- An account with administrator privileges
- Internet access

LAB PREPARATION

Before the lab begins, the instructor or lab assistant needs to do the following:

- Verify Windows starts with no errors; for the best student experience, try to use systems that are not optimized and need the benefits of this lab. For example, you can do this lab using your own or a friend's computer, or one your instructor assigns to you that gets heavy student use.

◢ Verify each student has access to a user account with administrator privileges

◢ Verify Internet access is available

ACTIVITY BACKGROUND

A troubleshooting problem you'll often face as an IT support technician is a sluggish Windows system. Customers might tell you that when their Windows computer was new, it ran smoothly and fast, with no errors, but that it now hangs occasionally, is slow to start up or shut down, and is slow when working. One particular problem doesn't stand out above the rest. The customer just wants you to make the system work faster. When solving these types of general problems, it helps to have a game plan. This activity gives you just that. You'll learn how to speed up Windows, ridding it of unneeded and unwanted processes that are slowing it down.

ESTIMATED COMPLETION TIME: 60 MINUTES

Activity

Use an administrator account to log on to the system each time you need to log on during this lab. Before you make any changes to the system, first get a benchmark of how long it takes for Windows to start up. Do the following:

1. Power down the computer, and then turn it back on. Using a watch with a second hand, note how many minutes it takes the system to start. Startup is completed after you have logged on to Windows, the hard drive activity light has stopped, and the mouse pointer looks like an arrow. How long does startup take?

_____

2. Describe any problems you observed during startup:

_____

_____

This lab assumes that Windows might be slow starting, but that it does start up without errors. If you see error messages on screen or the system refuses to boot, you need to solve these problems before you continue with a general cleanup in the following steps.

When you're ready to begin a general cleanup, do the following:

1. If valuable data on the hard drive is not backed up, back up that data now.

2. Run anti-malware software. Here are your options:

   ◢ If anti-malware software is not installed and you have the anti-malware software setup CD, install it. If it fails to install (some malware can block software installations), boot into Safe Mode, and install and run it from there.

   ◢ If you don't have access to the anti-malware software setup CD, you can download software from the Internet. If your computer cannot connect to the Internet (possibly because Internet access is being blocked by malware), try to connect to the Internet using the Safe Mode with Networking option on the Advanced Boot Options menu. (This option might disable malware that is preventing Internet access.) If that doesn't work, then download the software on another computer, and burn a CD with the downloaded file.

◢ If you don't have anti-malware software installed and don't have access to an anti-malware software setup CD, but you can connect the computer to the Internet, you can run an online anti-malware scan from an anti-malware website. For example, Trend Micro (*trendmicro.com*) offers a free online anti-malware scan. (This free online scan has been known to find malware that other scans do not.)

◢ List the steps you took to run the anti-malware software:

_____

_____

_____

◢ List any malware the anti-malware software found:

_____

_____

_____

3. Reboot the system. Is there a performance improvement? How long does startup take?

_____

_____

4. If the system is still running so slowly you find it difficult to work, you can temporarily turn off startup processes that are hogging system resources. In Windows 8, use Task Manager to manage startup processes, and in Windows 7, use the System Configuration utility.

5. You can keep services from starting by unchecking them on the Startup tab. List all of the services that are run at startup, and use the Internet to determine the purpose of each of them:

_____

_____

_____

_____

_____

_____

_____

6. Uncheck all the services except the ones associated with your anti-malware program. Reboot the system to cause these changes to take effect.

7. Is there a performance improvement? How long does startup take?

_____

8. Clean up the hard drive. Delete temporary files, and check the drive for errors. If the system is slow while doing these tasks, do them from Safe Mode. Note that you need about 15 percent free hard drive space to defragment the drive. If you don't have that much free space, find some folders and files you can move to a different media. Windows requires this much free space to run well.

9. Reboot the system. Is there a performance improvement? How long does startup take?

_____

10. Check Device Manager for hardware devices that are installed but not working as well as those devices that are no longer needed and should be uninstalled. Did you find any devices that need fixing or uninstalling? How did you handle the situation?

_____

_____

4

Challenge Activity (Additional 15 Minutes)

Task Manager in Windows 8 and System Configuration in Windows 7 do not necessarily show all the processes that run at startup. So, to get a more thorough list, you need to use a more powerful startup manager such as Autoruns from Sysinternals.

1. Go to **http://technet.microsoft.com/en-us/sysinternals/bb963902**, and download and install the latest version of Autoruns.

2. Run Autoruns, and then select the **Logon** tab, as shown in Figure 4-6.

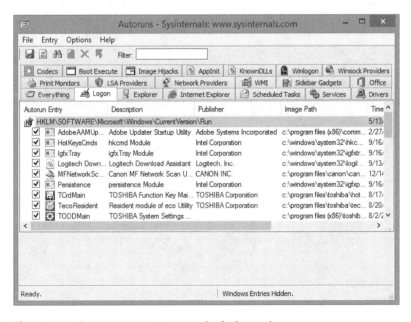

Figure 4-6 Autoruns startup manager by Sysinternals

3. How does the list of startup processes differ from the list generated by System Configuration? List any additional processes identified:

_____

_____

_____

_____

REVIEW QUESTIONS

1. If anti-malware software is not installed and you don't have access to the Internet, how can you install it?

_____

2. Which window or dialog box is used to check a hard drive for errors?

_____

3. What two folders can contain programs to be launched when a specific user logs on to the system?

_____

4. When cleaning up startup, why should you not delete a program file you find in a startup folder?

_____

5. What utility lists all currently running processes?

_____

CHAPTER 5

Supporting Customers and Troubleshooting Windows

Labs included in this chapter:

- **Lab 5.1:** Understand IT Codes of Ethics
- **Lab 5.2:** Provide Customer Service
- **Lab 5.3:** Practice Help-Desk Skills
- **Lab 5.4:** Practice Good Communication Skills
- **Lab 5.5:** Understand How to Create a Help-Desk Procedure
- **Lab 5.6:** Apply a Restore Point
- **Lab 5.7:** Update Drivers with Device Manager
- **Lab 5.8:** Find a Driver for an Unknown Device
- **Lab 5.9:** Research Data Recovery Software
- **Lab 5.10:** Use the Problem Steps Recorder

LAB 5.1 UNDERSTAND IT CODES OF ETHICS

OBJECTIVES

The goal of this lab is to become familiar with the concept of a code of ethics for IT professionals. After completing this lab, you will be able to:

◢ Examine a code of ethics for IT professionals

◢ Consider different values when making an ethical decision

MATERIALS REQUIRED

This lab requires the following:

◢ A Windows 8 or Windows 7 workstation

◢ Internet access

◢ A workgroup of two to four students

LAB PREPARATION

Before the lab begins, the instructor or lab assistant needs to do the following:

◢ Read through the IEEE code of ethics and be prepared to discuss it with each group

◢ Verify Windows starts with no errors

◢ Verify Internet access is available

ACTIVITY BACKGROUND

Most companies and professional organizations have a code of ethics or a code of conduct that they expect their employees or members to uphold. The code typically outlines the rights and responsibilities of employees/members as well as their customers. Certain practices, such as respecting confidentiality and avoiding conflicts of interest are common to most codes, while other behaviors are industry specific. In addition, many businesses publish a Statement of Values that outlines the values or qualities that guide their actions. In this lab, you examine a code of ethics developed by the Institute of Electrical and Electronics Engineers (IEEE), and consider the values it represents.

ESTIMATED COMPLETION TIME: 60 MINUTES

 Activity

To develop your own code of ethics that you think professionals in the computer industry should follow, complete these steps:

1. In your opinion, what are the three most important ethical issues professionals in the computer industry regularly face?

_____

_____

_____

2. Develop an ethical standard that professionals in the computer industry should use when faced with each of the three issues you identified above:

_____

_____

_____

3. Discuss your ideas in your workgroup, and, as a group, create a code of ethics using the five ethical standards your group thinks are most important for professionals in the computer industry:

_____

_____

_____

_____

_____

To learn more about computer industry ethics and values, follow these steps:

1. To begin, go to the IEEE website (**ieee.org**) and search for the IEEE code of ethics. Review the code, and then do the following:

◢ Discuss this code with your group. What do you, as a group, consider to be the most important guideline in the list?

_____

◢ Describe any significant similarities or differences between the IEEE code and the code of ethics your workgroup created:

_____

_____

◢ Find at least one other technological organization or company that posts a code of ethics on its website. Write down the name of the organization and its URL below:

_____

_____

◢ Describe any significant similarities or differences between the IEEE code and the code from the other technological organization:

_____

_____

_____

Ethical decisions are often constructed around a set of priorities or values, such as fairness, equality, and honesty. Further evaluate values by following these steps:

1. On your own, write down as many unique values as you can come up with in 10 minutes. You might want to research "ethical values" on the Internet for inspiration.

_____

_____

_____

_____

_____

2. When you're finished, share your list of values with your group, and try to agree on what you consider to be the seven most important values for aiding ethical decision making. Remember that there are no right or wrong answers; you're just trying to determine what's most important to the members in your group.

◢ List the values below:

1. _____

2. _____

3. _____

4. _____

5. _____

6. _____

7. _____

3. What values from your group's list are also represented by the IEEE code of ethics?

_____

_____

_____

_____

Case study: You are working in the IT Department of a large company. Your employer has asked you to monitor the email and Internet activity of select individuals in the company, and to submit a report on those activities at the end of the week. Answer the following questions:

1. Does your employer have the right to monitor this information? Does it have a responsibility to do so? Explain your answer:

_____

_____

_____

2. Does your employer have a responsibility to inform its employees that their email and Internet activity are being monitored? Explain your answer:

_____

_____

3. What should you do if you discover an illegal activity during your investigation? What if your employer doesn't agree with your decision?

_____

_____

_____

4. What would you do if you discovered that your employer was engaged in illegal activity, such as using pirated software?

_____

_____

_____

5. If a coworker who is a close friend is found to be using the Internet for job hunting, would you mention it in your report? Explain your answer:

_____

_____

_____

REVIEW QUESTIONS

1. Did your group have any trouble agreeing on the seven most important values? Why did you agree or disagree?

_____

_____

2. Do you think having a company code of ethics makes ethical decisions any easier? Why?

_____

_____

3. Do you think most people share a fundamental set of values? Why?

_____

_____

4. What can you do in cases where your personal values conflict with the values of your employer?

_____

_____

LAB 5.2 PROVIDE CUSTOMER SERVICE

OBJECTIVES

The goal of this lab is to develop an understanding of some of the issues involved in providing excellent customer service. After completing this lab, you will be able to:

◢ Evaluate the service needs of your customers

◢ Plan for good customer service

◢ Respond to customer complaints

MATERIALS REQUIRED

This lab requires the following:

◢ A workgroup of two to four students

LAB PREPARATION

Before the lab begins, the instructor or lab assistant needs to do the following:

◢ Read through the customer service scenarios and be prepared to discuss them with each group

ACTIVITY BACKGROUND

An IT technician needs to be not only technically competent, but also skilled at providing excellent customer service. Acting in a helpful, dependable, and, above all, professional manner is a must—whether the technician deals directly with customers or works with other employees as part of a team.

To complete this lab, work through the following customer service scenarios. When you are finished, compare your answers with the rest of your group and see whether you can arrive at a consensus. Keep in mind that there might not be a single right answer to each question.

ESTIMATED COMPLETION TIME: 60 MINUTES

 Activity

Working with a group, review the following customer service scenarios, and answer the accompanying questions:

    1. A customer returns to your store complaining that the upgraded computer he just picked up doesn't boot. You remember testing the computer yourself before the pickup, and everything was fine.

        ◢ What can you do to remedy the situation?

        _____

        _____

        ◢ How can you avoid this kind of problem in the future?

        _____

        _____

2. You're working in a call center that provides support to customers who are trying to install your company's product at home. While working with an inexperienced customer over the telephone, you realize that she's having trouble following your directions.

    ◢ What are some ways you can help customers even when they can't see you in a face-to-face environment?

_____

_____

_____

_____

_____

    ◢ How can you communicate clearly with your customers while avoiding the impression that you're talking down to them?

_____

_____

_____

3. You arrive on a service call, and the overly confident office supervisor shows you the malfunctioning computer. She begins to explain what she thinks is the problem, but you can tell from the computer's operation that it's something else. You suspect that the office supervisor might have caused the malfunction.

    ◢ How can you troubleshoot the problem without offending your customer?

_____

_____

_____

    ◢ Would it be a mistake to accuse the customer of causing the problem? Why?

_____

_____

4. An irate customer calls to complain that he's not satisfied with service he has received from your company, and he tells you he plans to take his future business elsewhere.

    ◢ Should you apologize even if you don't think your company acted improperly?

_____

_____

    ◢ How can you give the customer the impression that you and your company are listening to his complaints?

_____

_____

REVIEW QUESTIONS

1. What other viewpoints did the other members of your group have that you hadn't considered?

_____

_____

_____

2. Did you have any trouble coming to a consensus about how to deal with each situation? Explain your answer:

_____

3. Why is an understanding of good customer service important for a technician who doesn't work directly with customers?

_____

_____

4. How can you improve your listening skills when working with customers?

_____

_____

_____

LAB 5.3 PRACTICE HELP-DESK SKILLS

OBJECTIVES

The goal of this lab is to learn how to work with a customer via a chat session and a telephone conversation. After completing this lab, you will be able to:

◢ Use help-desk skills in a chat session and on the phone to solve customer problems

MATERIALS REQUIRED

This lab requires the following:

◢ Two or more Windows 8 or Windows 7 operating systems

◢ Internet access

◢ Access to instant messaging software such as Skype

◢ A phone (or cell phone) for each student

LAB PREPARATION

Before the lab begins, the instructor or lab assistant needs to do the following:

◢ Verify Windows starts with no errors

◢ Verify Internet access is available

◢ Verify messaging software is available

◢ Instruct students to bring their cell phones to the lab, or provide telephones in the lab

ACTIVITY BACKGROUND

In the past, help-desk support was provided solely by telephone; however, most hardware and software companies now also offer technical support for their products through chat sessions with the company's help-desk staff. Help-desk personnel need to know how to ask questions, connect with customers in a friendly and personal tone, and solve problems via a telephone conversation or a chat session. Typically, a customer can initiate a chat session by clicking a link on a company's website. For example, in Figure 5-1, you can see where to click to start a live chat session with NETGEAR support.

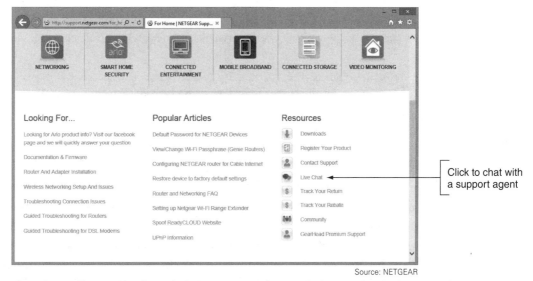

Source: NETGEAR

Figure 5-1 Chat sessions for technical support are often available through manufacturer websites

ESTIMATED COMPLETION TIME: 60 MINUTES

 Activity

Imagine that Jesse is having problems securing his home wireless network. The router that serves as his wireless access point was not working, so he pressed the Reset button on the router. The router began working, but Jesse then discovered he had reset the router back to the factory default settings, undoing all his wireless security settings. When Jesse tried to reconfigure the router, he could not find the router documentation, which included the user name and password to the router firmware utility. After giving up his search for the documentation, he has decided to contact NETGEAR for help.

Jesse goes to the NETGEAR website and clicks the Support link, which opens the page shown earlier in Figure 5-1. He clicks the Live Chat link, and on the next page, enters his name, phone number, email address, and product name. After he submits this information, a chat window opens, similar to the one in Figure 5-2. Farly is working the help desk at NETGEAR and responds to Jesse.

Source: NETGEAR

Figure 5-2 Sample technical support chat window

Working with a partner in your workgroup, use network and chat software such as Skype, and complete the following steps:

1. Select one person in your workgroup to play the role of Jesse, the customer. Select another person to play the role of Farly, the help-desk technician.

2. Jesse initiates a chat session with Farly. What is the first thing Farly says to Jesse in the chat session?

_____

3. In your chat session between Jesse and Farly, communicate the following:

   Farly asks Jesse for the serial number of the router. This number is embedded on the bottom of the router.

   Farly knows that the default user name for this router is a blank entry with "admin" for the password. Farly wants Jesse to know it would have been better for him to have reset the router by unplugging it and then plugging it back in, rather than using the Reset button. Farly also tells Jesse that, for security reasons, he needs to enter a new user name and password for the router.

4. Print the chat session. If your chat software does not have a print option, then copy and paste the chat session text into a document, and print the document. As a courtesy, many companies send the customer a transcription of the chat session via email.

5. Critique the chat session with others in your workgroup. Make suggestions that might help Farly to be more effective, friendly, and helpful.

Use telephones to simulate a help-desk conversation. Use the same troubleshooting scenario, but this time, switch players between Jesse and Farly. Do the following:

1. Jesse calls Farly, and Farly answers, "Hello, this is Farly Jackson with the NETGEAR help desk. May I please have your name, the product you need help with, your phone number, and email address?"

2. After the necessary information is collected, Farly allows Jesse to describe the problem and then steps him through the solution.

3. When the problem is solved, Farly ends the call politely and positively.

4. Ask your workgroup to make suggestions that might help Farly to be more effective, friendly, and helpful.

In the next help-desk session, Joy contacts technical support for her company, complaining of too many pop-up ads on her desktop. Do the following:

1. Select someone to play the role of Joy and another person to play the role of Sam, the help-desk technician. Assume that Joy is a novice user who needs a little extra help with keystrokes.

2. Using chat software, Joy starts a chat session with Sam, and Sam solves the problem.

3. Sam decides to have Joy turn on the Internet Explorer pop-up blocker, use previously installed anti-malware software to scan for viruses, and in Windows 8 run Windows Defender and in Windows 7 download, install, and run Microsoft Security Essentials software from the Microsoft website.

4. Print the chat session, and discuss it with your workgroup. Do you have any suggestions for Sam to improve his help-desk skills?

_____

_____

5. Using telephones, switch players for Joy and Sam, and solve the same problem. Do you have any suggestions for Sam to improve his help-desk skills?

_____

_____

CHALLENGE ACTIVITY (ADDITIONAL 30 MINUTES)

Do the following to get more practice supporting users on the phone:

1. Think of a computer problem you or a friend has encountered that you or your friend could not quickly solve. Describe the problem as a user would describe it when he first calls a help desk:

_____

_____

2. Working with a partner, the partner plays the role of a help-desk technician and you play the role of the user. Call the "help desk," and describe your problem. Work with your partner toward a solution. Answer the following questions:

   ◢ Was your partner able to help you solve the problem?

   _____

   ◢ Assess how well your partner handled the call. How would you assess the service you received?

   _____

   _____

3. Switch roles with your partner, and repeat Steps 1 and 2. You become the help-desk technician as your partner gets help with a problem she or a friend has encountered in real life.

REVIEW QUESTIONS

1. After doing your best, but finding you still cannot solve a customer's problem, what is the appropriate next step?

   _____

   _____

2. Your cell phone rings while working with a customer. You look at the incoming number and realize it's your sister calling. How do you handle the call?

   _____

   _____

   _____

3. Why is it not a good idea to tell a customer about the time you were able to solve the computer problem of a very important person?

   _____

   _____

4. A customer is angry and tells you he will never buy another product from your company again. How do you respond?

   _____

   _____

LAB 5.4 PRACTICE GOOD COMMUNICATION SKILLS

OBJECTIVES

The goal of this lab is to help you learn how to be a better communicator. After completing this lab, you will be able to:

◢ Listen better

◢ Work with a customer who is angry

◢ Act with integrity toward customers

MATERIALS REQUIRED

This lab requires the following:

◢ Paper and pencil or pen

◢ A workgroup of two or more students

LAB PREPARATION

No lab preparation is necessary.

ACTIVITY BACKGROUND

IT support technicians are expected to be good communicators; however, technical people often find this to be a difficult skill to master, so practice and training are very important. In this lab, you discover some ways to be an active listener and a better communicator.

ESTIMATED COMPLETION TIME: 60 MINUTES

 Activity

Work with a partner to learn to be a better listener. Do the following:

1. Sit with paper and a pencil in front of another student who will play the role of a customer. As the customer describes a certain computer problem he or she is having, take notes as necessary.

2. Describe the problem back to the customer. Were you able to describe the problem accurately, without missing any details? Have the customer rate you from one to ten, with ten being the highest rating, for good listening skills. What rating did you receive?

   _____

3. Switch roles as you, the customer, describe a problem to the support technician. Then have the technician repeat the problem and its details. Rate the technician for good listening skills on a scale of one to ten.

4. Choose a somewhat more difficult problem, with more details, and describe it to the support technician. Rate the technician on a scale of one to ten for good listening skills.

5. Switch roles, and listen as the customer describes a more detailed and difficult problem. Then repeat the problem and its details back to the customer, and have the customer rate your listening skills. What rating did you receive?

   _____

Being a good communicator requires being able to deal with people who may be angry and difficult. Make suggestions as to the best way to handle these situations:

1. An angry customer calls to tell you that she has left you numerous phone messages that you have not answered. She is not aware that you receive about 25 voice messages each day and are trying hard to keep up with the workload. What do you say?

   _____

   _____

2. A customer who is frustrated and angry begins to use abusive language. What do you say?

   _____

   _____

3. You have tried for over two hours, but you cannot fix the customer's boot problem. You think the motherboard has failed, but you are not sure. Before you make your conclusions, you want to try a POST diagnostic card. The customer demands that you fix the problem immediately, before she leaves the office at 4:45 p.m.—about 10 minutes from now. What do you say to her?

   _____

   _____

Discuss in your workgroup the ethical thing to do in each situation below. Write down the group consensus to each problem:

1. You work on commission in a computer retail store. One day, you spend over an hour working with a very difficult customer who then leaves without buying anything. As he walks out the door, you notice he dropped a twenty-dollar bill near where you were talking. What do you do?

_____

_____

2. A customer is yelling at a coworker in a retail store. You can see that your coworker does not know how to handle the situation. What do you do?

_____

_____

3. You are working in a corporate office as a technical support person, trying to fix a scanner problem at an employee's workstation. You notice the employee has left payroll database information displayed on the screen. You know this employee is not authorized to view this information. What do you do?

_____

_____

4. Your supervisor has asked you to install a game on his computer. The game is on a CD-R and is obviously a pirated copy. What do you do?

_____

_____

5. You work for a retail store that sells a particular brand of computers. A customer asks your opinion of another brand of computer. What do you say?

_____

_____

6. You are asked to make a house call to fix a computer problem. When you arrive at the appointed time, a teenage girl answers the door and tells you her mother is not at home, but will return in a half hour. What do you do?

_____

_____

Have a little fun with this one! Working in a group of three, one member of the team plays the role of tech support. A second team member writes down a brief description of a difficult customer and passes the description to a third team member. (The tech support person cannot see this description.) The third team member plays out the described customer role. Use the following scenarios or make one up:

1. A customer calls to say his notebook will not start. The LCD panel was broken when the customer dropped the notebook, but he does not willingly disclose the fact that the notebook was dropped.

2. A customer complains that her CD drive does not work. The CD is in the drive upside down, and it is clear that the customer sees herself as a techie and does not want the tech to ask her about such a simple issue.

REVIEW QUESTIONS

1. When working at a retail store that also fixes computers, what five pieces of information should you request when a customer first brings a computer to your counter?

_____

_____

_____

_____

_____

2. List three things you should not do while at a customer's site:

_____

_____

_____

3. When is it acceptable to ask a customer to refrain from venting about a problem?

_____

_____

_____

4. When is it appropriate to answer a cell phone call while working with a customer?

_____

_____

5. When is it appropriate to install pirated software on a computer?

_____

LAB 5.5 UNDERSTAND HOW TO CREATE A HELP-DESK PROCEDURE

OBJECTIVES

The goal of this lab is to explore the process of creating help-desk procedures. After completing this lab, you will be able to:

⬧ Identify problems that would prevent users from browsing the network

⬧ Determine which types of problems can be solved over the telephone

◢ Decide which types of problems require administrative intervention

◢ Create a help-desk procedure that includes a support matrix for telephone instruction

MATERIALS REQUIRED

This lab requires the following:

◢ Windows 8 or Windows 7 operating system

◢ A network connection

◢ Paper and pencil or pen

◢ Internet access (optional)

◢ Two workgroups, with two to four students in each group

LAB PREPARATION

Before the lab begins, the instructor or lab assistant needs to do the following:

◢ Verify Windows starts with no errors

◢ Verify the network connection is available

◢ Verify Internet access is available (optional)

ACTIVITY BACKGROUND

When a company sets up a help desk for computer users, it establishes a set of procedures to address common troubleshooting situations. Well-written help-desk procedures ensure that help-desk workers know each and every step to perform in a given situation, which means they can solve problems more quickly and confidently. These procedures should include instructions that the average user can be expected to carry out with telephone support from help-desk staff. In this lab, you create help-desk procedures for resolving a common problem: the inability to connect to a network. Assume you're working at a company help desk. If you can't solve the problem, you escalate it to the network administrator or an onsite technician who actually goes to the computer to fix the problem.

ESTIMATED COMPLETION TIME: 60 MINUTES

 Activity

Work with a group to better understand how to create help-desk procedures. Do the following:

1. Assume that your company network is designed according to the following parameters. (Note that your instructor might alter these parameters so that they more closely resemble your network's parameters.)

   ◢ Ethernet LAN is using only a single subnet

   ◢ TCP/IP is the only protocol

   ◢ The workgroup name is ZEBRA

   ◢ The DHCP server assigns IP information

2. Assume that all users on your company network use computers with the following parameters. (Note that your instructor might alter these parameters so that they more closely resemble your computer.)

   ◢ Core i7 2.9 GHz

   ◢ Windows 8 operating system

◢ Internal NIC

◢ Category 5e cabling with RJ-45 connectors

3. As a group, discuss the reasons a user might not be able to connect to the network, and then make a list of the four most common reasons. In your list, include at least one problem that would be difficult to solve over the phone and would require the network administrator or another technician to go to the computer to solve the problem. Order the four problems from the least difficult to solve to the most difficult to solve. The one problem that requires administrator intervention should be Problem 4. If your group has trouble completing the list, ask your instructor or search the web for ideas. List the source of these problems, both hardware and software, on the following lines:

◢ Source of Problem 1:

_____

◢ Source of Problem 2:

_____

◢ Source of Problem 3:

_____

◢ Source of Problem 4:

_____

For each problem, describe the symptoms as a user would describe them:

◢ Symptoms of Problem 1:

_____

_____

◢ Symptoms of Problem 2:

_____

_____

◢ Symptoms of Problem 3:

_____

_____

◢ Symptoms of Problem 4:

_____

_____

As a group, decide how to solve each problem by following these steps:

1. On separate sheets of paper, list the steps to verify and solve each problem. (This list of steps is sometimes referred to as a procedure, support matrix, or job aid.)

2. Double-check the steps by testing them on your computer. (In real life, you would test the steps using a computer attached to the network you're supporting.) When making your list of steps, allow for alternatives, based on how the user responds to certain

questions. For example, you might include one list of steps for situations in which the user says others on the network are visible in the Network window and another list of steps for situations in which the user says no remote computers can be seen in the Network window.

3. For any problem that can't be solved by the procedure, the last step should be for help-desk personnel to escalate the problem. In your procedure, include questions to the user when appropriate. As you work, you might find it helpful to use a diagram or flowchart of the questions asked and decisions made. Here's an example of one step that involves a question:

◢ Question: Is your computer on?

◢ Answer: Yes, go to Step 3; no, go to Step 2.

Now it is time to test your help-desk procedures by using them on another workgroup. Follow these steps:

1. Introduce one of your four problems on a computer connected to a network.

2. Have someone from another workgroup sit at your computer. The remaining steps in this step sequence refer to this person as "the user."

3. Sit with your back to the user so that you can't see what he or she is doing. Place your step-by-step procedures in front of you, either on paper or on screen. (It's helpful if you can sit at a computer connected to the network so that you can perform the same steps you ask the user to perform. However, make sure you can't see the other computer screen or see what the user is doing.)

4. The user should attempt to access the network and then "call" your help desk for assistance.

5. Follow your procedure to solve the problem.

6. Revise your procedure as necessary.

7. Test all four help-desk procedures.

REVIEW QUESTIONS

1. Can all users' computer problems be solved with remote help-desk support? Why or why not?

_____

_____

2. After you design and write your help-desk procedures to solve problems, what should you do next?

_____

3. How should help-desk procedures address complex problems that require administrative intervention?

_____

_____

_____

4. How should you write your procedures based on your users' technical experience?

_____

5. Why do you need to consider what the network and computer configuration are when creating your procedures?

_____

_____

6. What has been your experience when calling a help desk? How well did the technician walk you through the process of solving your problem?

_____

_____

LAB 5.6 APPLY A RESTORE POINT

OBJECTIVES

The goal of this lab is to restore the system state on a Windows 8 or Windows 7 computer. After completing this lab, you will be able to:

◢ Create a restore point by using System Restore

◢ Change system settings

◢ Restore the system state with the restore point you created

MATERIALS REQUIRED

This lab requires the following:

◢ Windows 8 or Windows 7 operating system

LAB PREPARATION

Before the lab begins, the instructor or lab assistant needs to do the following:

◢ Verify Windows starts with no errors

ACTIVITY BACKGROUND

Using the System Restore tool in Windows, you can restore the system to the state it was in when a snapshot, called a "restore point," was taken of the system state. The settings recorded in a restore point include system settings and configurations and files needed for a successful boot. When the system state is restored to a restore point, user data on the hard drive isn't affected, but software and hardware might be. Restore points are useful if, for example, something goes wrong with a software or hardware installation and you need to undo these changes. In this lab, you create a restore point, make changes to system settings, and then use the restore point to restore the system state.

Activity

To use the System Restore tool to create a restore point, follow these steps:

1. Click **Start, All Programs, Accessories, System Tools,** and, finally, **System Restore.** The System Restore dialog box opens.

2. In Windows 8, use the information on this screen or search Windows Help and Support. In Windows 7, click **Is this process reversible?** to open Windows Help and Support. Answer the following questions:

   ◢ Can changes made by System Restore be undone?

   _____

   ◢ What type of data does System Restore leave unaffected?

   _____

   _____

3. Close Windows Help and Support if necessary. In the System Restore box, click **Next.** Check **Show more restore points.** (If this check box is not available, your system has no more restore points to show.)

   ◢ What are the dates of the three most recent restore points?

   _____

   ◢ What types of recent events prompted Windows to automatically create restore points?

   _____

   _____

4. To create a new restore point, open **Control Panel** and click **System.** Click **System protection** in the left pane of the System window to open the System Properties dialog box.

5. To create a restore point, click **Create.** Name your restore point, and then click **Create.** A restore point is created.

6. Close any open windows.

Next, you make a change to the system by changing the display settings. Follow these steps:

1. Open **Control Panel** and click **Personalization.** Using the Personalization window, change the desktop background or the desktop theme.

2. Close the Control Panel window. Notice that the desktop background or desktop theme has changed to the one you selected.

Follow these steps to use the restore point you created to restore the system state:

1. Open the **System Restore** tool. Click **Next.**

2. Select the restore point you created earlier in the lab, and then click **Next.**

3. When a confirmation window is displayed, click **Finish** to continue. If necessary, click **Yes** to proceed.

◢ Describe what happens when you proceed with a restore:

_____

_____

4. After the system restarts, log on to the Windows desktop. A message is displayed stating that the restoration is complete. Click **Close**.

◢ Did the display settings change back to their original settings?

_____

REVIEW QUESTIONS

1. List three situations in which you might want to create a restore point:

_____

_____

_____

2. What types of restore points are created by the system, and what types are created by users?

_____

_____

3. How often does the system create restore points automatically?

_____

4. Can more than one restore point be made on a specific date?

_____

5. Does Windows track more than one restore point? Why?

_____

_____

_____

LAB 5.7 UPDATE DRIVERS WITH DEVICE MANAGER

OBJECTIVES

The goal of this lab is to explore the functions of Device Manager. After completing this lab, you will be able to:

◢ Use Device Manager to find information about your display adapter and update the display adapter drivers

◢ Explore alternative methods to update a driver

MATERIALS REQUIRED

This lab requires the following:

⊿ Windows 8 or Windows 7 operating system

⊿ Updated driver files for the display adapter (optional)

⊿ Internet access

LAB PREPARATION

Before the lab begins, the instructor or lab assistant needs to do the following:

⊿ Verify Windows starts with no errors

⊿ Verify Internet access

⊿ Locate or download updated driver files for the display adapter or video card, if newer driver files are available

ACTIVITY BACKGROUND

With Device Manager, you can update device drivers as well as monitor resource use. If you find a new driver for a device, you can use Device Manager to select the device and update the driver. In this lab, you use Device Manager to update the driver for your display adapter.

ESTIMATED COMPLETION TIME: 30 MINUTES

 Activity

In this lab, you first use Device Manager to update a driver, and then you explore alternative ways to update drivers.

PART 1: USE DEVICE MANAGER TO UPDATE A DRIVER

1. To open Device Manager, open **Control Panel**, and then click **Device Manager**.

2. Click the arrow next to **Display adapters** to expand this category, and then click your display adapter to select it. What is the name of your display adapter?

   _____

3. To open the Properties dialog box for your display adapter, right-click the **adapter** and select **Properties**. What is the manufacturer of your display adapter?

   _____

4. Click the **Driver** tab, and answer the following questions:

   ⊿ What company is the provider for your driver?

   _____

   ⊿ What is the driver date?

   _____

   ⊿ What is the driver version?

   _____

5. Click the **Driver Details** button, and answer the following questions:

   ⊿ Which folders contain the drivers used by your display adapter?

   _____

   _____

◢ What is the file version?

6. Click **OK** to return to the Driver tab in the display adapter's Properties dialog box. Click **Update Driver**. A dialog box appears asking where to find the drivers (see Figure 5-3).

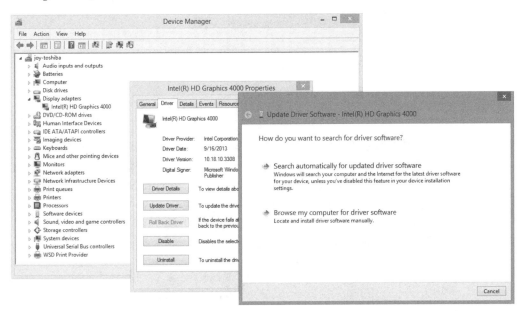

Figure 5-3   Use Device Manager to find and update drivers

7. If your instructor has provided the updated driver in a specific location on your computer, click **Browse my computer for driver software**. If your instructor has not provided the drivers, you can allow Windows to search the web for the drivers. To do so, click **Search automatically for updated driver software**.

8. If you are using the web to update your driver, follow the on-screen instructions to search for and install drivers. If your driver is already up to date, Windows displays a message saying the best driver software for your device is already installed. If Windows finds a newer version, it installs the update. When the update is finished, you might be asked to restart your computer. Then, proceed to Part 2 of this lab.

9. If your instructor has provided the drivers, type the location of the driver installation file, or click the **Browse** button to select the location your instructor has designated. After you have specified a location, click **Next**. Windows searches the location and reports its findings.

10. If the wizard indicates it has found a file for the display adapter, click **Next** to continue. If the wizard reports that it can't find the file, verify you have entered the installation file's location correctly.

11. After Windows locates the drivers, it copies the driver files. If a file being copied is older than the file the system is currently using, you're prompted to confirm that you want to use the older file. Usually, newer drivers are better than older drivers. However, you might choose to use an older driver if you experience problems after updating drivers. In this case, you might want to reinstall the old driver that wasn't causing problems.

12. When the files have been copied, click **Finish** to complete the installation.

13. Close all open windows, and restart the computer if prompted to do so.

PART 2: EXPLORE ALTERNATIVE WAYS TO UPDATE DRIVERS

1. Device Manager should now show updated driver information for your display adapter. Return to Device Manager. Record the new driver information below, and compare it with the information you collected earlier.

  ◢ Driver date:

  _____

  ◢ Driver version:

  _____

  ◢ File version:

  _____

Windows will not always have access to drivers through Device Manager, especially drivers for accessories or other after-market hardware. In these situations, you can do one of the following:

  ◢ Install a driver from a disc that comes with the new hardware. You can use the Browse option in Device Manager, as described above, or you can open File Explorer/Windows Explorer and double-click an installation program on the disc.

  ◢ Download a driver directly from the hardware manufacturer's website. To install a driver from a manufacturer's website, you need information about your system in order to search online for the correct driver. After the driver file is downloaded, you install the driver by double-clicking the downloaded file and following the on-screen directions.

To collect the information you need to find a driver online, follow these steps:

1. In the Run box, type **msinfo32** and press **Enter**.

2. Using the System Information dialog box, collect the following information:

  ◢ OS name: _____

  ◢ System manufacturer:_____

  ◢ System model: _____

  ◢ System type: _____

When downloading and running a program from the web, always download the file to your hard drive and then use File Explorer/Windows Explorer to execute the downloaded file. To avoid accidentally installing malware, do not run the file from your browser. Also, always reboot your system after installing a new driver, even if not instructed to do so. This last precaution helps identify any problems with the boot process or with Windows that might be caused by a new device or driver.

CRITICAL THINKING (ADDITIONAL 30 MINUTES)

Open Device Manager, and select other devices to update. Device drivers that you might want to update include your motherboard and audio drivers. If an update does not work properly, you can use the Roll Back Driver button on the Driver tab of the device's Properties dialog box to return the device to a previously installed driver.

REVIEW QUESTIONS

1. Describe the steps to access Device Manager:

_____

_____

2. What are the steps to view the properties of a device using Device Manager?

_____

_____

3. What tab in the Properties dialog box do you use to update a driver?

_____

4. Besides typing the path, what other option can you use to specify a driver's location?

_____

_____

5. Why might you want to use an older driver for a device rather than the latest driver?

_____

_____

LAB 5.8 FIND A DRIVER FOR AN UNKNOWN DEVICE

OBJECTIVES

The goal of this lab is to learn how to find the drivers for an unknown device. After completing this lab, you will be able to:

◢ Use third-party software to determine brand and model information of an unknown device

◢ Use the Internet to find and download a driver

MATERIALS REQUIRED

This lab requires the following:

◢ A Windows 8 or Windows 7 computer designated for this lab

◢ Internet access

◢ A burnable CD and a marker to label the CD

◢ A USB flash drive with at least 1-GB capacity (all data on the flash drive will be erased in this lab) (optional)

LAB PREPARATION

Before the lab begins, the instructor or lab assistant needs to do the following:

◢ Verify Windows starts with no errors

◢ Verify Internet access is available

◢ Download files before the lab starts and make these files available to students

> **Notes** The instructor or lab assistant is encouraged to download the required files to a local server and make these available to students locally so students are not required to perform this long download during the lab.

ACTIVITY BACKGROUND

Someone has come to you for help with her computer. She is unable to connect to the Internet and is not sure why. After some investigation, you realize that she has just replaced her computer's network adapter, but has lost the driver CD for the adapter, along with its documentation. Windows does not recognize the device type and there is no model information on the device itself. To find the correct drivers on the web, you need to know the exact brand and model of the device.

Software that runs from a bootable CD or USB flash drive sometimes does a better job of identifying an unknown device than software installed in Windows. In this lab, you use Hiren's BootCD to identify your network adapter. To save time in this lab, your instructor might have already downloaded the program. Ask your instructor if the file is available, and record its location and file name here:

> **Notes** The Hiren's BootCD software sometimes causes anti-malware software to give a false positive alert. The software, however, is safe to use.

ESTIMATED COMPLETION TIME: 45 MINUTES (NOT INCLUDING DOWNLOAD TIME)

 Activity

In this lab, you create and use the Hiren's BootCD to find out the brand and model of an unknown device. This tool can be a valuable utility to add to your computer repair kit, and it can be installed on a burnable CD or a USB flash drive. Follow these steps to create and use a bootable CD using the Hiren's BootCD software:

1. Later in the lab, you use Hiren's BootCD to identify the network adapter installed on your computer. So that you can later compare its results with what Windows reports, open **Device Manager**.

2. Find your network adapter, and open its **Properties** dialog box. Find the tab that displays the brand and model of your NIC and the provider and version number of its driver. Record the following information:

   ◢ What is the brand and model of your NIC?

   ◢ Who is the driver provider, and what is the version number of the driver?

   ---

3. If your instructor has made the Hiren's BootCD download file available, skip to Step 4. If you need to download the file, go to the Hiren's BootCD download page at **hirensbootcd.org/download** and download the Hiren's BootCD Zip file. (For version 15.2, the file name is **Hirens.BootCD.15.2.zip**, although the current version might be different. The link to download the file is located near the bottom of the page. Be careful to not download other free software from this website.) This file is large and will take a while to download. Save the file in your Downloads folder or on your desktop. Answer the following:

   ◢ What is the exact path, file name, and file extension of the downloaded file?

   ---

4. The downloaded file is a Zip file. Extract the contents of the Zip file, and open the extracted folder in File Explorer/Windows Explorer. Compare the contents of the folder with the list shown in Figure 5-4 in the right pane of Explorer.

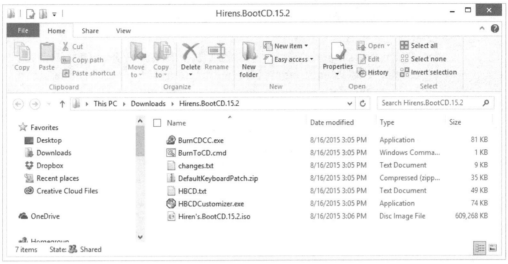

Source: Hiren's BootCD

Figure 5-4   Contents of the extracted Hiren's BootCD folder

◢ Do the contents of your extracted folder differ from the list shown in the figure? If so, record the differences here:

_____

◢ One of the files extracted is an ISO disc image, which has an .iso file extension. When using version 15.2, that file name is Hiren's.BootCD.15.2.iso. What is the name of the ISO file in your extracted folder?

_____

◢ In these instructions, we are using version 15.2. What version of the Hiren's BootCD are you using?

_____

5. With Windows 8 or Windows 7, you can burn an .iso disc image to a CD. To do so, in Windows 8, right-click the Hiren's.BootCD.15.2.iso file, and select **Burn disc image** in the shortcut menu. In Windows 7, right-click the **Hiren's.BootCD.15.2.iso** file, and select **Open with** in the shortcut menu. The Open with dialog box appears. Click **Windows Disc Image Burner**, and then click **OK**. The Windows Disc Image Burner Wizard opens.

> **Notes** If you don't see Windows Disc Image Burner listed in the Open with dialog box, another disc image burner program is probably installed on your computer. You can uninstall that program in order to enable the Windows disc image burner, or you can use the other program to burn the image.

6. Insert a blank CD in the optical drive, check **Verify disc after burning**, and then click **Burn**. The CD is burned. Click **Close** when finished, and then close any open windows.

7. If your computer automatically ejects the CD when the burn is complete, reinsert the CD into your disc drive. If necessary, close the AutoPlay dialog box.

8. Reboot the computer from the CD. To boot from a CD, you might need to access the UEFI/BIOS setup and change the boot sequence to list the optical drive first in the boot priority order.

9. When the computer boots from the CD, the Hiren's BootCD menu appears. In this menu, select **Mini Windows Xp**, and then press **Enter**. The computer displays a graphical user interface similar to that of Windows XP.

10. From the desktop, click **Start**, and then click **HBCD Menu**. The Hiren's BootCD 15.2 – Program Launcher dialog box appears.

11. On the menu bar, click **Programs**, and then answer the following questions:

    ◢ What are two utilities included on the CD for partitioning hard drives?

    _____

    _____

    ◢ Name three utilities on the CD that provide system information:

    _____

    _____

    _____

    ◢ What are two utilities included for backup of data?

    _____

    _____

12. From the Program menu, point to **Device Drivers**, and then click **UnknownDevices (device info)**. This program scans your computer hardware and displays a report in the Unknown Devices window. Use this window to find the make and model number of the NIC installed in your system, and record that information:

    _____

    _____

13. Close all open windows, remove the CD, and reboot your system. Using a permanent marker, label the CD **Hiren's BootCD**, and include the version number that you downloaded.

14. Using the information you collected from the Hiren's BootCD about your NIC, search the web for the correct NIC driver. What is the name of this driver, and where did you find it on the web?

    _____

    _____

15. Earlier in the lab, you recorded the information that Windows offered about the make and model of your NIC and the current driver installed on your computer.

   ◢ Do the make and model of the NIC reported by Windows and the Hiren's BootCD match? Describe any differences.

   _____

   ◢ Does the driver information you collected by your research match the driver currently installed on your system? Describe any differences.

   _____

CHALLENGE ACTIVITY (ADDITIONAL 60 MINUTES)

As you build your arsenal of tools that can take your diagnostic skills to the next level, you might find that creating a version of the Hiren's BootCD on a USB flash drive is not only convenient but necessary in case you are called on to troubleshoot a computer that does not have an optical drive. Follow these steps to create a bootable Hiren's BootCD on a USB flash drive:

1. Connect a 1-GB or larger USB flash drive to your computer. (Be aware that all data on the flash drive will be erased.)

2. Using File Explorer/Windows Explorer, right-click on the flash drive. In the shortcut menu, click **Format**. The Format Wizard opens.

3. Leave Capacity at its default setting, select **FAT32** for File system, select **4096 bytes** (or the next closest size) for Allocation unit size, and then type **USB DISK** for Volume label. In the Format options, unselect **Quick Format** and then click **Start**. If a warning displays indicating that all the information will be deleted, click **OK**. A progress bar is displayed right above where you clicked Start. When formatting is complete, click **OK** and then close the Format Wizard box.

4. Next you'll need to prepare your flash drive with an MBR (Master Boot Record) environment, which makes it bootable. Using your web browser, go to one of these URL locations to download the Zip file named grub4dos.zip:

   ◢ **hirensbootcd.org/files/grub4dos.zip**

   ◢ **hirensbootcd.org/usb-booting/**

5. Once the file is downloaded, extract the contents of the folder to your desktop.

6. Open the **grub4dos** folder created on your desktop, and double-click **gubinst_gui. exe**. If a UAC dialog box appears, click **Yes** to continue. The Grub4Dos Installer 1.1 displays.

7. Under Device Name, select **Disk**. In the drop-down list beside Disk, select your flash drive. To determine which disk is your flash drive, match the size of the disk to the size of your flash drive.

8. To the right of Part List, click **Refresh**.

> **Notes** If you receive an error message like the one on the right side of Figure 5-5, it means that your flash drive has an MBR record that Grub4dos does not recognize. (Most likely this is because your flash drive has a large capacity.) To get around the problem, first click OK to close the message box, and then type skip-mbr-test in the Extra box, as shown on the left side of Figure 5-5.

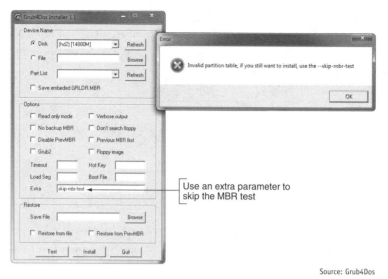

Source: Grub4Dos

Figure 5-5   Grub4Dos does not recognize the MBR record on the flash drive

9. In the drop-down list beside Part List, select **Whole disk (MBR)**. Click **Install**. A command window displays. Press **Enter** to close this window. In the Grub4Dos Installer dialog box, click **Quit**. The dialog box closes.

10. Insert the previously created Hiren's BootCD into your CD drive. Copy all files and folders from the Hiren's BootCD to the flash drive.

> **Notes**   Alternately, you can mount the Hiren's BootCD image using an ISO disk mounting utility such as MagicDisc, ISODisk, or slysoft Virtual Clone Drive.

11. Now you need to give the bootable flash drive a boot loader program and a startup menu. Open the HBCD folder in the Hiren's BootCD, and copy and paste the following files to the root folder of your flash drive.

   ◢ grldr

   ◢ menu.lst

Figure 5-6 shows all the correct files on the USB flash drive.

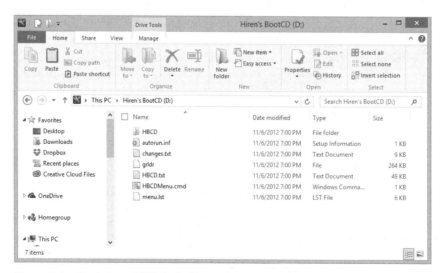

Figure 5-6   Final view of USB flash drive contents

12. Close all open windows, and remove the Hiren's BootCD disc from the optical drive. Shut down your computer.

13. Boot the computer from the USB flash drive. To do so, you might need to change the boot priority sequence using the UEFI/BIOS setup. (Some older computers do not provide USB boot capability, so you might not be able to boot from the USB device.)

14. Using the Hiren's BootCD menu, launch Mini Windows Xp, and verify the desktop loads. Then shut down the system.

15. After removing the USB flash drive, label it with a tag (or write directly on the casing), using the name Hiren's BootCD, and give the version number you used.

REVIEW QUESTIONS

1. When trying to identify an unknown device, what are some advantages to using a boot CD over running diagnostic programs in Windows?

   _____

   _____

2. What are ISO images, and can Windows use them to burn a CD or DVD without additional software?

   _____

   _____

   _____

   _____

3. Other than the situation described in this lab, describe two other situations in which the Hiren's BootCD would be useful:

   _____

   _____

   _____

   _____

4. How much does the Hiren's BootCD software cost?

   _____

5. When you need to boot from the optical drive or a USB flash drive, what must you do to prevent the computer from booting from Windows on the hard drive?

   _____

   _____

LAB 5.9 RESEARCH DATA RECOVERY SOFTWARE

OBJECTIVES

The goal of this lab is to explore different methods of recovering deleted data from a hard disk drive. After completing this lab, you will be able to:

◢ Restore files from the Recycle Bin

◢ Identify the benefits of third-party data recovery software and services

◢ Recover deleted files using Recuva (optional)

MATERIALS REQUIRED

This lab requires the following:

◢ Windows 8 or Windows 7 operating system

◢ An account with administrator privileges

◢ Internet access

LAB PREPARATION

Before the lab begins, the instructor or lab assistant needs to do the following:

◢ Verify Windows starts with no errors

◢ Verify each student has access to a user account with administrator privileges

◢ Verify Internet access is available

ACTIVITY BACKGROUND

A client has contacted you because she accidentally deleted a group of files that hold very important financial information. She is unable to find the files in the Recycle Bin and is panicked because her job may depend on retrieving the files, which contain sensitive financial information. To retrieve the data, you will need to install third-party data recovery software to scan the drive and attempt retrieval.

ESTIMATED COMPLETION TIME: 30 MINUTES

 Activity

Let's first see how to recover files from the Recycle Bin. To begin, you need to create a folder and files. Follow these steps to create the folder and files, delete them, and then recover them from the Recycle Bin:

1. To create a new folder on your desktop, right-click your desktop, and in the shortcut menu select **New** and then click **Folder.** A new folder is created. Name the newly created folder **Important Files**.

2. Double-click the **Important Files** folder to open it. Right-click in the white space in the right pane of File Explorer/Windows Explorer, select **New** in the shortcut menu, and then click **Text Document.** Name this document **Monthly budget.** Open the text file, type your name in the document, and close the file, saving your changes.

3. Create a second text document, naming this document **Financial statement**. Enter some text in the document, and then save and close the document.

4. Select both files and right-click your selection. In the shortcut menu, click **Delete**. If necessary, confirm your deletion. The files are deleted and placed in the Recycle Bin.

5. Double-click the Recycle Bin on your desktop, and search for the deleted files. In Windows 8, you can use the View ribbon to change the Sort by selection and the View selection to more easily find your deleted files. In Windows 7, click a column heading to sort by that field. Right-click one of the files you just deleted. In the shortcut menu, click **Restore**. The file is restored to the Important Files folder. Restore the second file in the same way.

6. Check the Important Files folder and confirm the two files are restored. You may need to click the Refresh icon in File Explorer/Windows Explorer.

Sometimes deleted files cannot be found in the Recycle Bin. In this situation, third-party data recovery software, such as Recuva by Piriform, might help. To learn about the Recuva (pronounced recover) data recovery software, follow these steps:

1. Open your browser and go to **piriform.com/recuva**.

2. Review the features and information provided about Recuva, and answer the following questions:

   ◢ What is a deep scan?

   _____

   _____

   ◢ How can you use a portable version of Recuva if you can't or don't want to install the software on the computer on which you're trying to recover files?

   _____

   _____

   ◢ What are the editions of Recuva and their respective prices?

   _____

   _____

3. Save this website to your browser's Favorites or Bookmarks under a new folder called Recovery Programs.

Another company that offers data recovery software is Paragon. To learn about this third-party software, follow these steps:

1. Go to **paragon-software.com/home/rk-free**.

2. Review the features and information provided, and answer the following questions:

   ◢ Does your computer meet the minimum system requirements? If not, explain why.

   _____

   _____

◢ Paragon's Rescue Kit offers an ISO image. Why is this significant when considering data recovery?

_____

_____

_____

◢ Are you allowed to use this free software on your personal computer? Can you use it in a corporate environment?

_____

3. Add the website to your list of Favorites or Bookmarks in the Recovery Programs folder.

Sometimes, storage devices experience mechanical failure or are damaged by fire or a natural disaster. Occasionally, someone even intentionally tries to destroy data to cover a crime. Third-party software might not be able to retrieve data that has been damaged to this point. In these situations, special, almost surgical, procedures are needed to retrieve the data. To learn about these processes, follow these steps:

1. Go to **drivesaversdatarecovery.com**.

2. Point to **Why DriverSavers?** on the menu bar, and then click **Data Recovery You Can Trust**.

   ◢ What level of clean room does DriveSavers maintain?

   _____

   ◢ What security compliance qualifies DriveSavers to handle confidential medical records?

   _____

3. Point to **Why DriveSavers?** on the menu bar, click **Virtual Tour**, and then play the virtual tour video. Answer the following questions:

   ◢ What are two kinds of devices that DriveSavers can recover data from?

   _____

   _____

   ◢ If DriveSavers opens your hard drive, what happens to your manufacturer's warranty?

   _____

   _____

4. Point to **Data Recovery Services** on the menu bar, and then click **Data Recovery Service Plans**. What is one Security Type offered by DriveSavers?

   _____

CHALLENGE ACTIVITY (ADDITIONAL 45 MINUTES)

Recuva is a powerful freeware utility that can be used to restore files that have been deleted and cannot be restored from the Recycle Bin. To practice using Recuva, follow these steps:

1. Create a new Microsoft Word Document in the Important Files folder titled **My Resume**. (If you don't have Microsoft Word installed, create a Text Document file instead.) Open the file, type **This is a test of My Resume**, and then save and close the file.

2. Delete the **My Resume** file in the Important Files folder.

3. To empty the Recycle Bin, right-click the **Recycle Bin** on your desktop. In the shortcut menu, click **Empty Recycle Bin**. When prompted to confirm deletion, click **Yes**.

4. Open your browser and go to **piriform.com**. Download the latest version of Recuva and install it. As you install it, be careful to not install other freeware offered during the installation. Close all open windows.

5. Launch Recuva. If a UAC dialog box appears, click **Yes**. The Recuva Wizard opens. Click **Next**. If you created a Microsoft Word Document file, select **Documents** for the File type. If you created a Text Document file, select **All Files** for the File type. Click **Next**.

6. On the next screen in the wizard, select **In the Recycle Bin** for the file location (see Figure 5-7). Click **Next**.

Source: Recuva

Figure 5-7　Recuva asks where to search for files to recover

7. Click **Start**. Recuva will run a scan on your computer, which might take several minutes depending on the size of your drive(s). If Recuva does not find any files, it offers to perform a deep scan. If you see this message, you can click **Yes** to allow a deep scan. If this was not an option, close and then relaunch Recuva. Rescan your computer using the deep scan option available on the final screen, where you click Start.

8. When the program presents its scan results, look for a .docx or .txt file created at the same time you created the My Resume file. Figure 5-8 shows one search results window, but yours might look different. The file name might be an unintelligible mix of letters, numbers, and symbols, but you can identify the correct file by checking the date and time it was last modified. (To sort the list by date last modified, click the Last Modified column heading.) Check the box next to the file, and then click **Recover**.

9. In the Browse For Folder dialog box, select the **Important Files** folder, and then click **OK**. When asked if you want to restore to the same drive, click **Yes**. When the operation is completed, click **OK**.

10. Go back to the Important Files folder in File Explorer/Windows Explorer, and double-click the recovered file. Confirm that the text you typed in the file earlier has been successfully recovered.

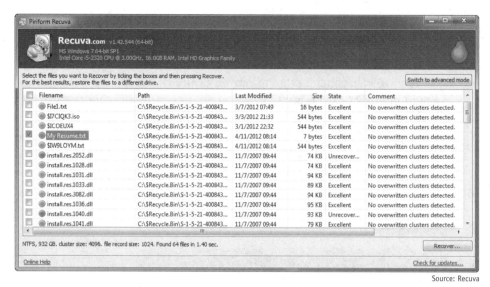

Source: Recuva

Figure 5-8   In this example, the file name is the same as the original, but sometimes it is altered

> **Notes** Sometimes the data in a deleted file is corrupted and cannot be recovered easily by Recuva. A red dot next to the file indicates it is corrupted, and a green dot indicates a good file. If your file has a red dot, you can still go through the steps of recovering the file, but you will get an error message when you try to open the file.

REVIEW QUESTIONS

1. What happens to files when you delete them?

   _____

   _____

2. How do you recover a deleted file using the Recycle Bin?

   _____

   _____

3. What is a clean room, and how is it used by data recovery services?

   _____

   _____

4. What are three methods of restoring data you learned about in this lab?

   _____

   _____

   _____

LAB 5.10 USE THE PROBLEM STEPS RECORDER

OBJECTIVES

The goal of this lab is to use the Windows 8 Steps Recorder. After completing this lab, you will be able to:

◢ Record steps using Steps Recorder

◢ Review steps recorded

MATERIALS REQUIRED

This lab requires the following:

◢ Windows 8 operating system

LAB PREPARATION

Before the lab begins, the instructor or lab assistant needs to do the following:

◢ Verify Windows starts with no errors

ACTIVITY BACKGROUND

When you're troubleshooting a problem in Windows, recording the steps you take can be crucial to proper documentation. Recording steps is also helpful when you're documenting how to do something or when a user needs to show you what he or she is doing. Fortunately, Microsoft provides Steps Recorder to record steps and generate a report with all actions recorded.

ESTIMATED COMPLETION TIME: 20 MINUTES

 Activity

Follow these steps to use Steps Recorder:

1. On the Start screen, start typing **Steps Recorder**. Click **Steps Recorder** in the search results. The Steps Recorder program opens on the desktop.

2. Click **Start Record**. The Steps Recorder begins recording all actions taken on the computer.

3. Return to the **Start** screen, and type **paint**. Click **Paint** in the search results. The Paint program opens on the desktop. Note that when you click, a red dot appears. This indicates that this action was recorded.

4. Draw a mark or shape on the Paint window.

5. In the Steps Recorder program, click **Stop Record**. The Steps Recorder automatically opens a file containing all the steps and information that was recorded. See Figure 5-9. Scroll down the window to review the scripted steps and images that were recorded while you opened the Paint program and drew an image in the Paint window.

6. In the Steps Recorder window showing the file containing the steps, click **Save**.

7. Save this report to your computer, and name it **UsingPaint.zip**. Close the Steps Recorder and Paint windows (no need to save changes in Paint).

8. Open the UsingPaint.zip file, and then open the recording file. Review your recording, and close the file.

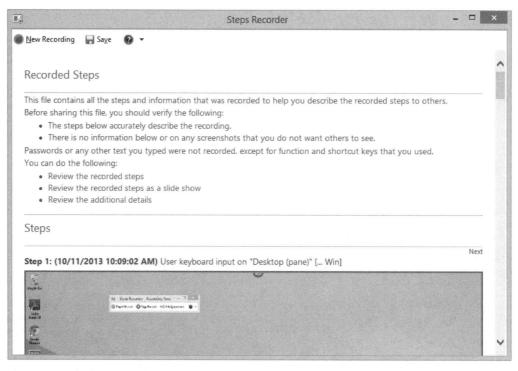

Figure 5-9   The Steps Recorder records screen captures and detailed steps of user activity

REVIEW QUESTIONS

1. How do you know an action using the mouse is recorded?

2. What type of folder contains the file of recorded steps?

3. What type of file contains the recorded steps? By default, which program is used to view the file?

4. Does Steps Recorder record a script of the actions taken or images of the actions taken?

5. Imagine you have a job working on a help desk. What is a possible situation in which you might use the Steps Recorder?

CHAPTER 6

Troubleshooting Windows Startup

Labs included in this chapter:

- **Lab 6.1:** Investigate Startup Processes
- **Lab 6.2:** Explore Tools to Solve Windows 8 Startup Problems
- **Lab 6.3:** Create and Use a Custom Refresh Image
- **Lab 6.4:** Create a Windows 7 Repair Disc
- **Lab 6.5:** Explore the Repair Disc and Windows Recovery Environment (RE)
- **Lab 6.6:** Reimage the Windows Volume
- **Lab 6.7:** Recover Data from a Computer That Will Not Boot
- **Lab 6.8:** Critical Thinking: Sabotage and Repair Windows

LAB 6.1: INVESTIGATE STARTUP PROCESSES

OBJECTIVES

The goal of this lab is to identify malicious software running on your computer by examining all running processes. After completing this lab, you will be able to:

▲ Identify all processes running on your computer at startup

▲ Use the Internet to determine the function of each process

MATERIALS REQUIRED

This lab requires the following:

▲ Windows 8 or Windows 7 operating system

▲ An account with administrator privileges

▲ Internet access

LAB PREPARATION

Before the lab begins, the instructor or lab assistant needs to do the following:

▲ Verify Windows starts with no errors

▲ Verify each student has access to a user account with administrator privileges

▲ Verify Internet access is available

ACTIVITY BACKGROUND

As more add-ons, utilities, and applications are installed on a system over time, they can cause Windows to slow down and give errors. When a program automatically launches at startup, it takes up valuable computer resources behind the scenes and can cause startup errors. In this lab, you learn to investigate all the startup processes on your computer and to identify those you should remove.

ESTIMATED COMPLETION TIME: 45 MINUTES

 Activity

Follow these steps to investigate the startup processes on your computer:

1. Restart your computer, and log on as an administrator.

2. Use Task Manager to display all the running processes on your machine. In Windows 8, use the Details tab in Task Manager, and in Windows 7, use the Processes tab. Be sure to show processes for all users.

3. How many processes are running? Note that many processes are listed twice, but you should count each process only once. To help you identify processes listed more than once, click the **Name** column in Windows 8, or the **Image Name** column in Windows 7 to sort the processes by process name. Figure 6-1 shows the running processes for one system, but yours will be different. On a separate piece of paper, make a list of each process running on the computer, or create and print screen shots that show these processes.

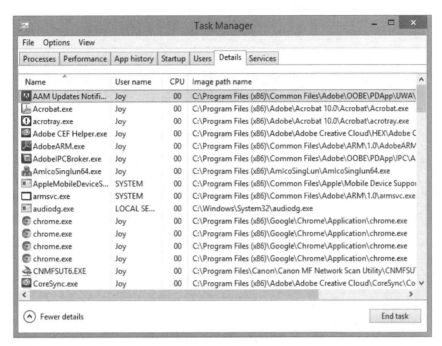

Figure 6-1 The Name and Image path name columns on the Details tab can help you identify a process and how it is loaded

4. Now reboot the computer in Safe Mode, and use Task Manager to list the running processes for all users again. How many processes are running now? (Remember: Count each process only once.)

_____

5. Which processes didn't load when the system was running in Safe Mode?

_____

_____

_____

_____

6. Research each process identified in Step 5 on the web, and write a one-sentence explanation of each process on a separate piece of paper.

   ◢ Did you find any malicious processes running? If so, list them:

_____

_____

_____

◢ Did you find any programs that should be uninstalled from the system? If so, list them:

_____

_____

_____

◢ Suppose one of the processes running on your computer is named whAgent.exe. What program is associated with this process?

_____

◢ How could you use the System Configuration utility to temporarily disable a process?

_____

_____

◢ List the steps you could take to remove this program from your computer:

_____

_____

_____

_____

7. To improve the computer's performance, use the System Configuration utility to temporarily disable any program that you decide is not necessary. Which program, if any, did you disable?

_____

8. If the system works fine with the program disabled, go ahead and uninstall the program. Which program, if any, did you uninstall?

_____

REVIEW QUESTIONS

1. Why is it a good idea to temporarily disable a program before removing it altogether?

_____

2. Why might anti-malware software not detect malicious software?

_____

_____

3. Why would you expect fewer processes to be running in Safe Mode?

_____

_____

4. Why is disabling the Lsass.exe process not a good idea?

_____

5. What key do you press during startup to launch Safe Mode?

_____

LAB 6.2 EXPLORE TOOLS TO SOLVE WINDOWS 8 STARTUP PROBLEMS

OBJECTIVES

The goal of this lab is to explore tools to solve Windows 8 startup problems. After completing this lab, you will be able to:

◢ Find troubleshooting tools for Windows startup problems

◢ Use the Startup Repair process

◢ Enable and disable the Advanced Boot Options menu

◢ Boot to Safe Mode with Networking

MATERIALS REQUIRED

This lab requires the following:

◢ Windows 8 operating system

◢ Windows 8 setup DVD or recovery drive

◢ An account with administrator privileges

◢ Internet access

LAB PREPARATION

Before the lab begins, the instructor or lab assistant needs to do the following:

◢ Verify Windows starts with no errors and the Windows 8 setup DVD or a recovery drive is available

◢ Verify each student has access to a user account with administrator privileges

◢ Verify Internet access is available

ACTIVITY BACKGROUND

Startup problems can be annoying, and Windows 8 has taken great effort to minimize this pain. Windows 8 is one of the most stable operating systems with the fewest errors at startup. On the third sequential reboot, Windows 8 automatically starts a self-healing process. If you still encounter a hang-up, error message, stop error, or hardware error after Windows 8 has attempted to heal itself, you can use the startup repair tools discussed in this lab to help you resolve startup problems.

ESTIMATED COMPLETION TIME: 45 MINUTES

 Activity

This lab is divided into two parts. In Part 1, you use the charms bar to explore several Windows 8 tools used to fix startup problems. You also use the Startup Repair tool, and you boot into Safe Mode with Networking. In Part 2 of the lab, you enable the Advanced Boot Options menu and boot into Safe Mode with Networking. As you work through this lab, reference Figure 6-2 to keep track of where you find each of the startup troubleshooting tools.

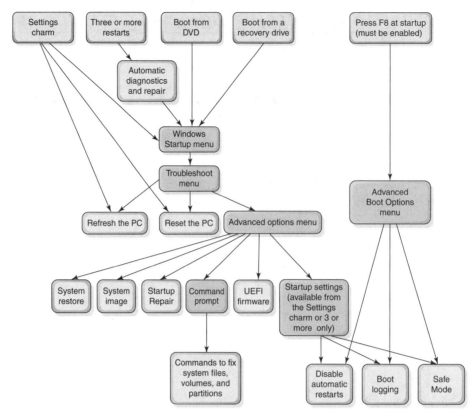

Figure 6-2   Methods to boot the system, including menus and tools for troubleshooting startup problems

PART 1: FIND TOOLS TO FIX STARTUP PROBLEMS

Follow these steps to locate startup repair tools:

1. Sign in to your system with an administrator account.

2. On the **charms bar**, select the **Settings** charm. Click **Change PC settings**.

3. On the PC settings page, click **Update and recovery** in the left pane.

4. On the Update and recovery page, click **Recovery** in the left pane. List the options for recovering your computer that can be accessed through the Settings charm, and briefly describe the purpose of each one:

   _____

   _____

   _____

5. Click **Restart now** under the Advanced startup option. Your computer restarts. When given an option, click **Troubleshoot**, and then click **Advanced options**. List the tools available under Advanced options for troubleshooting startup problems, and briefly describe the purpose of each:

   _____

   _____

   _____

_____

_____

6. Select **Startup Repair**. Your computer restarts into Startup Repair.

7. Choose your account name, and enter your password. Click **Continue**.

8. Startup Repair diagnoses your system, and reports its findings. Click **Advanced options**. This returns you to the Windows Startup menu.

9. Click **Troubleshoot**, and then click **Advanced options**.

10. Click **Startup Settings**, and then click **Restart**.

11. Listed are options for changing startup behavior. Press **5** or **F5** on your keyboard to select **Enable Safe Mode with Networking**. The system reboots. After you sign in, Safe Mode with Networking loads.

12. Open **Internet Explorer**, and make sure the Internet is available.

13. On the charms bar, click the **Settings** charm, and then click **Restart**.

If the hard drive is so corrupted you cannot boot to it, you must boot from another bootable media. Follow these steps to explore the troubleshooting tools available when booting from other bootable media:

1. Boot from the Windows setup DVD or a recovery drive, and select your language and keyboard layout. (Before you can boot to media other than the hard drive, you might need to first change the boot priority order in UEFI/BIOS setup.)

2. When the Windows Setup screen appears, click **Repair your computer**. On the next screen, select your keyboard layout. Next, select the correct troubleshooting options on each screen until you reach the Advanced options screen.

◢ List the tools available under Advanced options:

_____

_____

_____

_____

◢ Which tool is not available on this screen that was available in Step 5, when you used the Settings charm to restart the system?

_____

3. Launch Windows 8 normally, and remove the bootable media from your computer.

PART 2: ENABLE AND USE THE ADVANCED BOOT OPTIONS MENU

Safe Mode can be extremely useful when you're trying to solve a problem with a corrupted device driver or a problem caused by a malware infection because the malfunctioning driver or the malware may not load when Safe Mode is launched. By default in Windows 8, Safe Mode is launched only from the Settings charm. If you cannot start Windows properly, you cannot use the Settings charm to access Safe Mode.

> **Notes** This part of the lab will not work if your computer is set for dual boot.

Another way to launch Safe Mode is to press F8 at startup. This allows you to access the Advanced Boot Options menu. By default, this option is disabled. To use F8 at startup, you must enable it before you encounter a startup problem. Follow these steps to enable the use of F8 during startup:

1. On the Start screen, type **command**. Right-click the **Command Prompt** tile that appears, and select **Run as administrator** in the status bar. Respond to the UAC dialog box. The command prompt window opens on the desktop with administrator privileges.

2. In the command prompt window, enter this command: **bcdedit /set {default} bootmenupolicy legacy**. Press **Enter**.

3. Restart your system. When Windows first starts to load, press F8 to access the Advanced Boot Options menu. List the options available to change the boot behavior:

_____

_____

_____

_____

_____

_____

4. Select **Safe Mode with Networking**, and press **Enter**. The system reboots. After you sign in, Safe Mode with Networking loads.

5. On the charms bar, click the Settings charm, and then click **Restart**.

If your instructor asks you to disable the use of F8 at startup, follow these steps to disable the F8 option:

1. Open a command prompt window with administrator privileges.

2. In the command prompt window, enter this command: **bcdedit /set {default} bootmenupolicy standard**. Press **Enter**.

3. Close all open windows.

REVIEW QUESTIONS

1. Why is Windows 8 considered to be a more stable system than previous Windows editions in terms of startup problems?

_____

_____

2. List the steps you take to find the Refresh the PC option using the charms bar:

_____

_____

_____

_____

3. What is the difference between a refresh and a reset?

_____

_____

_____

4. Why would you want the F8 option at startup enabled on a system?

_____

_____

5. What is the command line you enter into the command prompt window to disable the F8 option at startup?

_____

6. If the hard drive is so corrupted that pressing F8 at startup cannot load the Advanced Boot Options menu, how should you boot the system so you can attempt to repair the Windows installation?

_____

LAB 6.3 CREATE AND USE A CUSTOM REFRESH IMAGE

OBJECTIVES

The goal of this lab is to create and use a custom refresh image. After completing this lab, you will be able to:

◢ Create a custom refresh image

◢ Refresh your system using your custom refresh image

MATERIALS REQUIRED

This lab requires the following:

◢ Windows 8 operating system

◢ Internet access

◢ An account with administrator privileges

LAB PREPARATION

Before the lab begins, the instructor or lab assistant needs to do the following:

◢ Verify Windows starts with no errors

◢ Verify Internet access is available

◢ Verify each student has access to a user account with administrator privileges

ACTIVITY BACKGROUND

If your system isn't running well, you might want to refresh or reset it. A refresh is preferred to a reset because a refresh retains user settings, data, and Windows 8 apps. A refresh works even better if you have created a custom refresh image to use during the refresh. Using the image, the system is restored to the point it was when the image was created, and then any user settings, data, or Windows 8 apps that were installed or changed since the image was created are also restored. After you refresh your system using a custom refresh image, you will need to reinstall any desktop applications that were not installed at the time you created the custom refresh image.

Best practice is to create a custom refresh image after you have the system configured just the way you want it. A custom refresh image takes a snapshot or image of the current system and stores in the image the Windows installation, all installed applications, and user settings and data.

In this lab, you make some changes to user settings, data files, and installed apps. Then, you create a custom refresh image, and make additional changes to user settings, data files, and installed apps. Next, you refresh the system, and then examine the system to find out which changes are retained by the refresh. By working your way through this lab, you can be confident you understand exactly how a refresh works and what to expect from one.

ESTIMATED COMPLETION TIME: 60–120 MINUTES

 Activity

Follow these steps to customize your computer:

1. Sign in using an administrator account.

2. From the Start screen, on the **charms bar**, click the **Settings** charm. Click **Personalize**. Select a picture for the Start screen background, and then select a **Background color**. Describe the picture and color you selected:

   _____

3. Visit **google.com/chrome**, and download and install the free web browser, Google Chrome.

4. Create a new document, and save it in your Documents folder. What is the file name and the path to your document?

   _____

Follow these steps to create a custom refresh image:

1. On the Start screen, move your pointer to the bottom of the screen, and click the **down arrow**. On the Apps screen, scroll to the right, and in the Windows System section, find the Command Prompt tile. Right-click **Command Prompt**. In the status bar, click **Run as administrator**. Respond to the UAC dialog box. The command prompt window opens.

2. Enter this command, substituting any drive and folder for that shown in the command line:

   recimg /createimage C:\MyImage

3. The image is created and registered. In the command prompt, enter this command:

   recimg /showcurrent

4. The location of the image is displayed. Write down the location of the image:

   _____

5. Close the command prompt window. Open File Explorer, and browse to the image file. What is the location given in your address bar? What is the size of the image file?

   _____

Follow these steps to make additional changes to your system:

1. From the Start screen, open the **Settings** charm, and click **Personalize**. Select a picture for the Start screen background and a background color different from those you selected at the beginning of this lab. Describe the new picture and color you selected:

   _____

2. Go to **mozilla.org/firefox**, and download and install the Mozilla Firefox browser.

3. Open the Store app, and install a Windows 8 app. Which application did you install?

   _____

4. Delete the file you stored in your Documents folder earlier in the lab.

Follow these steps to refresh the system using the custom refresh image you created earlier:

1. On the **charms bar**, select the **Settings** charm, and then click **Change PC settings**.

2. On the PC settings page, click **Update and recovery** in the left pane.

3. On the Update and recovery page, click **Recovery** in the left pane.

4. Under Refresh your PC without affecting your files, click **Get started**.

5. On the Refresh your PC screen, review what will happen when you perform a refresh. Click **Next**.

6. Click **Refresh**. During the refresh process, your system restarts.

Do the following to find out the results of the refresh:

1. Sign in to your system, and answer the following questions:

   ◢ Does the Start screen use the latest picture and background color you selected? Why or why not?

   _____

   ◢ Is the app you installed from the Windows Store still installed? Why or why not?

   _____

   ◢ Is the file you stored in your Documents folder there? Why or why not?

   _____

   ◢ Is Google Chrome installed as a desktop app? Why or why not?

   _____

   ◢ Is Mozilla Firefox installed as a desktop app? Why or why not?

   _____

2. Browse to the root of drive C:. What is the size of the Windows.old folder?

   _____

3. Open the file stored on the Windows desktop that lists the desktop applications that were removed from your computer during the refresh. Which application(s) were removed during the refresh?

   _____

Now it's time to clean up the system. Do the following:

1. To keep your hard drive clean, it's best to delete the Windows.old folder after you have confirmed that the refresh was successful. Delete the **Windows.old** folder.

2. Uninstall any Windows 8 apps or desktop applications that you installed in this lab that are still installed.

3. If your instructor requests it, delete the custom refresh image you created in this lab.

REVIEW QUESTIONS

1. What command line can you enter into the command prompt window to view the location of the active recovery image?

   _____

2. What is the file name of the refresh image?

   _____

3. When you perform a system refresh, how will your computer settings be changed?

   _____

4. When you perform a system refresh without the help of a custom refresh image, some apps are kept and some are removed. Which apps are kept? Which are removed? How do you know which apps were removed?

   _____

   _____

   _____

LAB 6.4 CREATE A WINDOWS 7 REPAIR DISC

OBJECTIVES

The goal of this lab is to learn to create a Windows 7 repair disc, which can be used in the event the hard drive will not boot and the Windows 7 setup DVD is not available. After completing this lab, you will be able to:

◢ Create a Windows 7 repair disc

◢ Verify the disc boots without errors

MATERIALS REQUIRED

This lab requires the following:

◢ Windows 7 operating system

◢ A computer with a CD-R drive or other optical drive that will burn a CD

◢ Blank CD-R disc

◢ Permanent marker to label the disc

LAB PREPARATION

Before the lab begins, the instructor or lab assistant needs to do the following:

◢ Verify Windows starts with no errors

◢ Verify the boot priority order in UEFI/BIOS is set so that the system can boot to a CD before turning to the hard drive; if you expect the students to change the boot priority order during the lab, verify the key to press at startup to access setup UEFI/BIOS.

ACTIVITY BACKGROUND

Windows 7 allows you to create a bootable repair disc that holds the Windows Recovery Environment (RE). The repair disc can be used in place of the Windows 7 setup DVD to fix a corrupted Windows installation. When Windows creates the repair disc, a 32-bit version of Windows creates a 32-bit version of Windows RE, and a 64-bit version of Windows creates a 64-bit version of Windows RE. These discs are not interchangeable; you must use a 32-bit repair disc to repair a 32-bit installation of Windows, and a 64-bit repair disc must be used to repair a 64-bit installation. You can, however, use a repair disc created by one edition of Windows 7 to repair another edition. For example, a repair disc created by Windows 7 Home Premium can be used to repair a Windows 7 Ultimate installation.

In this lab, you create the repair disc. Then in the next lab, you will use the repair disc to explore Windows RE.

ESTIMATED COMPLETION TIME: 15 MINUTES

6

 Activity

Follow these steps to create a Windows 7 repair disc:

1. To find out if your version of Windows 7 is a 32-bit or 64-bit OS, open the System window, and answer these questions:

   ◢ Is your system type a 32-bit operating system or a 64-bit operating system?

   _____

   ◢ What edition of Windows 7 is installed?

   _____

2. Insert a blank CD in your CD-R drive or other optical drive that has the ability to burn a CD.

3. There are several ways to launch the utility to build the repair disc. In this lab, you use the Backup and Restore window. Click **Start**, type **Backup and Restore** in the Search box, and then press **Enter**. The Backup and Restore window opens.

4. In the left pane, click **Create a system repair disc**, and follow the on-screen directions to create the disc.

5. When the process is finished, remove the CD from the drive, and label it "Windows 7 32-bit Repair Disc" for a 32-bit version of Windows or "Windows 7 64-bit Repair Disc" for a 64-bit version of Windows. Also include on the label the edition of Windows 7 used to create the disc.

Follow these steps to test the repair disc, verifying you can use it to boot the system and launch Windows RE:

1. Insert the repair disc in the optical drive, and restart the system. A message might appear that says, "Press any key to boot from DVD or CD." If so, press any key.

2. If the system does not boot from the disc, chances are UEFI/BIOS setup is configured to look first to the hard drive before turning to the optical drive for a boot device. Check UEFI/BIOS setup, and change the boot sequence so that it looks to the optical drive before it turns to the hard drive for an OS. The method for accessing UEFI/BIOS setup varies, depending on your computer. Look for a message that says "Press Del to access setup" or "Press F2 for setup," or a similar message when the system is first started. After you have made your changes, save your UEFI/BIOS settings and reboot. This time you should be able to boot from the disc.

3. After you have booted from the CD, the first screen shows the System Recovery Options window where you can select your keyboard input method. When you see this window, you know you have successfully created a bootable repair disc.

4. Remove the disc, and restart the system to the Windows 7 desktop.

5. Save the repair disc to use in the next lab.

REVIEW QUESTIONS

1. What Windows utility is used to create a Windows 7 repair disc?

   _____

2. Is your system a 32-bit or 64-bit operating system?

   _____

3. Why do you think it is important to label the Windows repair disc as a 32-bit or 64-bit version?

   _____

   _____

4. Sometimes a computer boots directly to the hard drive even when a bootable CD is inserted in the optical drive. Explain why this happens and how you can fix the problem so that the computer boots from the CD:

   _____

   _____

   _____

   _____

5. What key on your computer do you press to access UEFI/BIOS setup to change the boot sequence?

   _____

LAB 6.5 EXPLORE THE REPAIR DISC AND WINDOWS RECOVERY ENVIRONMENT (RE)

OBJECTIVES

The goal of this lab is to learn how to use the repair disc and the Windows Recovery Environment (RE) to solve problems with Windows startup. After completing this lab, you will be able to:

⊿ Boot to the Windows RE user interface using two methods

⊿ Use the tools in Windows RE to solve startup problems

MATERIALS REQUIRED

This lab requires the following:

⊿ Windows 7 operating system

⊿ An account with administrator privileges

⊿ Repair disc created in the previous lab

LAB PREPARATION

Before the lab begins, the instructor or lab assistant needs to do the following:

⊿ Verify Windows boots with no errors

⊿ Verify each student has access to a user account with administrator privileges

⊿ Verify the repair disc created in the previous lab is available

ACTIVITY BACKGROUND

Windows RE is an operating system designed to be used to recover from a corrupted Windows installation. Windows RE can be loaded from the Windows setup DVD, the repair disc, or the hard drive. It contains graphical and command-line tools used to troubleshoot a failed Windows startup. In a real troubleshooting situation, first try to load Windows RE from the hard drive using the Advanced Boot Options menu. If that does not work, you can start Windows RE from the Windows setup DVD or the repair disc.

ESTIMATED COMPLETION TIME: 45 MINUTES

 Activity

Even if Windows will not start, you can load Windows RE from the hard drive if the hard drive is still healthy. Follow these steps to load the Windows RE operating system from the hard drive using the Advanced Boot Options menu:

1. If necessary, shut down the computer.

2. Start the computer, and, as it boots up, press **F8**. The Advanced Boot Options menu appears. (In a real troubleshooting situation, the menu might not appear if the hard drive is badly corrupted.)

> **Notes** If the F8 option has been disabled on your computer, open an elevated command prompt, and use this command to enable the F8 option: **bcdedit /set {default} bootmenupolicy legacy**.

6

3. On the Advanced Boot Options menu, use the arrow keys to highlight **Repair Your Computer**, and then press **Enter**. Windows RE loads and the System Recovery Options menu appears. Click **Next**.

4. On the next screen, enter a password to an administrator account.

5. The System Recovery Options menu appears (see Figure 6-3). Click **Shut Down** to shut down the system. (You will explore the System Recovery Options menu later in this lab.)

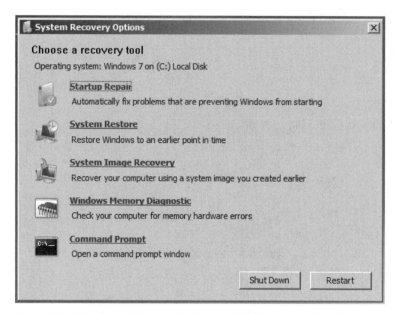

Figure 6-3 The System Recovery Options window lists troubleshooting tools

Starting Windows RE from the hard drive will not work if the hard drive is corrupted. In this situation, you must use either the repair disc or the Windows setup DVD to load Windows RE. Follow these steps to use the repair disc you created in the previous lab to launch Windows RE:

1. Insert the repair disc in the optical drive, and power up the system. A message might appear that says, "Press any key to boot from DVD or CD." If so, press any key.

2. If the system does not boot from the disc, reboot the system, press a key to launch setup UEFI/BIOS, and change the boot sequence to list the optical drive first. Then reboot using the disc.

3. On the first screen, click **Next**. Windows RE searches for Windows installations.

4. On the next screen, Windows RE lists the installations of Windows it was able to detect. (If Windows cannot detect an installation, it gives you the option to restore the system from a previously created system image.) Select your installation, and confirm that the **Use recovery tools that can help fix problems starting Windows** option is selected. Click **Next**. The System Recovery Options menu appears, as shown earlier in Figure 6-3.

5. The first tool to try in almost every troubleshooting situation is Startup Repair, which examines key system files used to start the system and replaces or rebuilds them if a problem is detected. It's easy to use, and you can't do any harm using it. Click **Startup Repair**.

6. The system is checked for errors, and an error report is generated. Click **Finish** to return to the System Recovery Options window.

7. Sometimes a problem can be resolved by applying a restore point. To explore this option, click **System Restore**, and then click **Next**. A list of restore points appears.

   ◢ What types of problems can you solve by successfully applying a restore point?

   _____

   _____

   ◢ What problems might you create when you successfully apply a restore point?

   _____

   _____

8. To continue without applying a restore point, click **Cancel**. You are returned to the System Recovery Options window.

9. In a troubleshooting situation, you might decide to completely restore the volume on which Windows is installed to the time the last system image was created. To explore this option, click **System Image Recovery**. If a system image is found, information about the system image appears, and you can continue with the restore. Describe what changes you would make to the system if you continued with the System Image Recovery:

   _____

   _____

10. If no system image is found, a message indicating that appears. Click **Cancel** to close the message. Another window appears, giving you another opportunity to provide the backup media that contains a system image. Click **Cancel** to return to the System Recovery Options window.

11. Problems with memory can often present themselves as Windows or application problems. To test memory for errors, click **Windows Memory Diagnostic**. A message appears saying that the utility wants to restart the system to test memory.

    ◢ What type of symptoms might a system exhibit if memory is bad?

    _____

    _____

    ◢ If Windows Memory Diagnostic reports bad memory, what should you do next?

    _____

12. Click **Cancel** to skip performing the memory test.

13. Some problems can be resolved by using commands in a command prompt window. To explore the command prompt window, click **Command Prompt**. A command prompt window opens where you can enter commands.

    ◢ What is the default drive and path showing in the command prompt?

    _____

14. At the command prompt, enter the command to list the contents of the current folder. What command did you use?

    _____

6

15. Enter the command to move up one level in the directory tree to the parent folder of the current folder. What command did you use?

_____

16. Enter the command to close the command prompt window. What command did you use?

_____

17. In the System Recovery Options window, click **Restart** to restart the system and load the Windows desktop.

REVIEW QUESTIONS

1. Which System Recovery Option should you use to solve a problem with a corrupted device driver that was just installed and causes the system to not boot?

_____

2. Which System Recovery Option should you use if Microsoft Word documents continue to get corrupted?

_____

3. Suppose that after you insert the repair disc in the drive and restart the system, the Windows desktop loads. Why did the system not boot from the disc?

_____

4. Which System Recovery Option should you use if the system hangs at odd times and is generally unstable?

_____

5. What can you conclude if you cannot load the Advanced Boot Options menu by pressing F8 at startup, but you can load Windows RE by booting from the repair disc?

_____

_____

6. Which System Recovery Option will make the least intrusive changes to the system, System Restore or Startup Repair?

_____

LAB 6.6 REIMAGE THE WINDOWS VOLUME

OBJECTIVES

The goal of this lab is to learn how to create a system image and use it to restore the Windows volume. After completing this lab, you will be able to:

◢ Create a system image using a second hard drive installed in a system

◢ Use the system image to reimage the Windows volume

MATERIALS REQUIRED

This lab requires the following:

◢ Windows 7 operating system

◢ A second internal or external hard drive

◢ Alternately, you can use Windows 7 installed in a virtual machine (If you are using a VM, this lab creates a second virtual hard drive in the VM. Instructions in this lab are given for both Windows Virtual PC and Oracle VirtualBox.)

LAB PREPARATION

Before the lab begins, the instructor or lab assistant needs to do the following:

◢ Verify Windows starts with no errors and a second hard drive is available

◢ Alternately, if you plan to use a VM for this lab, verify Windows 7 is installed in the VM

ACTIVITY BACKGROUND

A system image backs up the entire Windows volume and can be stored on an external or internal hard drive or on DVDs. (For Windows 7 Professional, Ultimate, and Enterprise editions, you can install the system image on a network location.) When the Windows volume is corrupted or data on the drive is totally lost, you can use a system image to restore the entire Windows volume to the time the system image was last updated.

You can do this lab using a Windows 7 computer with a second hard drive. Alternately, you can use Windows 7 installed in a virtual machine and create a second hard drive in the VM. Directions for both methods are included.

6

> **ESTIMATED COMPLETION TIME: 45 MINUTES**

 Activity

If you are using a Windows 7 computer and a second hard drive, follow the steps in Part 1 of this lab. If you are using Windows 7 in a VM, follow the steps in Part 2 of this lab.

PART 1: USE A WINDOWS 7 COMPUTER TO CREATE AND USE A SYSTEM IMAGE

1. Plug in an external hard drive or install a second internal hard drive in your computer.

2. If the hard drive is new and needs to be partitioned and formatted, open Disk Management, and partition and format the hard drive using the NTFS file system.

3. Using Windows Explorer, find out how much space is used on drive C:. Find out how much space is free on the second hard drive. The free space needed to hold the system image on the second hard drive will be about 80 percent of the space used on drive C:.

   ◢ How much space is used on drive C:?

   _____

   ◢ How much space is free on the second hard drive? Do you have enough room on the second drive for the system image?

   _____

4. To create the system image, open the Backup and Restore utility, and then click **Create a system image**. Follow the on-screen directions to create the image.

   ◢ Other than the second hard drive, what locations or devices can you use for the image?

   _____

   ◢ What is the name of the subfolder in the WindowsImageBackup folder that holds the system image? What is the size of this subfolder?

   _____

5. Now let's make some changes to the Windows volume. Use Windows Explorer to go to your user profile in C:\Users*username*. Record below the exact path to your My Documents, My Music, My Pictures, and My Videos folders, and then delete these four folders.

   _____

   _____

6. Shut down Windows.

7. Boot up the computer, and load the Advanced Boot Options menu. Click **Repair Your Computer** to launch Windows RE. What responses did you need to make to launch Windows RE?

   _____

8. In the System Recovery Options window, click **System Image Recovery**. Follow the on-screen directions to reimage the drive. What decisions and responses did you need to make during this process?

   _____

   _____

   _____

9. When the imaging is complete, Windows restarts and the Windows desktop loads. Look in your user profile. Are the deleted folders restored?

   _____

PART 2: USE WINDOWS 7 IN A VM TO CREATE AND USE A SYSTEM IMAGE

1. Using Windows Virtual PC or Oracle VirtualBox, select a VM that has Windows 7 installed. If necessary, install in the VM a second virtual hard drive (VHD). Make the VHD a dynamically expanding drive with a maximum capacity of at least 50 GB.

2. Start the VM. If you have just installed a new VHD, use Disk Management to partition and format this drive using the NTFS file system.

3. Open Windows Explorer or Disk Management to help you answer these questions:

   ◢ How much space is used on drive C:?

   _____

◢ How much space is free on the second hard drive? Do you have enough room on the second drive for the system image?

_____

4. Open the Backup and Restore utility, and use it to create a system image on the second hard drive.

◢ What other locations or devices can you use for the image other than the second hard drive?

_____

◢ What is the name of the subfolder in the WindowsImageBackup folder that holds the system image? What is the size of this subfolder?

_____

5. Now let's make some drastic changes to the Windows volume. List the exact paths to several folders on drive C:, and then delete these folders. Include Windows subfolders and Users subfolders in your list of folders to delete.

_____

_____

_____

6. Shut down the Windows 7 VM.

7. Start the VM again and load the Advanced Boot Options menu. Launch Windows RE. What responses did you need to make to launch Windows RE?

_____

8. In the System Recovery Options window, click **System Image Recovery**. Follow the on-screen directions to reimage the drive. What decisions and responses did you need to make during this process?

_____

_____

_____

9. When the imaging is complete, the VM restarts and the Windows desktop loads. Did Windows launch successfully? Are the deleted folders restored?

_____

CHALLENGE ACTIVITY (ADDITIONAL 20 MINUTES)

Interestingly enough, Windows stores the system image in a VHD. If you drill down into the WindowsImageBackup subfolders, you will find a very large VHD file, which contains the image. Mount (attach) this VHD file as a virtual hard drive installed on your computer or virtual machine. Then, use Windows Explorer to explore the VHD. Copy a file from the C:\Users\Public\Public Music\Sample Music folder in the system image to the Windows desktop.

Answer the following questions:

◢ What utility did you use to attach the VHD file to your system as an installed virtual hard drive? What drive letter did Windows assign the VHD?

_____

◢ What is the size of the VHD file in the WindowsImageBackup folder that holds the system image you created in this lab?

_____

◢ Why is it unreasonable to ask you the name of the VHD file?

_____

REVIEW QUESTIONS

1. If you were using single-sided recordable DVDs to hold the system image you created in this lab, how many DVDs would be required? How did you arrive at your answer?

_____

_____

2. What Windows utility is used to create a system image? To restore the system using a system image? To mount a VHD to the Windows system?

_____

_____

_____

3. Why is it useful to know that you can mount into the Windows system the VHD that holds the system image?

_____

_____

4. Describe one situation in the field when you might want to recover the Windows volume using the system image. Describe a situation when you might want to mount into the Windows system the VHD that holds the system image:

_____

_____

LAB 6.7 RECOVER DATA FROM A COMPUTER THAT WILL NOT BOOT

OBJECTIVES

The goal of this lab is to learn how to recover data from a computer that will not boot. After completing this lab, you will be able to:

◢ Copy data from a nonbooting computer

MATERIALS REQUIRED

This lab requires the following:

◢ Two Windows 8 or Windows 7 computers designated for this lab

◢ An account with administrator privileges

◢ Internet access

LAB PREPARATION

Before the lab begins, the instructor or lab assistant needs to do the following:

◢ Verify Windows works with no errors

◢ Verify each student has access to a user account with administrator privileges

◢ Verify Internet access is available

ACTIVITY BACKGROUND

If Windows is corrupted and the system will not boot, recovering your data might be your first priority. One way to get to the data is to remove your hard drive from your computer and install it as a second nonbooting hard drive in another working system. After you boot up the system, you should be able to use File Explorer/Windows Explorer to copy the data to another medium, such as a USB flash drive. If the data is corrupted, you can try to use data recovery software. In this lab, you will remove the hard drive from a computer and attempt to recover information from it.

ESTIMATED COMPLETION TIME: 45 MINUTES

 Activity

First you need to create some data on the first computer that will need to be rescued:

1. Boot the first computer, and log on as administrator.

2. Using Control Panel, create a new user called **User1**.

3. Log on as User1.

4. You will now create some files to represent important information that might be saved in various locations on this computer. Use Notepad to create three text files, named **file1.txt**, **file2.txt**, and **file3.txt**, and save one in each of the following locations:

   ◢ Save **file1.txt** in User1's My Documents folder.

   ◢ Save **file2.txt** in the Public Documents subfolder in the \Users\Public folder.

   ◢ Save **file3.txt** in the root (probably C:\).

5. Open Internet Explorer, and bookmark at least three locations on the web.

6. Log off and shut down this computer.

Now pretend this computer is no longer able to boot. Because a backup or restore point has not been created recently, you will remove the hard drive and attempt to recover your important files before attempting to determine why the computer won't boot.

1. Remove the main hard drive, and install it as a second hard drive in another Windows machine. If you are not trained to work inside a computer, ask your instructor for assistance.

> **Notes** You can save time by purchasing an external IDE/SATA-to-USB converter kit (for about $30), which can be used to temporarily connect a hard drive to a USB port on a working computer.

2. Boot this computer, and log on as an administrator.

3. Use File Explorer/Windows Explorer to locate the three text files on the hard drive you just installed.

4. List the path where each of these files can be found:

   ◢ file1.txt

   _____

   ◢ file2.txt

   _____

   ◢ file3.txt

   _____

5. Determine the name and location of the file containing your Internet Explorer bookmarks:

   _____

6. Can you think of any other locations that could contain information a user might want to recover?

   _____

   _____

In some cases, the files you are trying to recover might be corrupt, or you might not be able to access the drive at all. In these cases, you can attempt to use file-recovery software.

1. Open a command prompt window. Use the chkdsk command to check the hard drive on which you have important data for errors, and attempt to fix them. What chkdsk command line did you use?

   _____

2. Shut down the system you're using and return the hard drive to its original computer.

3. Boot both computers back up, and ensure that everything is working before shutting them both down.

CHALLENGE ACTIVITY (ADDITIONAL 45 MINUTES)

You can simulate this lab using two virtual machines. Go through the steps in the lab again using Windows 8 or Windows 7 installed in a virtual machine using either Virtual PC or VirtualBox. Then "move" the virtual hard drive (VHD) to a second VM that has Windows 8 or Windows 7 installed. Install the VHD as the second hard drive in this VM. Then use Windows 8 or Windows 7 on this second VM to recover the data on your virtual hard drive. Finally, return the VHD to the original VM, and start up both VMs to make sure everything is working as it should. Answer the following questions:

1. List the steps you took to "move" the VHD in the first VM to the second VM:

   _____

   _____

2. List the steps you took to locate and use the second virtual hard drive when you started the second VM:

_____

_____

_____

3. List the steps you took to return the VHD to the first VM:

_____

_____

_____

4. What problems did you encounter while performing this Challenge Activity, and how did you solve them?

_____

_____

REVIEW QUESTIONS

1. Why might you want to recover lost data before attempting to resolve a boot problem?

_____

_____

2. How could scheduled backups save you a lot of time if your system will not boot?

_____

_____

3. What type of errors might cause a computer to not boot? List three possible causes:

_____

_____

_____

4. If you suspect the first computer is not booting because it is infected with a virus, what should you ensure before installing its hard drive in a second computer?

_____

_____

6

LAB 6.8 CRITICAL THINKING: SABOTAGE AND REPAIR WINDOWS

OBJECTIVES

The goal of this lab is to learn to troubleshoot Windows by repairing a sabotaged system. After completing this lab, you will be able to:

⊿ Troubleshoot and repair a system that isn't working correctly

MATERIALS REQUIRED

This lab requires the following:

⊿ Windows 8 or Windows 7 installed on a computer designated for sabotage

⊿ Windows 8 or Windows 7 setup DVD or installation files

⊿ A workgroup of two to four students

> **Notes** This lab works great on Windows 8 or Windows 7 installed in a VM.

LAB PREPARATION

Before the lab begins, the instructor or lab assistant needs to do the following:

⊿ Verify Windows starts with no errors

⊿ Provide each workgroup with access to the Windows 8 or Windows 7 installation files, if needed

ACTIVITY BACKGROUND

You have learned about several tools and methods you can use to recover Windows when it fails. This lab gives you the opportunity to use these skills in a troubleshooting situation. Your group will sabotage another group's system while that group sabotages your system. Then your group will repair its own system.

ESTIMATED COMPLETION TIME: 45 MINUTES

 Activity

Follow these steps to sabotage a Windows 8 or Windows 7 system for another group, and then repair your Windows 8 or Windows 7 system that the other group has sabotaged:

1. If your system's hard drive contains important data, back it up to another medium. Is there anything else you would like to back up before another group sabotages the system? Record the name of that item here, and then back it up:

   _____

2. Trade systems with another group, and sabotage the other group's system while they sabotage your system. Do one thing that will cause the system to fail to boot, display errors after the boot, or prevent a device or application from working. The following list offers some sabotage suggestions. Do something in the following list, or think of another option. (Do not alter the hardware.)

◢ Find a system file in the root directory that's required to boot the computer, and rename it or move it to a different directory. (Don't delete the file.)

◢ Using the Registry Editor (Regedit.exe), delete several important keys or values in the registry.

◢ Locate important system files in the Windows folder or its subfolders, and rename them or move them to another directory.

> **Notes** To move, delete, or rename a Windows system file, you might need to first take ownership of the file using the takeown and icacls commands. The Microsoft Knowledge Base Article 929833 at *support.microsoft.com* explains how to use these two commands.

◢ Put a corrupted program file in the Windows folder that will cause the program to launch automatically at startup. Record the name of that program file and folder here:

_____

◢ Use display settings that aren't readable—such as black text on a black background.

◢ Disable a critical device driver or Windows service.

3. Reboot the system and verify a problem exists.

4. How did you sabotage the other team's system?

_____

_____

5. Return to your system and troubleshoot it.

6. Describe the problem as a user would describe it to you if you were working at a help desk:

_____

_____

_____

7. What is your first guess as to the source of the problem?

_____

8. As you troubleshoot the system, list the high-level steps you are taking in the troubleshooting process:

_____

_____

_____

_____

9. How did you finally solve the problem and return the system to good working order?

_____

_____

REVIEW QUESTIONS

1. What would you do differently the next time you encountered the same symptoms that you encountered in this lab?

   _____

   _____

2. What Windows utilities did you use—or could you have used—to solve the problem in the lab?

   _____

3. What might cause the problem in the lab to occur in real life? List three possible causes:

   _____

   _____

   _____

4. If you were the IT support technician responsible for this computer in an office environment, what could you do to prevent this problem from happening in the future or at least limit its impact on users if it did happen?

   _____

   _____

CHAPTER 7

Connecting To and Setting Up a Network

Labs included in this chapter:

- **Lab 7.1:** Understand the OSI Model
- **Lab 7.2:** Convert Binary and Hexadecimal Numbers
- **Lab 7.3:** Network Two Computers
- **Lab 7.4:** Demonstrate Homegroup Security
- **Lab 7.5:** Set Up a Wireless Router
- **Lab 7.6:** Secure a Wireless LAN

LAB 7.1 UNDERSTAND THE OSI MODEL

OBJECTIVES

The goal of this lab is to understand some of the concepts and principles of networking technology. After completing this lab, you will be able to:

◢ Describe the OSI layers

◢ Apply the OSI layer principles to networking

MATERIALS REQUIRED

This lab requires the following:

◢ Windows 8 or Windows 7 operating system

◢ Internet access

LAB PREPARATION

Before the lab begins, the instructor or lab assistant needs to do the following:

◢ Verify Windows starts with no errors

◢ Verify Internet access is available

ACTIVITY BACKGROUND

Network architects use a variety of principles and concepts for communication when designing and implementing networks. Collectively, this architectural model is called the OSI (Open Systems Interconnection) model. The OSI model consists of seven layers. As an IT support technician, you do not need to understand network architecture. However, you might find it interesting to know a little about these fundamental concepts, which can help you better understand how the TCP/IP protocols work. Understanding these concepts will also help you better communicate with network specialists.

ESTIMATED COMPLETION TIME: 30 MINUTES

 Activity

Using the Internet for your research, answer the following questions:

1. What are the seven OSI layers? Enter their names in the empty boxes on the left side of Table 7-1.

2. The OSI model is easier to understand if you memorize the seven layers. You can use a phrase mnemonic, in which the beginning letter of each layer is used to create a memorable phrase, to help you with this task. Research online for a mnemonic to help you memorize the OSI layers, and record it here:

_____

3. TCP/IP is a suite of protocols that follow the concepts of the OSI model. The four layers of the TCP/IP model are shown on the right side of Table 7-1. Email is one example of a TCP/IP application that works at the Application layer. What are two more examples of applications that work at this layer?

_____

OSI Layer		TCP/IP Protocol Stack Layer
7		**Application layer** (For example, email using SMTP and IMAP protocols)
6		
5		
4		**Transport layer** (TCP protocol)
3		**Internet layer** (IP protocol)
2		**Network interface layer** (Network card using Ethernet protocol)
1		

Table 7-1 Describing the OSI model and the TCP/IP model

4. The TCP protocol works at the Transport layer of TCP/IP. Briefly describe the function of the TCP protocol as used in Internet communications:

_____

_____

5. The IP protocol, working at the Internet layer, is responsible for locating the network and host for a data packet being transmitted by TCP. What type of address does the IP protocol use to identify a unique network and host?

_____

6. Other than a network card (NIC), what is an example of a device that works at the Network layer of the TCP/IP stack?

_____

7. Other than IP, what is an example of a protocol that works at the Internet layer of TCP/IP?

_____

8. At which TCP/IP layer does a MAC address function?

_____

9. At which TCP/IP layer does the TLS protocol work?

_____

10. At which TCP/IP layer does the HTTPS protocol work?

_____

7

11. Why do you think TCP/IP is often called a protocol stack rather than a protocol suite?

_____

_____

REVIEW QUESTIONS

1. What mnemonic can you use to help you remember the seven OSI layers?

_____

2. List all of the OSI layers used when an email client requests email over the Internet:

_____

_____

3. What protocol does a web browser normally use? At which OSI layer does this protocol work?

_____

4. When more than one application is running on a server, how does IP know which service should be presented an incoming data packet?

_____

5. When configuring a network connection to the Internet, you might need to enter the IP address of the computer, the DNS server, the subnet mask, and the default gateway. Of these four items, which are used to determine whether a remote computer is on the same network or a remote network?

_____

_____

6. Of the four items listed in Question 5, which is used to relate a domain name to an IP address?

_____

LAB 7.2 CONVERT BINARY AND HEXADECIMAL NUMBERS

OBJECTIVES

The goal of this lab is to practice converting numbers between decimal, binary, and hexadecimal forms. After completing this lab, you will be able to:

◢ Convert decimal numbers (base 10) to hexadecimal and binary form

◢ Convert hexadecimal numbers (base 16) to binary and decimal form

◢ Convert binary numbers (base 2) to decimal and hexadecimal form

MATERIALS REQUIRED

This lab requires the following:

◢ A pencil and paper and/or Windows Calculator

◢ Access to the online content "The Hexadecimal Number System" that accompanies this lab manual; for instructions on how to access this content at *cengagebrain.com*, see the Preface.

◢ Windows 8 or Windows 7 operating system

LAB PREPARATION

Before the lab begins, the instructor or lab assistant needs to do the following:

◢ Announce to students that, before they come to lab, they should read the online content "The Hexadecimal Number System." It is also suggested that students bring this content to class in printed form.

ACTIVITY BACKGROUND

Sometimes you need to know what resources, such as memory addresses, are being reserved for a device. This information is often displayed on a computer using the binary or hexadecimal (hex) number system, which, while useful to the computer, is difficult for humans to read and understand. In another example, IPv4 addresses are displayed and written in decimal and often need to be converted to binary. In addition, IPv6 addresses are written and displayed in hex, and you need to write them in binary or decimal. It's also interesting to know that MAC addresses are displayed in hex.

As an IT support technician, you are likely to encounter the need to convert numbers from one number system to another, such as when you are comparing an IP address with a subnet mask in order to decide if the IP address is in a particular subnet. This lab gives you that practice.

ESTIMATED COMPLETION TIME: 60 MINUTES

7

 Activity

Follow these steps to practice converting numbers from one number system to another:

1. Convert the following decimal numbers to binary numbers using a calculator or by following the instructions in the online content "The Hexadecimal Number System." (To access Windows Calculator in Windows 8, press **Win+S**, type **calculator**, and press **Enter**. To access Windows Calculator in Windows 7, click **Start**, **All Programs**, **Accessories**, and then click **Calculator**. If necessary, click **View** on the Calculator menu bar, and then click **Programmer** to access the function you need to perform the conversions in these steps.)

   ◢ 14 = _____

   ◢ 77 = _____

   ◢ 128 = _____

   ◢ 223 = _____

   ◢ 255 = _____

2. Convert the following decimal numbers to hexadecimal notation:

   ◢ 13 = _____

   ◢ 240 = _____

   ◢ 255 = _____

   ◢ 58880 = _____

   ◢ 65535 = _____

3. Convert the following binary numbers to hexadecimal notation:

- 100 = _____
- 1011 = _____
- 111101 = _____
- 11111000 = _____
- 10110011 = _____
- 00000001 = _____

4. Hexadecimal numbers are often preceded by "0x." However, when converting a hexadecimal number, do not include the "0x" in the entry on the calculator. Convert the following hexadecimal numbers to binary numbers:

- 0x0016 = _____
- 0x00F8 = _____
- 0x00B2B = _____
- 0x005A = _____
- 0x1234 = _____

5. Convert the following hexadecimal numbers to decimal:

- 0x0013 = _____
- 0x00AB = _____
- 0x01CE = _____
- 0x812A = _____

6. Convert the following binary numbers to decimal:

- 1011 = _____
- 11011 = _____
- 10101010 = _____
- 111110100 = _____
- 10111011101 = _____
- 11111000001111 = _____

A network card, also called a network adapter or NIC, is assigned a MAC address (or physical address) at the factory. Windows assigns to a network connection an IPv4 address, a subnet mask, and possibly an IPv6 address each time the connection is created. In the following steps, you find these assigned values for your computer, and then convert them to binary numbers:

1. Open the command prompt window, type **ipconfig /all**, and then press **Enter**.

2. Write down the following information for your system's active network connection (most likely either Ethernet or Wi-Fi):

- Physical address in paired hexadecimal form:

_____

- Physical address expressed in binary pairs:

_____

- IPv4 address in decimal form:

_____

- IPv4 address expressed as four octets in binary form:

_____

◢ Subnet mask in decimal form:

_____

◢ Subnet mask expressed as four octets in binary form:

_____

◢ IPv6 address in decimal form:

_____

◢ IPv6 address expressed as eight blocks of hexadecimal numbers (some of these blocks might contain a zero):

_____

◢ IPv6 address expressed as eight blocks of binary numbers:

_____

Memory addresses are displayed in hexadecimal form. Do the following to find out the memory address range assigned to the NIC on your computer, and then convert this range to decimal:

1. Open **Device Manager**, and then open the **Properties** dialog box for the network adapter. Click the **Resources** tab. What is the memory address range for the NIC?

_____

2. Convert the numbers in the network adapter's memory range, and determine how many bytes, expressed in a decimal number, are in its memory address range:

_____

CRITICAL THINKING (ADDITIONAL 15 MINUTES)

1. A typical video card uses a color depth of 8 bits to define the screen color in Safe Mode. Eight bits can form 256 different numbers from 00000000 to 11111111 in binary (0 to 255 in decimal) so 256 different colors are possible. How many colors are available with a 16-bit color depth? How many are available with a 24-bit or a 32-bit depth?

_____

_____

_____

REVIEW QUESTIONS

1. How long, in bits, is a typical MAC address?

_____

2. Computers often express numbers in _____ format, which is a base 16 number system.

3. Most people are more comfortable working with a(n) _____, or base 10, number system.

4. In the hexadecimal system, what decimal value does the letter A represent?

_____

5. Hexadecimal numbers are often preceded by _____ so that a value containing only numerals is not mistaken for a decimal number.

6. Write the following IPv6 address using a short hand method: 2001:0:4147:0:0:1c32:0:fe99.

_____

7. The IP address of Computer 1 is 192.168.200.10, and it has a subnet mask of 255.255.240.0. The IP address of Computer 2 is 192.168.195.200, and the IP address of Computer 3 is 192.168.230.40.

   a. How many bits of the IP address for Computer 1 are used to define its subnet?

   b. Are Computer 1 and Computer 2 part of the same subnet? Explain your answer.

   c. Are Computer 1 and Computer 3 part of the same subnet? Explain your answer.

_____

_____

_____

_____

_____

LAB 7.3 NETWORK TWO COMPUTERS

OBJECTIVES

The goal of this lab is to install and configure a network interface card (NIC) and configure the TCP/IP settings to connect two computers. After completing this lab, you will be able to:

◢ Uninstall and install a NIC

◢ Configure TCP/IPv4 settings

◢ Share files and folders between two computers

◢ Configure IP addressing

MATERIALS REQUIRED

This lab requires the following:

◢ Windows 8 or Windows 7 operating system

◢ An account with administrator privileges

◢ A wireless NIC and the associated drivers

◢ Wi-Fi network access

◢ A workgroup partner

LAB PREPARATION

Before the lab begins, the instructor or lab assistant needs to do the following:

◢ Verify Windows starts with no errors

◢ Verify each student has access to a user account with administrator privileges

◢ Verify drivers for the NIC and wireless equipment to connect two computers
are available

ACTIVITY BACKGROUND

Computers on a network have the ability to communicate with one another and share
resources, such as files and devices. A computer connects to a network through a network
interface card (NIC). In this lab, you install a NIC, configure necessary network settings,
and verify the NIC is functioning correctly. Working with a partner, you create a simple
network of two computers and work through the basics of networking.

ESTIMATED COMPLETION TIME: 45 MINUTES

 Activity

As an IT technician, you need to be able to set up, configure, and troubleshoot the hardware involved in
networking. A key hardware piece is the network interface card (NIC). This card allows the computer to
communicate on the network. Follow these steps to learn to uninstall and reinstall the NIC:

1. Power on your computer, and then sign in to Windows.

2. Disconnect any network cable, and then disable Wi-Fi.

3. Open **Device Manager**. Expand the **Network adapters** listing. What are the names of the
network adapters installed on your system?

_____

4. Right-click the **Wi-Fi network adapter,** and then click **Uninstall** in the shortcut menu.
Click **OK** to confirm the device uninstall.

5. Restart the computer, and install the NIC. The installation process might take a few
minutes because there might be several layers to the drivers.

6. After installation is complete, return to **Device Manager,** and verify your NIC has been
reinstalled and that Device Manager reports no problems with the device.

Now that the network adapter is working, you need to configure the computer to gain access to shared
resources on the network. It is important for you to know where to locate and how to modify settings that
control network communication. These settings make your computer unique on the network and easily
identified by other computers. Let's explore the configuring of the network settings.

To verify and configure the current TCP/IP settings, follow these steps:

1. Open **Network and Sharing Center** (see the left side of Figure 7-1). In the left panel,
click **Change adapter settings**. Right-click **the Wi-Fi network connection,** and click
Properties in the shortcut menu. The Wi-Fi Properties dialog box opens.

7

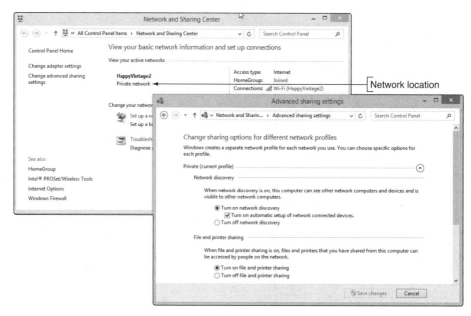

Figure 7-1 The Network and Sharing Center reports the network location and gives options for adjusting the network profile

2. In the list of connection items, click **Internet Protocol Version 4 (TCP/IPv4)**, and then click **Properties**. The Properties dialog box that opens can be used to configure the IP settings for the connection.

3. For this part of the lab, you use static IP addressing. With your lab partner, determine who will use the Partner #1 information in the grid below and who will use the Partner #2 information:

	Partner #1	**Partner #2**
IP address	192.168.1.1	192.168.1.2
Computer name:	Lab1	Lab2
Workgroup name:	NIC LAB	NIC LAB

4. Select the **Use the following IP address** option, and then enter your chosen IP address.

5. Use the **Tab** key to move to the Subnet mask box. If Windows doesn't automatically populate the subnet mask, enter a subnet mask of 255.255.255.0.

6. Click **OK**, and then close all windows.

Now that your computer has a unique IP address on the network, it is time to assign a computer name and workgroup name to your computer. These assignments will give the computer an identity on the network. Follow these steps:

1. Open the System window. In the Computer name, domain, and workgroup settings area, click **Change settings**. The System Properties dialog box opens.

2. Click **Change**. The Computer Name/Domain Changes dialog box opens.

3. Enter the computer name for your machine from the chart.

4. If necessary, click **Workgroup** to select it. Enter the Workgroup name from the chart. Other than Workgroup, what is a second choice for membership?

5. Click **OK**. A Welcome to the workgroup dialog box appears. Click **OK**. Windows displays a message with instructions about applying the change. What must you do next to apply the change?

_____

6. Click **OK**, and close all windows. Restart your computer, and then sign in to Windows.

7. Connect the computer to the Wi-Fi network. Make sure to configure the connection as a public network. In Windows 8, set the connection as public by clicking **No** when asked if you want to find PCs and other devices and content on the network. In Windows 7, set the connection as public by clicking **Public network** in the Set Network Location dialog box. Refer to the chapter, "Survey of Windows Features and Support Tools," for details on how to change this setting in either Windows 8 or Windows 7.

8. Open the **Network and Sharing Center**, and then click **Change advanced sharing settings** (see the right side of Figure 7-1). The Advanced sharing settings window opens. Here you can change your network profiles for each network location.

9. At the top of this window, hide the profile for Private in Windows 8 or for Home or Work in Windows 7, and expand the profile for Guest or Public in Windows 8 or for Guest in Windows 7. Verify the Guest or Public profile (in Windows 8) or the Public profile (in Windows 7) is labeled as the current profile.

10. Under Network discovery, select **Turn on network discovery**.

11. Under File and printer sharing, select **Turn on file and printer sharing**.

12. In Windows 8, expand the All Networks profile. In either Windows 8 or Windows 7, under Public folder sharing, select **Turn on sharing so anyone with network access can read and write files in the Public folders**.

13. Under Password protected sharing, select **Turn off password protected sharing**.

14. Click **Save changes**.

15. Open File Explorer or Windows Explorer. In the left pane, scroll down and then click **Network**.

◢ What machines show up in the Computer section?

_____

16. Close all windows.

Now let's see what happens when there is a conflict in IP addresses on your small network. Follow these steps:

1. Partner #1: Return to your Internet Protocol Version 4 (TCP/IPv4) Properties dialog box, and change the IP address of your machine to **192.168.1.2**.

2. Partner #1: Click **OK** and close all windows. If you're using a Windows 7 computer, what is the error message that appears on the Partner #1 computer?

_____

If you're using a Windows 8 computer, you have to do a little more detective work (which can also be done on a Windows 7 computer). With either Windows 8 or Windows 7, open a command prompt window, type **ipconfig**, and then press **Enter**. What is the IPv4 address for your computer? What does this information tell you?

_____

_____

3. Partners #1 and #2: Close all windows, reboot your computers, and sign in. If necessary, connect to the network. Wait for the Network icon in the taskbar to finish processing network discovery.

4. Partners #1 and #2: Open File Explorer or Windows Explorer, and drill down into the **Network** group.

    ◢ What computers have been discovered? (You might need to refresh this screen a couple of times. To refresh a selected window, press **F5**.)

    _____

    ◢ Explain the importance of using correct IP addressing when networking computers.

    _____

    _____

5. Partner #1: Return your IP address to 192.168.1.1, reboot your computer, and sign in. If necessary, connect to the network.

With the computers communicating with each other on the network, you can now view shared resources on each other's computer through the network. Follow these steps:

1. Open File Explorer or Windows Explorer, and drill down into the **Network** group. What computers are identified in the right pane?

    _____

2. Double-click your partner's computer icon to open that computer. What folder is presented to you?

    _____

3. Open the folder from Step 2. What folders are now presented to you?

    _____

4. Open the **Public** folder, and then open **Public Documents**.

    ◢ What files or folders do you find inside?

    _____

    ◢ What files or folders do you find in the Public Pictures folder?

    _____

5. Close all windows.

6. To open WordPad, type **WordPad** in the Search box, and then press **Enter**. Using WordPad, create a document with a single line of text, and save this document in your **Documents** library with a name of **Test Document**. What file extension did WordPad automatically assign the file?

    _____

7. Display your partner's computer in the Network listing of the Computer window.

8. Explore your partner's computer.

    ◢ Are you able to see your partner's WordPad document?

    _____

◢ What theory do you have as to why you can or cannot see the document?

Follow these steps to find out what changes are made to shared resources when you turn off Public folder sharing:

1. Return to the **Network and Sharing Center**, and access **Advanced sharing settings**.

2. Under Public folder sharing, select **Turn off Public folder sharing**, and save your changes.

3. Using File Explorer or Windows Explorer, look in the **Network** group for your partner's computer. Explore the user profile folders for your partner's user account. What has changed?

Follow these steps to find out what happens to shared resources when you change the network location:

1. To change the network location on a Windows 8 computer, open PC Settings, and click **Network, Connections**, and then click the name of the network. Turn on Find devices and content to change the network location to the private profile. Alternatively, force the computer to forget the network, and then re-create the network connection. On a Windows 7 computer, return to the **Network and Sharing Center**. In the View your active networks section, change the network location to **Work network**. Close all open windows.

2. Open File Explorer or Windows Explorer and view your partner's computer folders in the Network group. What has changed when viewing your partner's resources?

Now let's configure each computer to use dynamic IP addressing. If there is no DHCP server available to provide an IP address to your computer and Windows is set for dynamic IP addressing, Windows will use Automatic Private IP Addressing (APIPA). Follow these steps to investigate this situation:

1. Open an elevated command prompt window. List the exact steps you took to do so:

2. At the command prompt, enter **ipconfig /all** and press **Enter**. What are the following values for your network connection?
   ◢ IPv4 address: _____
   ◢ Subnet mask: _____
   ◢ Default gateway: _____
   ◢ DNS server: _____

3. Close the command prompt window.

4. Open the Internet Protocol Version 4 (TCP/IPv4) Properties dialog box.

5. Select **Obtain an IP address automatically** and **Obtain DNS server address automatically**. Click **OK**, and close all windows.

6. Reboot the computer and launch a command prompt window. Enter the **ipconfig /all** command, and record the results here:

   ▲ IPv4 address: _____

   ▲ Subnet mask: _____

   ▲ Default gateway: _____

   ▲ DNS server: _____

7. Compare these results with those recorded in Step 2. What are your conclusions about the TCP/IP values assigned to your computer?

   _____

   _____

REVIEW QUESTIONS

1. What dialog box do you use to configure TCP/IPv4 settings for the network adapter?

   _____

2. What are the two types of addresses or names used in this lab that can uniquely identify a computer on the network?

   _____

   _____

3. If there is no DHCP server to provide a computer a unique IP address, how is a computer able to acquire an IP address?

   _____

4. What is the exact path to the Documents folder (My Documents folder in Windows 7) for a user named John Smith?

   _____

5. What is the name of the window you can use to configure the network discovery and file sharing settings?

   _____

LAB 7.4 DEMONSTRATE HOMEGROUP SECURITY

OBJECTIVES

The goal of this lab is to learn how a Windows homegroup is used to provide security for shared resources on a small network. After completing this lab, you will be able to:

▲ Create and use a homegroup

▲ Change the homegroup settings

MATERIALS REQUIRED

This lab requires the following:

◢ Two computers using Windows 8 or Windows 7, networked together

◢ An account with administrator privileges

◢ A workgroup of two students

LAB PREPARATION

Before the lab begins, the instructor or lab assistant needs to do the following:

◢ Verify both computers start with no errors

◢ Verify the local network is working

◢ Verify students have access to a user account with administrator privileges

ACTIVITY BACKGROUND

Earlier versions of the Windows operating system (prior to Windows 7) support Windows workgroups to secure networked resources on a peer-to-peer network. Windows 7 and Windows 8 support both workgroups and homegroups. A homegroup is an easy method of sharing folders and printers on a small peer-to-peer network. The primary difference between a homegroup and a workgroup is that a password is assigned to the homegroup, and the password applies to all computers in the homegroup. In contrast, in a workgroup, a password is assigned to each user of a computer in the workgroup.

In this lab, you and your partner set up a homegroup between two computers and see how shared resources are managed by the homegroup. In Part 1 of this lab, you set up two user accounts, each on a different computer. In Part 2, you join Computer1 to the homegroup, and in Part 3, you join Computer2 to the homegroup.

ESTIMATED COMPLETION TIME: 45 MINUTES

 Activity

PART 1: SET UP USER ACCOUNTS

In this part of the lab, you set up two user accounts: User1 on Computer1 and User2 on Computer2. Working with a partner, designate one computer as Computer1 and the other computer as Computer2. Follow these steps to set up a user account on each computer:

1. Sign in to Computer1 and Computer2 with user accounts that have administrator privileges.

2. If Computer1 is running Windows 8, open PC Settings, click **Accounts, Other accounts**, and then **Add an account**. Click **Sign in without a Microsoft account (not recommended)**, and then click **Local account**. If Computer1 is running Windows 7, open Control Panel, and then click **Add or remove user accounts**. For either Windows 8 or Windows 7, follow the on-screen instructions to create a Standard user account named **User1**.

3. On Computer2, create a Standard user account named **User2**.

PART 2: JOIN COMPUTER1 TO THE HOMEGROUP

Follow these steps to set up a new homegroup or join Computer1 to an existing homegroup:

1. On Computer1, in the Search box, type **homegroup**, and then click **HomeGroup** in the search results. The HomeGroup window opens. If the window reports the computer already belongs to a homegroup, click **Leave the homegroup**. On the next screen, click **Leave the homegroup** again. Click **Finish**, and close all windows.

2. On Computer2, if the computer already belongs to a homegroup, leave the homegroup, and close all windows.

3. To create or join a homegroup, the network location must be set to Private on a Windows 8 computer or Home on a Windows 7 computer. On Computer1, to verify the network location, open the **Network and Sharing Center**.

The network location is reported under the View your active networks category. For example, in Figure 7-1 shown in the previous lab, the network location is a Private network.

If the network location is a Private (Windows 8) or Home (Windows 7) network, follow these steps to create a homegroup or join an existing homegroup, and then verify the homegroup settings:

1. In the left pane of the Network and Sharing Center window, click **HomeGroup**. The HomeGroup window opens (see Figure 7-2). If the window reports "There is currently no homegroup on the network," click **Create a homegroup**, and proceed to Step 2. If Windows detects and reports a homegroup on the network, go to Step 5 to join the existing homegroup.

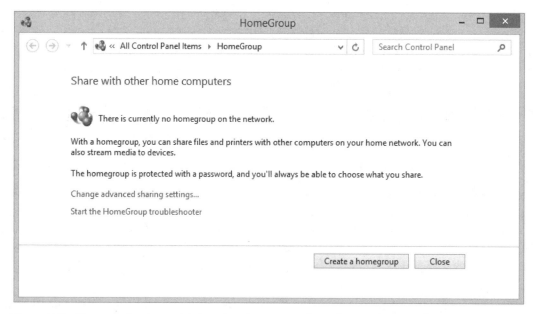

Figure 7-2   The computer does not belong to a homegroup that exists on the network

2. For Windows 8 systems, click **Next**. For either Windows 8 or Windows 7, you can select what you want to share in the homegroup. Make sure that **Documents, Pictures, Music, Videos,** and **Printers** are all shared, and then click **Next**.

3. The next screen provides a suggested password to the homegroup.

   ◢ Write down the password, being careful to record the correct case because the password is case sensitive:

4. Click **Finish**. Proceed to Part 3 of this lab, "Join Computer2 to the Homegroup."

5. If Windows detected a homegroup on the network, click **Join now**.

6. For Windows 8 systems, click **Next**. On either Windows 8 or Windows 7, verify the **Documents, Pictures, Music, Videos,** and **Printers** resources are shared with the homegroup, and then click **Next**.

7. On the next screen, enter the password for the existing homegroup, click **Next**, and then click **Finish**. If you don't know the password, go to another computer on the network that belongs to the homegroup, open the **Network and Sharing Center** window, click **HomeGroup**, and then click **View or print the homegroup password**.

   ◢ What is the password of the existing homegroup?

___

If the current network is a Public network or Work network, follow these steps:

1. Change the network location to a Private network (Windows 8) or Home network (Windows 7), as you learned how to do in the previous lab.

2. Join an existing homegroup or create a new one, as described above.

PART 3: JOIN COMPUTER2 TO THE HOMEGROUP

1. On Computer2, sign in with the User2 account, verify the network location is a **Private or Home network**, and join the homegroup using the password you recorded earlier in this lab. Share **Documents, Pictures, Music, Videos,** and **Printers** with the homegroup.

2. On Computer1, still signed in as an administrator, open File Explorer or Windows Explorer. Under Libraries, click **Pictures**, and notice the Shared status for this library in the status bar at the bottom of the Explorer window.

3. To see how and with whom this library is shared, right-click **Pictures**, point to **Share with** in the shortcut menu, and then click **Specific people**. The File Sharing dialog box appears. Answer these questions:

   ◢ What permission level does the homegroup have for this library?

   ___

   ◢ Based on the current homegroup security, can a user on Computer2 copy a file to this library?

   ___

4. Close the File Sharing dialog box.

5. Using File Explorer or Windows Explorer, remove the Pictures library from the homegroup. List the steps you took to accomplish this:

   ___

   ___

   ___

6. Still in File Explorer or Windows Explorer, click **Homegroup** in the left pane. Record the resources you see available in the homegroup:

   ___

_____

_____

_____

_____

7. Using File Explorer or Windows Explorer, create a folder named Data under the C root directory.

8. Add the Data folder to the homegroup, giving the homegroup users permission to read and write to the folder. List the steps you took to accomplish that:

_____

_____

_____

_____

_____

Follow these steps to see how User1 can access resources in the homegroup:

1. On Computer1, sign in to the system as **User1** (rather than as an administrator).

2. Open File Explorer or Windows Explorer. In the left pane, click **Music**, and notice in the status bar this Music folder is not shared with the homegroup.

3. Click **Homegroup**. Record the resources you see available to User1 in the homegroup:

_____

_____

_____

_____

_____

4. Based on what you have learned in this lab about homegroups, answer the following questions:

  ◢ Can any user signed in to a computer in a homegroup access resources shared with the homegroup?

_____

  ◢ If an administrator shares her Documents folder with the homegroup, will the Documents folders of all the users of this computer also be shared with the homegroup? Why or why not?

_____

  ◢ If one user on a computer shares his libraries or folders with the homegroup, will another user of the same computer be able to access these resources?

_____

5. Close all open windows on Computer1 and Computer2.

REVIEW QUESTIONS

1. List the steps to change the password to the homegroup:

_____

_____

_____

_____

_____

_____

2. What type of network location is required for a homegroup in Windows 8? In Windows 7?

_____

3. What five resources can be shared by default in a homegroup?

_____

_____

4. How does Windows indicate in File Explorer or Windows Explorer that a folder is shared?

_____

_____

5. How many homegroups can you have on a local network?

_____

LAB 7.5 SET UP A WIRELESS ROUTER

OBJECTIVES

The goal of this lab is to install and configure a wireless router. After completing this lab, you will be able to:

◢ Install and configure a wireless router

◢ Configure computers to connect to a wireless router

MATERIALS REQUIRED

This lab requires the following:

◢ Windows 8 or Windows 7 computer designated for this lab

◢ An account with administrator privileges

◢ A wireless router with setup CD or user's manual

◢ A USB wireless NIC is recommended for this lab

LAB PREPARATION

Before the lab begins, the instructor or lab assistant needs to do the following:

◢ Verify Windows starts with no errors

◢ Verify each student has access to a user account with administrator privileges

◢ Verify a network connection is available

ACTIVITY BACKGROUND

A small office/home office (SOHO) router is the best device to use to set up a small network. A router can provide these basic functions on the network:

◢ It can serve as a gateway to the Internet. The router stands between the networked computers and a DSL or cable modem used for a broadband connection to an ISP and to the Internet.

◢ The router can add additional security by providing a hardware firewall and limiting access to the Internet.

◢ A router can provide wired and wireless access to the network.

◢ The router can serve other purposes, such as functioning as a DHCP server.

In this lab, you set up and configure a wireless router, and then connect to it from a remote computer.

ESTIMATED COMPLETION TIME: 30 MINUTES

 Activity

Follow these steps to set up your router:

1. If your router comes with a setup CD (see Figure 7-3), run the setup program on one of your computers on the network (it doesn't matter which one). Follow the instructions on the setup screen or in the accompanying user's manual to use network cables to physically connect the computer to the router, plug in the router, and turn it on either before or after you run the setup CD. A computer can connect directly to a network port (Ethernet port) on the router (see Figure 7-4), or you can connect through a switch or hub to the router.

For this router, you run the setup CD before you connect the computer and the router

Figure 7-3 A typical SOHO router with a setup CD

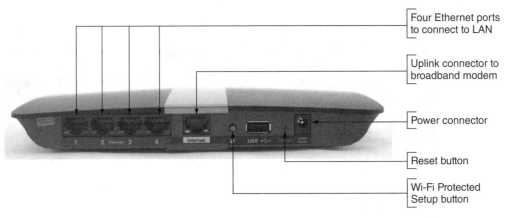

Figure 7-4 Connectors and ports on the back of a Cisco SOHO router

2. Connect the other computers on your network to the router.

3. Firmware on a router (which can be flashed for updates) contains a configuration program that you can access using a web browser from anywhere on the network. In your browser address box, enter the IP address of the router (for many routers, that address is 192.168.0.1 or 192.168.1.1), and then press **Enter**. What is the name and IP address for your router?

4. You'll probably be required to sign in to the router firmware utility using a default password. The first thing you want to do is reset this password so that others cannot change your router setup. What is your new router password?

5. After you change the password, a Setup or Quick Setup window appears, as shown in Figure 7-5. For most situations, the default settings on this and other screens should work without any changes required. The setup program will take you through the process of configuring the router. After you've configured the router, you might have to turn your cable or DSL modem off and back on so that it correctly syncs up with the router. What basic steps did the setup program have you follow to configure the router?

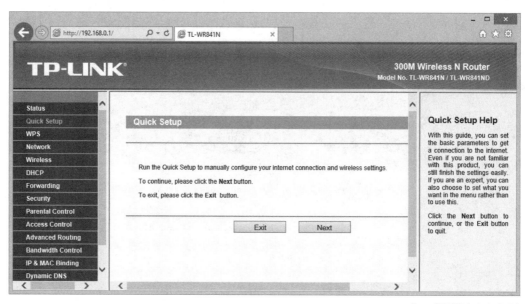

Figure 7-5   Quick Setup screen used to configure a TP-Link router

Source: TP-LINK Technologies Co., Ltd.

6. Spend some time examining the various features of your router. What security features does it have?

_____

_____

_____

7. What is the IP address of the router on the ISP network?

_____

8. Why is it necessary for the router to have two IP addresses?

_____

_____

Follow these steps to create a wireless connection to your wireless router from another computer:

1. Make sure you are signed in to Windows as an administrator. If you are using a wireless USB NIC, plug it into an available USB port. If necessary, install the drivers.

2. After the NIC has finished installing, click the **Network** icon in your taskbar. (If you don't see the Network icon, click the up arrow on the right side of the taskbar, and then click the **Network** icon, as shown in Figure 7-6a.)

3. Windows displays a list of wireless networks that are broadcasting availability (see Figure 7-6b for Windows 8). List all the networks that are available on your computer:

_____

4. Select the name of the network you would like to connect to. If you are comfortable with Windows automatically connecting to this network in the future, check **Connect automatically,** and then click **Connect.** If you are attempting to connect to a secured network, Windows will prompt you for the security key.

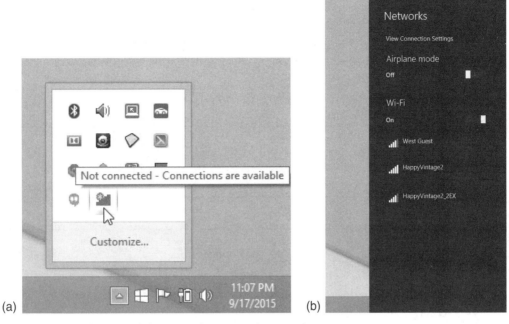

Figure 7-6 Use the Network icon to make a network connection

5. Windows reports the connection is being made. To see the network to which you are connected, click the **Network** icon in the taskbar or in the hidden icons box.

> **Notes** To add the Network icon to the taskbar, right-click the taskbar, and select **Properties**. In the Taskbar and Navigation properties dialog box (Windows 8) or Taskbar and Start Menu Properties dialog box (Windows 7), click **Customize**. In the Notification Area Icons window, select the option to show the Network icon, and then click **OK**.

6. Open the **Network and Sharing Center**. Verify Windows has configured the network as a Public network (see Figure 7-7). Click **Change advanced sharing settings** in the left pane.

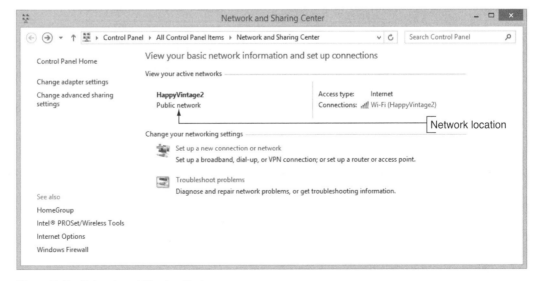

Figure 7-7 Network and Sharing Center

7. The Advanced sharing settings window appears. Verify that Network discovery, File and printer sharing, and Public folder sharing settings are all turned off.

8. To see the status of your wireless connection, click the **Back** arrow to return to the Network and Sharing Center. In the View your active networks section, click the wireless network connection.

◢ What speed is your wireless connection?

_____

◢ Fast Ethernet runs at 100 Mbps, and Gigabit Ethernet runs at 1000 Mbps. How does your wireless network speed compare with these two types of wired networks?

_____

_____

9. Open your browser to test the connection.

10. When you're finished, reset and uninstall the wireless router and NIC.

REVIEW QUESTIONS

1. What are some of the additional features available on your router that you would implement if you were setting up a small wired and wireless network?

_____

_____

2. Name two ways your router can limit Internet access:

_____

_____

3. Name one advantage and one disadvantage of a wireless connection compared with a wired connection:

_____

_____

4. Most wireless routers have a reset switch. Give an example of when this might be useful:

_____

_____

LAB 7.6 SECURE A WIRELESS LAN

OBJECTIVES

The goal of this lab is to learn how to set up and configure security options on a wireless router. After completing this lab, you will be able to:

◢ Download a manual for a wireless router

◢ Explain how to improve wireless security

◢ Describe a few methods for securing a wireless LAN

MATERIALS REQUIRED

This lab requires the following:

◢ Windows 8 or Windows 7 operating system

◢ Internet access

◢ Adobe Acrobat Reader installed for viewing PDF files

◢ Wireless router (optional)

◢ Laptop or desktop with compatible wireless access (optional)

LAB PREPARATION

Before the lab begins, the instructor or lab assistant needs to do the following:

◢ Verify Windows starts with no errors

◢ Verify Internet access is available

ACTIVITY BACKGROUND

Wireless networks are a simple way to include computers in a home or small office network. Without adequate security, however, you can open up your network to a wide range of threats. In this lab, you learn how to enable and configure some security features of a wireless router.

If you have a router, use your router in this lab. If you don't have a router to do this lab, you can still complete the lab. To do so, assume that your router is the Linksys EA4500 router, similar to the one shown earlier in Figure 7-3. If you are not using the Linksys EA4500 router, what router brand and model are you using?

7

ESTIMATED COMPLETION TIME: 45 MINUTES

 Activity

1. Open your web browser, and locate the support page for your router provided by the router manufacturer. For the Linksys EA4500 router, you go to the Linksys site for home routers at *linksys.com/us/shop-linksys/* and then search on the router model number.

   Follow links to view or download the user guide for your router. You might also find the user guide on the setup CD for your router. If you cannot find a user guide, then search the support documentation provided for the router on the manufacturer's website. Using any of these sources, answer the following questions:

   ◢ Most wireless routers can be configured with a web-based utility by entering the router's IP address in the browser address box. What's the default IP address of this router?

   ◢ Describe how you would log on to the router for the first time:

_____

_____

Most routers are easily configured with a setup utility that asks a series of questions about your network and your Internet service provider. The default settings, however, might not enable all your router's security features. Here are the four most important steps in securing your LAN:

- Update the router's firmware from the manufacturer's website so that any known security flaws are fixed.
- Set a password on the router itself so that other people can't change its configuration.
- Disable remote configuration of the router.
- Use some kind of wireless encryption. (WEP is better than nothing; WPA is better; and WPA2 is better still.)

Here are two more ways to secure a router. They are not considered strong security measures because they are easily hacked:

- Change the wireless network's name (called a service set identifier—SSID) and turn off the SSID broadcast to anyone who's listening.
- Enable MAC filtering so that only the computers whose MAC addresses are listed in your router table can access the network.

Continue to use the manual to answer the following additional questions:

- Which window in the router's web-based utility do you use to change the password needed to configure the router?

_____

- List the steps for changing the router's SSID:

_____

_____

_____

_____

- Does the router support Wi-Fi Protected Setup? If so, on which screen can it be enabled?

_____

- Describe the steps to limit access through MAC filtering to everything but the computer you are now using:

_____

_____

CHALLENGE ACTIVITY (ADDITIONAL 30 MINUTES)

If you have access to a wireless router, set up a secure wireless connection by following these steps:

1. Set up a nonsecure wireless connection with the router, as covered in the previous lab.

2. Go to the router manufacturer's website, and update the router's firmware (if necessary) to the latest version. Did your router require an update? What version of the firmware is it now running?

   _____

3. Set a strong password for the router. What password did you use?

   _____

4. Disable remote configuration for the router so the router cannot be configured wirelessly. List the steps you went through to complete this task:

   _____

   _____

   _____

   _____

5. Change the router's name (SSID). What was the router's default name, and what did you change it to?

   _____

6. Disable the broadcast of the new SSID.

7. Set up some kind of wireless encryption on the router. What form of encryption did you use?

   _____

8. Enable MAC filtering so that only the computer you are using can connect. How did you determine the MAC address of your computer?

   _____

   _____

9. Test your network connection by opening your browser and surfing the web.

10. When you're finished, reset the router to undo any changes you made to it.

REVIEW QUESTIONS

1. What client application on your computer is used to configure a home router?

   _____

2. Why should you update your router's firmware before making any other security changes?

   _____

   _____

3. How could not changing your router's password compromise all of your other security changes?

   _____

   _____

4. Why wouldn't "password" or "Linksys" make a good password for your router?

_____

5. How can you configure your router once you've disabled remote configuration?

_____

_____

CHAPTER 8

Supporting Mobile Operating Systems

Labs included in this chapter:

- **Lab 8.1:** Research the Latest Smart Phones
- **Lab 8.2:** Research Android Apps and Use Dropbox
- **Lab 8.3:** Explore How Android Apps Are Developed and Tested
- **Lab 8.4:** Configure Email and Dropbox on Mobile Devices
- **Lab 8.5:** Research Xcode and the iOS Simulator

LAB 8.1 RESEARCH THE LATEST SMART PHONES

OBJECTIVES

The goal of this lab is to explore the similarities and differences among iOS, Android, and Windows smart phones. Understanding the characteristics of different smart phones can help you make wise purchasing decisions for yourself or on behalf of a client. After completing this lab, you will be able to:

◢ Research different types of smart phones

◢ Summarize and compare the major features and capabilities of an Android, iOS, and Windows smart phone

MATERIALS REQUIRED

This lab requires the following:

◢ Windows 8 or Windows 7 computer

◢ Internet access

LAB PREPARATION

Before the lab begins, the instructor or lab assistant needs to do the following:

◢ Verify Windows starts with no errors

◢ Verify Internet access is available

ACTIVITY BACKGROUND

Smart phones are becoming more available and accessibly priced every day. New smart phones are constantly being released, and when you are ready to upgrade your phone, you need to do research to find the best option available to meet your needs. In addition, as a support technician, you will likely be called on to help a client decide which technology to purchase. Therefore, you need to be familiar with the technologies and options a client might want or need.

Deciding factors to consider when selecting your own smart phone or presenting options to a client are brand, capabilities, features, support provided by a manufacturer or apps vendor, and price. In this lab, you research iOS, Android, and Windows smart phones.

ESTIMATED COMPLETION TIME: 30 MINUTES

 Activity

In this lab, you research specifications for three different smart phones for comparison:

1. Use the Internet to research one example of a smart phone for each of the mobile operating systems named at the top of the columns of Table 8-1. You might find these phones on the manufacturers' websites or on service provider websites. Record in the table the specifications for each of the smart phones.

2. Use the Internet to research reviews for each of the phones that you selected in Step 1. Record the highlights of those reviews, as detailed below:

◢ Android advantages:

_____

_____

Specification	Android	iOS	Windows
Brand or manufacturer			
Model			
Price			
Version of OS installed			
Processor			
Types of network connections			
Storage capacity			
Screen size			
Screen resolution			
Camera pixels			
Website for cloud storage and app purchases			
Amount of free cloud storage			
Unique features			

Table 8-1   Fill in the specifications for three smart phones

◢ Android disadvantages:

_____

_____

◢ iOS advantages:

_____

_____

◢ iOS disadvantages:

_____

_____

◢ Windows advantages:

_____

_____

◢ Windows disadvantages:

_____

_____

3. Close all open windows.

REVIEW QUESTIONS

1. Assume that you are in the market to buy a new smart phone. Which of the smart phones you researched would you purchase? Why would you choose this smart phone over the other two smart phones?

   _____

   _____

   _____

2. What are some methods service providers use to offer lower prices on the devices they sell?

   _____

   _____

3. Some smart phones provide more flexible options for updating hardware than do others. Of the smart phones you researched, which (if any) allow for the battery to be replaced?

   _____

4. Other than the criteria given in this lab, what criteria might influence which smart phone you would purchase?

   _____

   _____

5. Give two reasons why you should research information about related apps and app stores when deciding which smart phone to buy:

   _____

   _____

LAB 8.2 RESEARCH ANDROID APPS AND USE DROPBOX

OBJECTIVES

The goals of this lab are to research and compare Android apps and to explore how to sync data between two sources using an Android app. This exploration is useful because, as an A+ certified technician, you will be expected to know how to service Android mobile devices and the apps installed on them. This service includes knowing how to sync data between two sources and back up data on an Android device. Android offers many data sync options to choose from, including the very popular Dropbox app. After completing this lab, you will be able to:

◢ Use the Google Play Store to research apps

◢ Find additional information on apps using other resources

◢ Install Dropbox, an Android-compatible app, on your computer

◢ Sync data between two sources using Dropbox

MATERIALS REQUIRED

This lab requires the following:

◢ Windows 8 or Windows 7 operating system

⊿ An account with administrator privileges

⊿ Internet access

⊿ Email account

⊿ Email addresses for your instructor and a classmate

LAB PREPARATION

Before the lab begins, the instructor or lab assistant needs to do the following:

⊿ Verify Windows starts with no errors

⊿ Verify each student has access to a user account with administrator privileges

⊿ Verify Internet access is working

⊿ Verify Dropbox is not already installed

ACTIVITY BACKGROUND

Because Android is open source software, Android-compatible apps are available from many different developers. It's not unusual to find several apps that do essentially the same tasks. Some developers produce excellent apps, and some produce only mediocre ones. Therefore, research is important in finding the best app for the job.

Most Android apps are available through the Google Play Store (*play.google.com/store/apps*) as seen in Figure 8-1, and this is a central location for information about those apps. Each app listed contains information on what access privileges the app needs, who the developer is, how much memory the app requires, and what other users think of the app. The 5-star rating system and the user reviews provide a wealth of feedback on the functionality and performance of apps, including how to address problems with the app features or installation.

One widely used file-sharing program available for Android is Dropbox. You can install Dropbox on nearly any current Windows, Mac, Linux, BlackBerry, or Android device, and share files between all those devices. Files saved in your Dropbox account are stored in

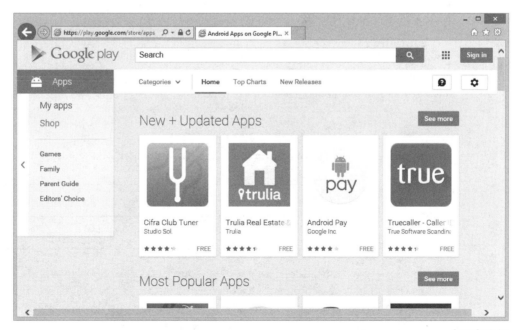

Source: Google, Inc.

Figure 8-1 The Google Play Store is one of many sources of Android apps

the cloud, and Dropbox automatically syncs these files with all of your Dropbox-enabled devices. Your Dropbox folders can be managed directly from any of these devices or through your online dashboard using a personal computer.

In this lab, you investigate some Android apps, and then you install and use the Dropbox software on your personal computer. If you have access to an Android device, you can also install and use the Dropbox app to sync data on your device with your other devices and computers, and with other users.

ESTIMATED COMPLETION TIME: 45 MINUTES

 Activity

The flashlight app can turn your smart phone or tablet into a flashlight. To collect information on flashlight apps, follow these steps:

1. Using a browser, go to Google Play at **play.google.com/store/apps**.

2. Click the **Categories** tab, and then click **Tools**.

3. Find three different flashlight apps, and collect the following information on these apps, as detailed in Table 8-2:

Specification	App 1	App 2	App 3
App name			
Rating			
Number of reviews			
Date last updated			
Three key features			
One negative issue raised by reviewers			

Table 8-2 Fill in the specifications for three apps

4. If you were to choose one of these flashlight apps, which one would you choose and why?

_____

_____

_____

5. Third-party websites can be an excellent source of information on apps you're researching. Do a quick search on **google.com** for the flashlight app you chose in Step 4; be sure to select **Past year** in the Search tools menu to ensure you find the latest information on the app. Is your selected app also available in the iTunes App Store?

_____

6. Next, research a different kind of app. A chromatic tuner is a device used by musicians to tune instruments. Do a Google search for chromatic tuner apps for Android, and answer the following questions:

  ◢ Based on your Google search results, what are three apps that can be used to tune a musical instrument?

  _____

  _____

  _____

  ◢ Besides Google Play, what is another source for one of the tuner apps you listed?

  _____

> **Notes** Different apps work with different devices. App listings online include a list of which devices are compatible with that app. However, when you surf the Play Store directly from your Android phone, only device-compatible apps show up in your search.

To install Dropbox on a mobile device, you download the Dropbox app from the device's primary application source (Google Play Store for an Android device or the App Store for an iOS device). To install Dropbox on your computer, do the following:

1. Go to **dropbox.com**, and click **Download the app**, as shown in Figure 8-2, and then save the download. What is the name of the downloaded file?

  _____

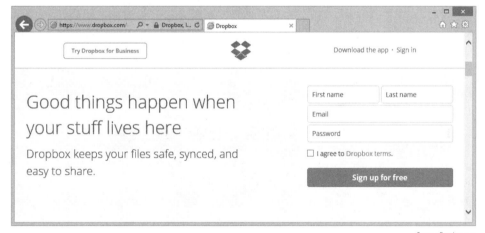

Source: Dropbox.com

Figure 8-2 At the time of this writing, you can get up to 2 GB of free online storage space with Dropbox

2. Locate the downloaded file, and install Dropbox.

3. In the Dropbox Setup dialog box, click **Sign up**, and enter the requested information to create an account. Write down the email address and password for your account:

  _____

4. Complete the installation process, and then click **Open my Dropbox**. In the Welcome to Dropbox dialog box, click **Get Started**. Proceed through the tour slides, and then click

Finish. Dropbox opens automatically in File Explorer/Windows Explorer. What item is included in your Dropbox folder by default? In the left pane of Explorer, where is the Dropbox shortcut located?

_____

_____

You can share Dropbox files and folders with other people. Anyone who has the link to a particular file or folder can view that item in a browser, even without using a Dropbox account. It's important to note that you have no control over who can use the link, so be sure you don't put private information in a shared folder. To practice sharing a file, do the following:

1. Create a text file using Notepad, and type a couple of lines of text. Click **File**, and then click **Save**. In the left pane of the Save As window, click **Dropbox** under Favorites. Name the file **MeetingNotes.txt**, and then click **Save**.

2. Close the file. Using File Explorer/Windows Explorer, find your file in the Dropbox folder.

3. Ensure the file shows a green check on its icon, indicating the file has been fully synced with Dropbox (see Figure 8-3). If the green check has not yet appeared, wait for the file to finish syncing.

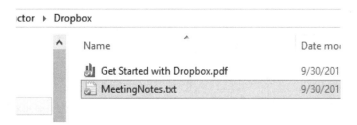

Figure 8-3   The green check shows that the file is fully synced

4. Right-click the **MeetingNotes.txt** file, and click **Share Dropbox link**, as shown in Figure 8-4. The link is copied to your Clipboard.

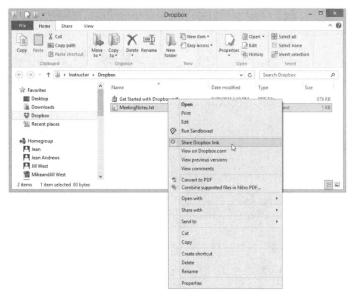

Figure 8-4   Copy the file's Dropbox link to your Clipboard

5. Paste the link into an email message to your instructor and to a classmate, and then send the email. When you receive your classmate's email, click the link. The file opens in your browser. Notice that you cannot change the text of your classmate's file, but you can copy the file to your computer and edit it there. You can also make comments on the file, and subscribe to notifications of future changes to the file.

Files placed in your Dropbox are automatically synced with your Dropbox on other devices linked to your account. To share files in your Dropbox with other people, it is not necessary to share your Dropbox account information. When you invite other Dropbox users to one of your folders, this folder, including all of its files and subfolders, is synced in their accounts and in your account (however, other folders in your Dropbox remain private unless you share them). To invite a classmate to one of your Dropbox folders, do the following:

1. Return to your Dropbox folder in File Explorer/Windows Explorer. Click **New folder**, and name the folder **Computer class**.

2. Right-click the folder you just created, and click **Share this folder**, as shown in Figure 8-5.

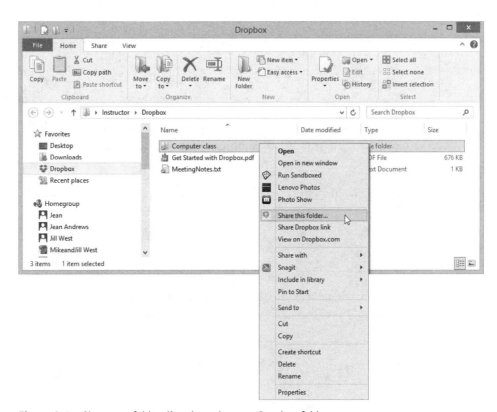

Figure 8-5 Share any folder directly under your Dropbox folder

3. The first time you associate your email address with Dropbox, Dropbox takes you to the Dropbox website and requests verification of your email address in order to share folders (see Figure 8-6). To verify your email address, click **Send Email**. Open the email sent by Dropbox (be sure to check your junk folder if you don't see the Dropbox email in your inbox), and click **Verify your email**. The Dropbox - Sign in webpage opens. Close the website (it's not necessary to sign in). Now that your email address is verified, repeat Step 2 to share the Computer class folder.

Figure 8-6 Access to your email account is needed to complete verification

4. In the Dropbox - Share Folder dialog box, enter a classmate's email address, and then click **Invite**. An invitation email is sent to your classmate. When your classmate accepts your invitation, you should receive a confirmation email.

5. To accept a Dropbox folder shared by your classmate, click the **View folder** link in the invitation email that you receive. Sign in if necessary, and then click **Accept** to add the folder to your Dropbox. Because you should now have two folders with the name Computer class, the new one will have a version number behind the name, such as Computer class (1).

> **Notes** Be aware that shared folders count toward a user's storage quota. Also, once a folder is shared, you cannot change the name or location of that folder as it is listed in another Dropbox. However, you can change the name or location of the folder in your own Dropbox.
> To unshare a folder, sign in on the Dropbox website. Open the folder, and then click **Settings**. Click **Unshare folder**. You can choose whether to allow collaborators to keep a copy of the files, and then click **Unshare folder**.

6. Take a moment to explore the online Dropbox dashboard. In the left pane, click **Get Started**. What steps do you still need to complete in order to earn extra, free storage space?

_____

_____

7. Next to your name, click the drop-down arrow, and then click **Settings**. Where can you find a listing of the devices linked to your account?

_____

8. Create a new text file using Notepad, and save the file to your shared 'Computer class' folder. Give it a silly name and write it here:

_____

9. Have your classmate execute Step 8 as well. When you receive your classmate's file in his or her shared Dropbox folder, write the name of that file here:

_____

10. Close any open windows.

If you want to use your Dropbox on a computer that has already been linked to another user's Dropbox, you can unlink the computer and add your own account. Follow these steps to set up your Dropbox account on another computer:

1. Go to another computer in the lab that has Dropbox installed. Click the **Dropbox** icon in the taskbar, click the cog settings icon, and then select **Preferences**.

2. From the Dropbox Preferences box, select **Account**. The email address currently linked to Dropbox on this computer appears. Click **Unlink This Dropbox,** and click **OK**. The Unlink Dropbox? dialog box opens.

3. Click **OK** to confirm that you want to unlink the computer from Dropbox. The Dropbox Setup dialog box, which you used earlier to create your account, opens. You can use this setup box to create a new Dropbox account or set up an existing Dropbox account on the computer. Follow directions on screen to set up your existing Dropbox account on this computer. Verify your Dropbox folders and files are present.

4. If you're working on a lab computer or public computer, go to the Programs and Features window in Control Panel and uninstall Dropbox.

5. Close any open windows.

REVIEW QUESTIONS

1. Besides apps and games, what other kinds of files can you download from Google Play?

   _____

2. Downloading apps on a mobile device can drain a user's cellular data allotment quickly. What is one way to avoid data charges when downloading apps?

   _____

   _____

3. In your online Dropbox dashboard, where can you find a record of the date and time you shared your folder with your classmate in Dropbox? *Hint:* Check the Dropbox menu in the left pane.

   _____

   _____

4. A file placed in a shared Dropbox folder is accessible by anyone with a link to that folder, no matter how they obtained the link. How can you remove the file from public access?

   _____

   _____

5. Do a quick Google search for another app other than Dropbox that can sync files between a mobile device and a personal computer. Which app did you find?

   _____

8

LAB 8.3 EXPLORE HOW ANDROID APPS ARE DEVELOPED AND TESTED

OBJECTIVES

The goal of this lab is to learn how Android apps are developed and tested using the Android Software Development Kit (SDK) and the Android emulator. If you have never used an Android device, this is your chance to learn about Android, by using an Android virtual device in the Android emulator. After completing this lab, you will be able to:

◢ Describe the tools and procedures used to develop and test Android apps

◢ Install and use the Android emulator to run an Android virtual device

MATERIALS REQUIRED

This lab requires the following:

◢ Windows 8 or Windows 7 operating system

◢ Internet access

LAB PREPARATION

Before the lab begins, the instructor or lab assistant needs to do the following:

◢ Verify Windows starts with no errors

◢ Verify Internet access is available

ACTIVITY BACKGROUND

The Android website at *android.com* by Google offers tools to develop and test Android apps. The process can be fun to learn but does require you download and install multiple pieces of software. The Android Software Development Kit (SDK) depends on Java to run. In this lab, you won't actually write an Android app, but you will learn much about the tools used and how the process works.

ESTIMATED COMPLETION TIME: 60 MINUTES

 Activity

How do you best like to learn a new computer skill? You might prefer to watch a video, read a book, search for online discussions or tutorials, or discuss and investigate the topic with your friends. The following steps will help you explore online videos and websites related to developing Android apps:

1. Go to **youtube.com** and search for tutorial videos. Possible search strings are "android application development," "make your first android app," and "android application tutorials."

2. Search the web for additional information and tutorials. Good search strings to use are "android app tutorial for beginners" and "how to develop android apps."

3. Explore websites that might help you with your research. Try researching on these useful websites: *techradar.com* and *androidcommunity.com*.

   ◢ What is Android Studio and where can you get it?

◢ What software should you install before you can install Android Studio?

_____

◢ What is the Android Emulator and how would you use it when developing an Android app?

_____

_____

◢ What programming language is used to write Android apps?

_____

◢ What file extension is used to hold an Android app after it is developed so that it can be tested in the Android Emulator?

_____

◢ What tool can you use to add an app to the Android Emulator?

_____

> **Notes** To run the Android Emulator on your computer, virtualization technology must be enabled in UEFI/BIOS, and Hyper-V must be disabled, which can be done through Programs and Features.

Now you're ready to install the software you need to run the Android Emulator. Android Studio requires Java Standard Edition (Java SE) Development Kit (also called JDK) to run. To download and install Java SE and Android Studio, follow these steps:

1. Go to **java.oracle.com** and drill down to the Java SE download page. Click the **Java Platform (JDK)** download link. Accept the license agreement, and download and install the Windows version of the JDK. Be sure you download the correct version for your Windows installation: 32-bit Windows or 64-bit Windows (see Figure 8-7). At the time of this writing, the link to the download is **oracle.com/technetwork/java/javase/downloads/jdk8-downloads-2133151.html**. However, your link might be different. After you download the file, double-click it to install the software, accepting all defaults, and then close all open windows.

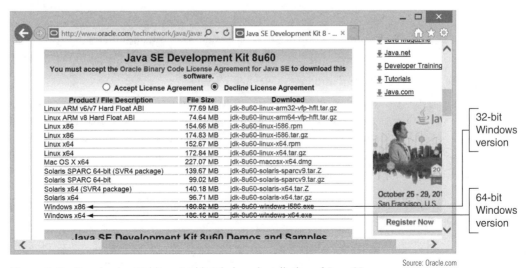

Source: Oracle.com

Figure 8-7 Download a 32-bit or 64-bit Windows installation of Java SE

2. Open File Explorer/Windows Explorer and locate the folder that contains the software. The folder name includes the version of Java SE installed. For the current version of Java, the folder is C:\Progam Files\Java\jdk1.8.0_60, but your Java version might install differently. What is the path to the Java software?

An environment variable is a string stored in the Windows registry that software can use to find other software or to know where to store its data. The Android SDK uses an environment variable to know where to look to find Java SE. Follow these steps to use the Environment Variables dialog box to create an environment variable that applies to the currently signed-on user and points to the Java SE path:

1. Open the System window of your computer, and click **Advanced system settings**. The System Properties box opens with the Advanced tab selected. Click **Environment Variables**. In the Environment Variables box, click **New** in the User variables group. The New User Variable box opens.

2. Enter **JAVA_HOME** as the Variable name and **C:\Program Files\Java\1.8.0_60** as the Variable value, substituting the path you recorded in Step 2 in the previous step sequence. See Figure 8-8. Click **OK** three times to close all boxes. Close the System window. The registry is immediately updated with this variable name and value.

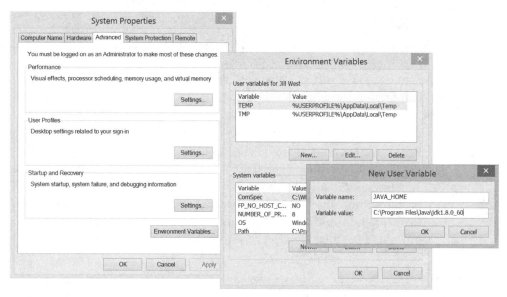

Figure 8-8 Create a user variable to point to the Java software

---

Follow these steps to download and install Android Studio:

1. Go to **developer.android.com** and locate and download Android Studio for Windows. What is the exact URL where you found the download? List the steps you took to download and install Android Studio, accepting all default settings:

2. Android Studio automatically launches and opens to the setup wizard (see Figure 8-9). If it does not launch, you can launch it from the Start screen (Windows 8) or the Start menu (Windows 7).

Source: Android Studio

Figure 8-9 Configure the Android Studio installation through the Android Studio Setup Wizard

3. To complete setup, in the Android Studio Setup Wizard dialog box, click **Configure**, and then click **SDK Manager**. The Android SDK Manager window opens with several packages selected by default. If your motherboard is made by Intel, you need one more item. Scroll down to the section under Extras, and select the **Intel x86 Emulator Accelerator** item. Click **Install packages** to install all the checked packages. Follow directions on screen to complete the installation, and then close the Android SDK Manager window.

4. Close the Android Studio Setup Wizard window and all other open windows.

5. To complete installation of the HAXM software on a system with an Intel motherboard, locate the application file in File Explorer/Windows Explorer. By default, the location is C:\Users*username*\AppData\Local\Android\sdk\extras\intel\Hardware_Accelerated_ Execution_Manager. (The file's location in your system might be different.) Double-click **intelhaxm-android.exe**, and follow the on-screen instructions. You do *not* need to launch the Intel HAXM documentation when you finish setup. After installation, close all open windows.

The AVD Manager is used to create and manage an Android Virtual Device (AVD), and is included in the Android SDK. Android app developers test an app on several AVDs, one for each type of Android device they expect the app to use. To access the AVD Manager, you first create a new project and then configure the virtual device. Follow these steps to use the AVD Manager program to set up an Android Virtual Device (AVD):

1. Open Android Studio, close the Tip of the Day box, and click **Start a new Android Studio project**. Follow the on-screen directions, accepting all default settings for your new app called My Application. Once your project is created, the My Application window shows an Android device (see Figure 8-10).

8

SDK Manager ⎯⎯
AVD Manager ⎯⎯

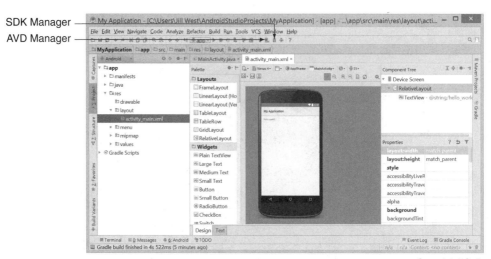

Source: Android Studio

Figure 8-10 Android Studio shows the new application on the virtual device's screen

2. Click the **AVD Manager** icon in the toolbar. The Android Virtual Device Manager window opens with one default device listed (see the left side of Figure 8-11).

3. Click **Create Virtual Device,** and select a device from the list (see the right side of Figure 8-11). Continue the device-creation process, keeping all default settings. Give your device a name, and click **Finish**. The new virtual device is now listed in the AVD Manager window.

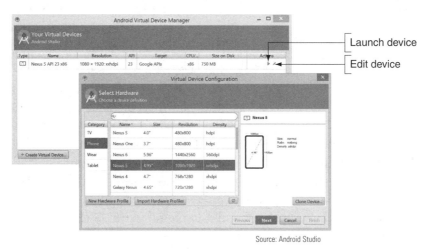

Launch device
Edit device

Source: Android Studio

Figure 8-11 Use the AVD Manager to create a new Android virtual device

For actual development and testing of Android apps, you would install several versions of Android and create one virtual device using each version so that you could test your apps on several Android platforms.

Let's see how a virtual Android device works. To find out, do the following:

1. In the Android Virtual Device Manager window, click the green launch arrow next to the AVD you just created. Depending on your system configuration, you might have to troubleshoot one or more error messages. Research online as necessary to determine the exact settings to use so the emulator will work on your system. For example, you might have to disable using the host GPU, which is enabled by default. Once you've resolved any error messages, relaunch the virtual device and wait a moment while the emulator boots the AVD.

2. Use the emulator as you would an Android device. What happens when you try to use it to surf the web?

3. Use the App Launcher to view the installed apps. See Figure 8-12. What apps are installed on the AVD?

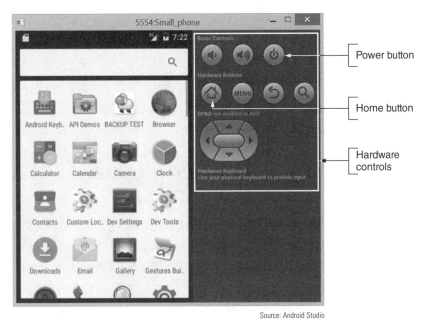

Source: Android Studio

Figure 8-12 The AVD showing installed apps.

4. List the steps to activate the camera on the AVD:

5. Check out the Settings app. Which settings can you adjust on the AVD?

6. Close any open windows.

REVIEW QUESTIONS

1. Why might an app developer want to test his apps on an AVD rather than on actual Android devices?

2. Which programming language is used to write Android apps?

3. When installing the Android SDK, what is the purpose of creating a user variable using the Environment Variables dialog box in Windows?

_____

4. Which program is used to create an Android virtual device?

_____

_____

_____

5. What would be the advantage of installing several AVDs when testing Android apps?

_____

_____

_____

LAB 8.4 CONFIGURE EMAIL AND DROPBOX ON MOBILE DEVICES

OBJECTIVES

The goal of this lab is to practice configuring various accounts, such as for email and Dropbox, on an Android device. After completing this lab, you will be able to:

◢ Create a new email account through the Email app on an Android virtual device

◢ Install Dropbox on a smart phone or tablet

◢ Sync Dropbox files from a smart phone or tablet

MATERIALS REQUIRED

This lab requires the following:

◢ Windows 8 or Windows 7 operating system

◢ Internet access

◢ Email account with password

◢ Email address for your instructor

◢ Dropbox account with sign-in information (created earlier in this chapter)

◢ Android Studio, as installed in the previous lab

◢ Android, iOS, or Windows Phone mobile device (optional)

LAB PREPARATION

Before the lab begins, the instructor or lab assistant needs to do the following:

◢ Verify Windows starts with no errors

◢ Verify Internet access is available

◢ Verify Android Studio is correctly installed

ACTIVITY BACKGROUND

Gone are the days when mobile devices had to be connected to a computer by cable in order to sync data. Email, files, and other data can be automatically synced over either Wi-Fi or cellular connections for any current Android, iOS, or Windows Phone mobile device.

In this lab, you add an email account to the Email app on your Android virtual device. Then you install the Dropbox app on your own or a classmate's Android, iOS, or Windows Phone mobile device, and then sync a file to Dropbox on your computer.

ESTIMATED COMPLETION TIME: 30 MINUTES

ACTIVITY

To add an email account on a virtual device in Android Studio, complete the following steps:

1. Open Android Studio. Click the **AVD Manager** icon to open the Android Virtual Device Manager window.

2. Click the green launch arrow on one of the devices listed.

3. After the device boots up, click the **Settings** icon (you might have to swipe to the left to view the second home screen—to swipe, press the mouse button and drag your cursor across the screen). Scroll down and click **Accounts**. Click **Add account**.

4. Click **Personal (IMAP)**, and then follow the on-screen directions to enter your email account information, keeping other default settings.

5. Swipe down to close the Settings app (alternately, click the **Home** hardware button, as shown earlier in Figure 8-12). Click the **Apps Drawer** icon, and then click **Email**.

6. In the Email app, complete any setup steps required. How far back in time did your email account sync on the virtual device?

   _____

7. Compose a new email and send it to your instructor.

8. To view server settings for this email account, click the **Menu** icon, scroll down, and then click **Settings**. Click the name of the email account.

9. Under Server settings, click **Incoming settings**. Answer the following questions:

   ◢ What port is the server using?

   _____

   ◢ What does this tell you about the protocol being used?

   _____

   ◢ What port would you have expected the server to be using here? Why?

   _____

   _____

10. To protect your privacy, be sure to remove your email account from any virtual devices. The most secure way to do this is to delete the AVD. Describe the steps to do this. Be sure to complete the deletion process so your information is protected.

    _____

    _____

    _____

Dropbox is compatible with many operating systems, including Android, iOS, and Windows Phone. Use your own smart phone or tablet for this portion of the lab, or team up with one or more classmates to use their mobile device(s). Alternatively, pair up with a classmate with a mobile device using a different OS than your own, and install Dropbox on both devices so you both can see how the app works on multiple mobile operating systems.

Complete the following steps:

1. Download Dropbox from your phone's primary app provider.
2. Sign in using the Dropbox account you created earlier in this chapter.
3. Take a screen shot of your phone's display that shows your Dropbox folders on your phone.
4. Open the screen shot, click the **Share** icon, and add the screen shot file to Dropbox. Save it to the Computer class folder you created in the Dropbox lab earlier in this chapter.
5. Open Dropbox on your computer. (If you're using a lab computer and Dropbox is not installed, use the online Dropbox dashboard at **dropbox.com**.) Sign in if necessary.
6. Open the **Computer class** folder. Click on the screen shot file to view it, and then click **Share**. Enter your instructor's email address to send the link, and then click **Send**.

REVIEW QUESTIONS

1. What port number is used by default to receive IMAP email? POP3 email?

_____

_____

2. What port numbers are used to receive email by IMAP and POP3 servers when using SSL?

_____

3. What are the steps to change how far back in time the Email app syncs with the email account?

_____

_____

_____

4. Why should you delete the AVD at the end of the lab?

_____

LAB 8.5 RESEARCH XCODE AND THE iOS SIMULATOR

OBJECTIVES

The goal of this lab is to explore the features and requirements of Xcode. After completing this lab, you will be able to:

◢ Describe the purpose of Xcode

◢ Explain the use of the Simulator tool in Xcode

MATERIALS REQUIRED

This lab requires the following:

◢ Internet access

LAB PREPARATION

Before the lab begins, the instructor or lab assistant needs to do the following:

◢ Verify Internet access is available

ACTIVITY BACKGROUND

When app developers create apps for iOS devices, they use Apple's Xcode application. The program is available only for Mac computers; however, you can learn about the application without downloading it by going to the iOS Developer website (*developer.apple.com*), which contains a wealth of useful information, resources, and community support. In this lab, you explore some of Apple's app developer tools contained within Xcode.

ESTIMATED COMPLETION TIME: 45 MINUTES

ACTIVITY

Do the following to find out more about Xcode:

1. In your web browser, go to **developer.apple.com**, and explore the resources on the main page. If necessary, use a search engine as you answer the following questions, and add the **site:developer.apple.com** tag to limit your search to Apple's website:

   ◢ How much does the Apple Developer Program individual membership cost?

   _____

   > **Notes** Some schools qualify for the free iOS Developer University Program, which provides a suite of tools for student development projects and collaboration between students and instructors. Learn more at *developer.apple.com/programs/ios/university*.

   ◢ What is Xcode? What is the current version of Xcode?

   _____

   _____

   ◢ What equipment and OS do you need to get Xcode from the App Store for free?

   _____

   ◢ What is Simulator?

   _____

   _____

   ◢ What is Swift?

   _____

   _____

2. Using your favorite search engine, search for the iOS Simulator User Guide. At the time of this writing, the Simulator User Guide is found at the following webpage: https://developer.apple.com/library/prerelease/ios/documentation/IDEs/Conceptual/iOS_Simulator_Guide/Introduction/Introduction.html

8

Answer these questions:

◢ What are the two ways to access iOS Simulator in Xcode?

_____

_____

◢ Other than iOS, what OSs can be simulated in Simulator?

_____

◢ How are gestures simulated on a virtual device in Simulator?

_____

_____

3. Search for online Xcode tutorial videos on *youtube.com* or by using a search engine. Answer the following questions:

◢ What is the playground?

_____

◢ What file type is used to store the code for a new app?

_____

◢ What is a storyboard?

_____

REVIEW QUESTIONS

1. What programming language does Apple currently use for iOS apps?

_____

_____

2. What OS is used on Apple Watch devices?

_____

3. Xcode is a free app from the App Store, so why might you need to pay for an Apple Developer Program membership?

_____

4. If you were to begin developing apps, which OS would you prefer to work with? Why?

_____

CHAPTER 9

Windows Resources on a Network

Labs included in this chapter:

- **Lab 9.1:** Map a Network Drive and Use Wake-on-LAN
- **Lab 9.2:** Use Remote Desktop
- **Lab 9.3:** Manage User Accounts in Windows 8
- **Lab 9.4:** Manage User Accounts in Windows 7
- **Lab 9.5:** Use NTFS Permissions to Share Files and Folders
- **Lab 9.6:** Work with Offline Files

LAB 9.1 MAP A NETWORK DRIVE AND USE WAKE-ON-LAN

OBJECTIVES

The goal of this lab is to learn to map a network drive and remotely power on your computer. After completing this lab, you will be able to:

◢ Map a network drive in Windows

◢ Set up Wake-on-LAN

MATERIALS REQUIRED

This lab requires the following:

◢ Two or more Windows 7 or Windows 8 computers on the same wired network (not wireless)

◢ Internet access (optional and used for research only)

LAB PREPARATION

Before the lab begins, the instructor or lab assistant needs to do the following:

◢ Verify Windows starts with no errors

◢ Verify Internet access is available

◢ Set up a peer-to-peer network with two or more computers

ACTIVITY BACKGROUND

When using more than one computer (for example, a laptop and a desktop), it is sometimes necessary to pass files between them. Having a mapped network drive on a computer makes it easy to access the files on another computer. On a small network, you might be accessing a resource on a desktop instead of a server, and the hosting computer might go to sleep. Setting up the Wake-on-LAN allows you to wake up the hosting computer and access your files. This can be useful if you're accessing your files remotely over a VPN from the other side of the country, or if you are just tired of getting up and walking across the room to turn on the computer.

ESTIMATED COMPLETION TIME: 45 MINUTES

 Activity

> **Notes** Sometimes HomeGroup does not play well with others when sharing. Before beginning this lab, open the **Network and Sharing Center**, and click **Change advanced sharing settings**. Make sure HomeGroup is turned off. Also, in Windows 8, open the **Settings** charm, and click **Change PC settings**. Click **Network**, and then click **HomeGroup**. If available, click **Leave**. Repeat these steps on the second computer.

In this lab, Computer 1 is acting as the server that is serving up a network resource (a folder named Downloads), and Computer 2 is acting as the client that is using this shared resource.

1. Begin with two networked Windows computers. Designate one computer to be Computer 1 and the other computer to be Computer 2.

2. On Computer 1, which will be your server, open File Explorer/Windows Explorer, navigate to your C: drive, and display the drive root.

3. To create a new folder in the root of drive C:, on the Home ribbon, click **New folder**, and name it **Resources.**

4. Right-click your new **Resources** folder, select **Share with,** and then click **Specific people** to open the File Sharing window.

5. To grant access to all users, select **Everyone** from the drop-down list, and then click **Add.** Under Permission Level, grant **Read/Write** access, and then click the **Share** button. Windows confirms that the folder is shared.

6. Make sure network discovery and file and printer sharing are turned on. To check these settings in the Network and Sharing Center, click **Change advanced sharing settings.**

7. To see a list of all network shares on this computer, open a command prompt window, and enter the **net share** command at the command prompt. Record on the following lines all the shared resources on the computer. Close the command prompt window.

_____

_____

_____

8. Go to Computer 2, and expand **Network** in the File Explorer/Windows Explorer navigation pane. Computer 1 should be in the list of available computers. If Computer 1 is not in the list, check Computer 1 and make sure its network discovery settings are correct. Record the names of all the computers visible on the network:

_____

9. To view the shared resources on Computer 1, open Computer 1. You might have to enter your user name and password if you haven't previously opened the network resource and saved your credentials.

10. You see a list of the shared resources on Computer 1. Does the list match the list of shared resources you wrote down in Step 7?

_____

11. Right-click the **Resources** folder, and select **Map network drive.** Windows assigns a drive letter by default, starting at Z and working backward through the alphabet. However, you can change this drive letter. What drive letter did you assign to the network drive? Check **Reconnect at sign-in** or **Reconnect at logon** if it is not already checked, and then click **Finish.**

_____

12. To test the functionality of your new network drive, create a test document on the mapped drive.

13. Go back to Computer 1, and verify the test document you created is in the Resources folder in the C: drive.

Now you will activate the Wake-on-LAN functionality. Follow these steps:

1. On Computer 1, open the **Network and Sharing Center.**

2. In the left pane, click **Change adapter settings.**

3. Right-click the network adapter for the wired connection, and select **Properties.**

4. Click **Configure**, and then select the **Power Management** tab. Which boxes are checked on the Power Management tab?

_____

_____

5. Make sure that the **Allow the computer to turn off this device to save power** option is selected. This enables power management in Windows.

6. Check **Allow this device to wake the computer**. Why shouldn't you select *Only allow a magic packet to wake this computer*?

_____

_____

_____

7. Click **OK**.

8. Shut down Computer 1.

9. Boot Computer 1, and access setup UEFI/BIOS. Find the power management configuration screen in UEFI/BIOS, and confirm that Wake-on-LAN is enabled. Did you need to enable Wake-on-LAN?

_____

10. Exit the UEFI/BIOS setup, and start Windows.

11. Put Computer 1 in sleep mode.

12. On Computer 2, go to File Explorer/Windows Explorer and try to open your mapped network drive. What happens?

_____

13. Shut down Computer 1.

14. On Computer 2, go to File Explorer/Windows Explorer and try to open your mapped network drive. What happens?

_____

REVIEW QUESTIONS

1. What is the purpose of the net share command? When network discovery and file and printer sharing are turned off, does the net share command still report a shared folder as shared?

_____

2. What drive letter does Windows first attempt to assign a mapped network drive? What is the second letter used?

_____

3. Why should you map a network drive rather than just access your network resource from the Network group in File Explorer/Windows Explorer?

_____

4. In what two locations must you enable Wake-on-LAN to use it?

_____

_____

5. Why is Wake-on-LAN typically disabled on laptops?

_____

_____

6. Why would you choose to disable the Wake-on-LAN functionality?

_____

_____

LAB 9.2 USE REMOTE DESKTOP

OBJECTIVES

The goal of this lab is to learn how to log on to another computer remotely by using Windows Remote Desktop. After completing this lab, you will be able to:

◢ Configure Remote Desktop

◢ Use Remote Desktop to log on to another computer remotely

MATERIALS REQUIRED

This lab requires the following:

◢ Windows 8 or Windows 7 Professional, Ultimate, or Enterprise edition

◢ An account with administrator privileges

◢ A network workgroup consisting of two or more computers

◢ A team of two or more students

LAB PREPARATION

Before the lab begins, the instructor or lab assistant needs to do the following:

◢ Verify Windows starts with no errors

◢ Verify a network connection is available

◢ Verify each student has access to a user account with administrator privileges

ACTIVITY BACKGROUND

Windows allows users to connect remotely from other Windows machines. With a remote connection, you can control a computer from another location, such as work or home. Remote Desktop is different than Remote Assistance because Remote Desktop does not need the end users' permission to connect their computer. Remote Desktop is also useful for connecting to servers, database servers, file servers, or other machines you access. For example, as a support technician, you might find Remote Desktop useful when you need to update or reset software on a server when you are working at your desk and the server is in the data center.

Remote Desktop is only available in Windows 8 or Windows 7 Professional, Ultimate, and Enterprise versions. Using Home editions of Windows 7, you cannot host the Remote Desktop, but you can remote in to a computer that is hosting Remote Desktop.

Remote Desktop is not enabled by default in the operating system. When enabled, members of the administrators group can connect to the computer from another machine. When you use Remote Desktop, you are logged on to the remote computer as if you were actually sitting in front of that machine with full rights and access. Standard users must be placed on a remote access list to use Remote Desktop.

In this lab, you configure one computer to accept a remote connection, and then allow someone in your class workgroup to connect to it from her machine.

ESTIMATED COMPLETION TIME: 30 MINUTES

 Activity

In this lab, you set up your computer to allow a remote connection. Then, you remote it to another computer in your workgroup that is also configured to use Remote Desktop. To configure your computer to accept a remote connection, follow these steps:

1. Log on using an account with administrator privileges.

2. To determine the computer name and IP address, open a command prompt window, and enter the **ipconfig /all** command. Write down the computer name (host name) and IP address:

_____

3. Open the **System** window, and click **Remote settings** in the left pane. The System Properties dialog box opens with the Remote tab selected.

4. Select the **Allow connections only from computers running Remote Desktop with Network Level Authentication** option. If a dialog box appears warning about a Power Options setting, click **OK** to continue. Click **Apply**.

5. Click **Select Users**. In the Remote Desktop Users dialog box, you can add or remove users who are allowed to use a Remote Desktop connection. The users listed here and the user currently signed in have access to Remote Desktop. On the following line, list those users:

_____

6. Close all windows.

Follow these steps to connect to a computer using Remote Desktop:

1. Find someone in your group who has set up Remote Desktop on his or her computer. Ask for the computer name and IP address of his or her computer so that you can connect to it using Remote Desktop. What computer name and IP address will you connect to?

_____

2. In Windows 8, on the Start screen, type and then select **Remote Desktop Connection**. In Windows 7, click **Start, All Programs, Accessories, Remote Desktop Connection**.

> **Notes** All local users are automatically logged off a computer when it is being remotely accessed. Also, only one computer can remotely access a single computer at a time.

3. In the Remote Desktop Connection dialog box, enter the IP address or computer name of the remote computer in the Computer text box, and click **Connect**.

4. A Windows security window appears asking for the logon credentials of the computer you are connecting to. Enter the credentials for one of the user accounts that is allowed access. For the user name, you might need to include the computer name, for example LenovoLaptop\Jean Andrews.

5. An identity warning window might pop up because the system cannot authenticate the certificate. If you see this window, click **Yes** to accept. You can also check the **Don't ask me again for connections to this computer** box so that the warning doesn't appear again.

6. After a moment, the screen of the computer to which you now have remote access appears.

Follow these steps to use the remote machine:

1. Notice the toolbar at the top of the screen. What is the name of the computer that you are accessing?

   _____

2. Open the **Documents** folder. Create a test document on the remote computer. What is the name of the document you created?

   _____

   _____

3. Using Control Panel, adjust the time by a half hour. What is the new time?

   _____

4. Click **OK**, and close all windows.

5. Close the Remote Desktop Connection window, which ends the remote connection session.

6. Log on to the remote machine you just used, change the time back to the correct time, and verify the file has been created.

REVIEW QUESTIONS

1. Describe two situations in which you might want to use Remote Desktop Connection:

   _____

   _____

   _____

2. How can you tell if you are connected remotely to another computer?

   _____

   _____

3. How can you determine the name of the remote computer before connecting? How can you determine the IP address of the remote computer?

   _____

   _____

9

4. How might other programs, such as firewalls, interfere with a remote connection?

_____

_____

5. When a connection was made to the remote computer in the lab, what changed on that computer?

_____

6. What is the advantage of a host computer not displaying the Windows desktop locally when a Remote Desktop session is active?

_____

_____

LAB 9.3 MANAGE USER ACCOUNTS IN WINDOWS 8

OBJECTIVES

The goal of this lab is to gain experience adding and modifying user accounts by using the PC settings page in Windows 8. After completing this lab, you will be able to:

▴ Add users

▴ Reset passwords

▴ Control user account access

MATERIALS REQUIRED

This lab requires the following:

▴ Windows 8 operating system

▴ An account with administrator privileges

LAB PREPARATION

Before the lab begins, the instructor or lab assistant needs to do the following:

▴ Verify Windows starts with no errors

▴ Verify each student has access to a user account with administrator privileges

ACTIVITY BACKGROUND

Maintaining Windows involves more than just managing physical resources like hard drives; you also need to manage users and their access to these resources. Managing users can be very time consuming, however. Much of this time is typically spent helping users who have forgotten their passwords or entered their passwords incorrectly multiple times, causing Windows to lock their accounts. In this lab, you practice managing user accounts and passwords using the PC settings page and the Manage Accounts window in Control Panel. For more advanced user account management, you can use the Computer Management console, which is not covered in this lab.

ESTIMATED COMPLETION TIME: 30 MINUTES

 Activity

To examine the user account information available via the PC settings page, follow these steps:

1. Sign in using an account with administrator privileges.

2. Open **Control Panel**. Click **User Accounts**, and then click **Manage another account**. The Manage Accounts window opens. Your screen will resemble Figure 9-1.

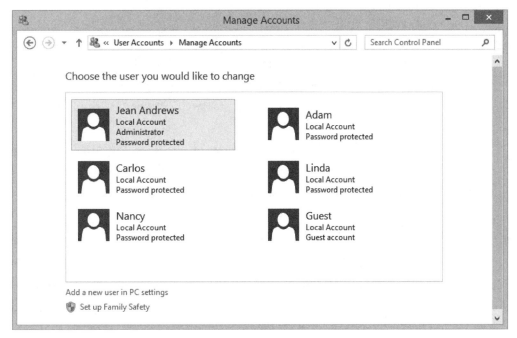

Figure 9-1   The Manage Accounts window lists all available user accounts

3. Examine the Manage Accounts window, click different user names, and answer the following questions:

◢ What types of user accounts are included on a Windows 8 system by default?

_____

_____

_____

◢ Does your system contain any individual user accounts? If so, list them here:

_____

_____

Windows 8 sends you to the PC settings page to add a new user. Add a new user on your local computer by following these steps:

1. In the Manage Accounts window, click **Add a new user in PC Settings**, or using the charms bar, click the **Settings** charm, and then click **Change PC settings**.

2. On the PC settings page, click **Accounts**, and then click **Other accounts**.

3. Click **Add an account**.

4. On the *How will this person sign in*? screen, click **Sign in without a Microsoft account** at the bottom of the screen. Review the two options for signing in, and then select **Local account**.

5. In the User name text box, type **James Clark**.

6. In the Password text box, type **changeme,** and confirm the password in the next text box. Enter a password hint in case the password is forgotten.

7. Click **Finish**.

New users in Windows 8 are set up as Standard user accounts by default. A Standard user account can't create, delete, or change other accounts; make system wide changes; change security settings; or install some types of software. To give the account administrator privileges, do the following:

1. On the Manage other accounts page, select the **James Clark** account, and then click **Edit**.

2. On the Edit account screen, change the account type to **Administrator**.

3. Click **OK**.

4. Sign out your computer, and sign in as James Clark. List the steps you took to accomplish this task:

_____

_____

_____

Occasionally, administrators have to reset user passwords. To reset a user's password, do the following:

1. Sign out of the James Clark account, and sign in again using the original administrator account.

2. Open the Manage Accounts window in Control Panel, and select the James Clark account.

3. Click **Change the password**. What information does a user lose when the password is changed by an administrator?

_____

_____

_____

4. Enter the password as **newpass**, confirm the password, enter a new password hint, and then click **Change password**.

5. Close all open windows, and try to sign in with the James Clark account using the old password. What error do you get? Click **OK**.

_____

6. If a user does not know his or her password, the user might be able to reset it using the sign-in screen. Under the password box on the sign-in screen, click **Reset password**. What does a user need to have to reset a password? Click **OK**.

_____

7. Sign in using the new password.

8. Finally, sign out of the James Clark account, sign in as the administrator, and delete the James Clark account. List the steps that you took to delete the account:

_____

_____

_____

REVIEW QUESTIONS

1. Besides adding, editing, and deleting users, what additional tasks can you perform in the Manage Accounts window of Control Panel in Windows 8?

_____

_____

2. Besides Administrator, Standard, and Guest account types, which are used to assign access, what is the fourth account type available in Windows 8? Why might you use this account type?

_____

_____

_____

_____

3. List the steps to change an account type using the PC settings page:

_____

_____

_____

_____

4. What user accounts management function can be performed on the PC settings page but not in the Manage Accounts window in Control Panel? What functions can be performed both on the PC settings page and in Control Panel?

_____

_____

_____

5. Why is it a good idea to primarily use a Standard account instead of an Administrator account for normal computer activity?

_____

_____

9

LAB 9.4 MANAGE USER ACCOUNTS IN WINDOWS 7

OBJECTIVES

The goal of this lab is to gain experience adding and modifying user accounts by using Control Panel in Windows 7. After completing this lab, you will be able to:

▲ Add users

▲ Control user account access

MATERIALS REQUIRED

This lab requires the following:

▲ Windows 7 operating system

▲ An account with administrator privileges

LAB PREPARATION

Before the lab begins, the instructor or lab assistant needs to do the following:

▲ Verify Windows starts with no errors

▲ Verify each student has access to a user account with administrator privileges

ACTIVITY BACKGROUND

Managing user accounts in Windows 8 is quite different than in Windows 7. In Windows 8, Microsoft moved some of the user management functions to the PC settings page. In Windows 7, you can access most of the necessary functions in just the Manage Accounts window in Control Panel. Because changing the password is almost exactly the same in Windows 7 as it is in Windows 8, you can refer to the previous lab, "Manage User Accounts in Windows 8," for those instructions. In this lab, you practice adding and editing user accounts using the Manage Accounts window in Control Panel. For more advanced user account management, you can use the Computer Management console, which is not covered in this lab.

> **ESTIMATED COMPLETION TIME: 30 MINUTES**

 Activity

To examine the user account information available via Control Panel, follow these steps:

1. Log on using an account with administrator privileges.
2. Click **Start**, **Control Panel**, and then click **Add or remove user accounts**. The Manage Accounts window appears.
3. Examine the Manage Accounts window, and answer the following questions:

   ▲ What three types of user accounts are included on a Windows 7 system by default?

   _____

   _____

   _____

   ▲ Does your system contain any individual user accounts? If so, list them here:

   _____

Using the Manage Accounts window, add and configure users on your local computer by following these steps:

1. In the Manage Accounts window, click **Create a new account**.

2. In the New account name text box, type **James Clark**.

3. Click **Standard user**, if it is not selected, and then click **Create Account**.

4. To create a password for the new account, click the **James Clark** account in the Manage Accounts window. Click **Create a password**.

5. In the New password text box, type **newuser**, and confirm the password in the next text box.

6. Click **Create password**, and then close all open windows.

A Standard user account can't create, delete, or change other accounts; make system wide changes; change security settings; or install some types of software. To give the account administrator privileges, do the following:

1. Open the Manage Accounts window in Control Panel, and select the **James Clark** account.

2. Click **Change the account type**, and select **Administrator**.

3. Click **Change Account Type**.

4. Log off your computer, and log on as James Clark. List the steps you took to accomplish this task:

_____

_____

_____

REVIEW QUESTIONS

1. Besides adding, editing, and deleting users, what additional tasks can you perform in the Manage Accounts window of Control Panel in Windows 7?

_____

2. What are the differences between Standard and Administrator accounts?

_____

_____

_____

_____

3. List the steps required to change an account type:

_____

_____

_____

_____

4. Why do you think new user accounts are not automatically assigned administrator privileges?

_____

_____

5. Why might it be a good idea to have users reset their passwords instead of having an administrator do it for them?

_____

_____

LAB 9.5 USE NTFS PERMISSIONS TO SHARE FILES AND FOLDERS

OBJECTIVES

The goal of this lab is to learn to use the advanced sharing and security tools in Windows to give folder permissions to specific local users and to control a network connection sharing specific folders with specific users and/or groups. After completing this lab, you will be able to:

◢ Configure how a network connection is controlled

◢ Share folders with others on the network using NTFS permissions

MATERIALS REQUIRED

This lab requires the following:

◢ Two computers networked together; one computer must use Windows 8 or Windows 7 Professional or higher, and the other computer can use any edition of Windows 8 or Windows 7

◢ An account with administrator privileges

◢ A workgroup of two students

LAB PREPARATION

Before the lab begins, the instructor or lab assistant needs to do the following:

◢ Verify both Windows computers start with no errors

◢ Verify the local network is working

◢ Verify each student has access to a user account with administrator privileges

ACTIVITY BACKGROUND

On a Windows 8 or Windows 7 Professional or higher computer, you can control which specific users or groups have access to specific folders. Microsoft best practices recommend that you set up a user group for each classification of data and assign permissions to a folder or other shared resources according to user groups. Assigning permissions to user groups is easier to maintain than assigning permissions to specific users because you can add or remove users from the group easier than you can change the permissions on each folder.

In this lab, you set up the security for a peer-to-peer network for a doctor's office. Two computers are connected to the small company network; one of these computers (Computer1) acts as the file server for the other computer (Computer2). You create two classifications of data, Financial and Medical. Two workers (Nancy and Adam) require access to the Medical data, and two workers (Linda and Carlos) require access to the Financial folder. In addition, the doctor, Lucas, requires access to both categories of data.

This lab is divided into four parts, which accomplish the following:

▲ Part 1: On Computer1, you create folders named Financial and Medical, and you create five user accounts, for Lucas, Nancy, Adam, Linda, and Carlos. All the accounts belong to the standard user group. You also create two new user groups, Financial and Medical.

▲ Part 2: You set the NTFS permissions on the Financial and Medical folders so that only the members of the appropriate group can access each folder.

▲ Part 3: You test your security settings for local users.

▲ Part 4: For each user on Computer2, you test the access to both folders across the network.

ESTIMATED COMPLETION TIME: 60 MINUTES

 Activity

Working with your partner, perform all four parts of this lab.

PART 1: CREATE FOLDERS, USER ACCOUNTS, AND USER GROUPS

Follow these steps to create the folders, user accounts, and user groups on Computer1 (the file server) that is using Windows 8 or Windows 7 Professional or higher edition:

> **Notes** Before beginning this lab, disable HomeGroup. In Windows 8, use the Network page under PC Settings page to leave the homegroup, and use the Advanced Sharing settings window in the Network and Sharing Center to turn off HomeGroup settings. In Windows 7, use the Network and Sharing Center and the Advanced Sharing settings window to turn off HomeGroup settings.

1. Log on to Computer1 as an administrator.

2. Create two folders: **C:\Financial** and **C:\Medical**. In each folder, create a test document. What is the name of the test document in the Financial folder? In the Medical folder?

_____

3. To open the Computer Management console, in Windows 8, right-click the **Start** button, and then click **Computer Management**, or in Windows 7, type **Computer Management** in the Search programs and files box, and then press **Enter**.

4. Using the console, create user accounts for Lucas, Nancy, Adam, Linda, and Carlos. To create the first new user, right-click **Users** under **Local Users and Groups**, and then select **New User** in the shortcut menu. Make the password for each user the same as the name of the user. Uncheck the **User must change password at next logon** check box. What are the other three check box options when creating user accounts?

_____

_____

_____

5. Click **Create**. The user will automatically be added to the Users group. Create all the user accounts, and click **Close** after the last user account is created.

9

6. To create the Financial user group, right-click **Groups** under Local Users and Groups, and then select **New Group** in the shortcut menu. The New Group dialog box appears. Enter **Financial** as the name of the group. Enter the description **Users have access to the Financial folder**.

7. To add members to the Financial group, click **Add**. The Select Users dialog box opens. In the *Enter the object names to select* box, enter the name of a user, and then click **OK**. Add all the user account names that need access to this folder, separated by semicolons, as in **Carlos; Linda; Lucas**. (Alternatively, you can click **Advanced** to open a new dialog box, and then click **Find Now** to view a list of user names. Then, hold down the **Ctrl** key and select multiple names, and then click **OK**.) To create the group, click **Create** in the New Group box.

8. Next, create the **Medical** group, and add Lucas, Nancy, and Adam to the group.

9. Close the Computer Management console.

PART 2: SET NTFS PERMISSIONS ON FOLDERS

Follow these steps to set the permissions for the two folders:

1. Open File Explorer/Windows Explorer, right-click the **Financial** folder, and then select **Properties** in the shortcut menu. The Properties dialog box for the folder appears. Click the **Security** tab (see the right side of Figure 9-2). What groups and users already have access to the C:\Financial folder?

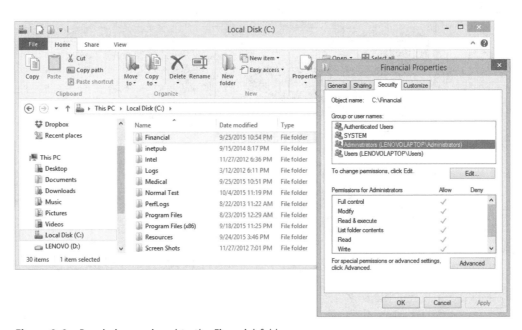

Figure 9-2   Permissions assigned to the Financial folder

2. When you select a user group in the Group or user name section, the type of permissions assigned to that group appears in the Permissions section. Note that the Administrators group has full control of the folder. Also notice the checks under Allow are dimmed. These permissions are dimmed because they have been inherited from the Windows parent object.

3. To remove the inherited status from these permissions so that you can change them, click **Advanced**. The Advanced Security Settings window appears. In Windows 8, click **Disable inheritance** (see Figure 9-3). In Windows 7, click **Change Permissions**. You can now uncheck **Include inheritable permissions from this object's parent**. A Windows Security

warning dialog box, also shown in Figure 9-3, appears. To keep the current permissions, but remove the inherited status placed on them, click **Convert inherited permissions into explicit permissions on this object** in Windows 8, or in Windows 7, click **Add**.

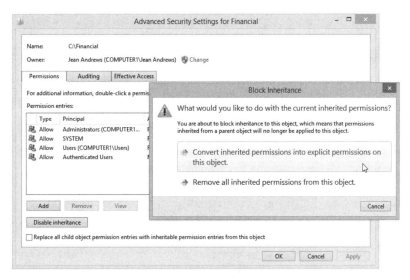

Figure 9-3 Remove the inherited status from the current permissions

4. Click **Apply**, and click **OK** to close the Advanced Security Settings window.

5. In the Financial Properties dialog box, notice the permissions are now checked in black, indicating they are no longer inherited permissions and can be changed. What permissions are allowed to the standard Users group by default?

_____

6. Click **Edit** to change these permissions.

7. The Permissions for Financial dialog box opens (see Figure 9-4). Select the **Users** group, and then click **Remove**. Also remove the **Authenticated Users** group. Don't remove the SYSTEM group or the Administrators group. That way, an administrator can always access the data.

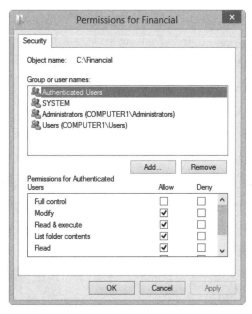

Figure 9-4 Change the permissions of a folder

9

8. To add a new group, click **Add**. The Select Users or Groups dialog box opens. In the *Enter the object names to select* box, type **Financial**, and then click **OK**. The Financial group is added to the list of groups and users for this folder.

9. In the Permissions for Financial section, check **Allow** for the **Full control** option to give that permission to this user group. Click **Apply**, and then click **OK** twice to close the Properties dialog box.

10. Following the same process, change the permissions of the C:\Medical folder so that Authenticated Users and Users are not allowed access and the Medical group is allowed full control. Don't forget to first disable inheritable permissions in the advanced settings.

PART 3: TEST YOUR SECURITY SETTINGS WITH LOCAL USERS

Do the following to test the share permissions on each shared folder:

1. On Computer1, log off and log back on as **Lucas** with the password set earlier in this lab. Verify Lucas can access both the Medical and Financial folders.

2. Log off and log back on as **Nancy**. Verify Nancy can access the Medical folder but not the Financial folder. What warning pops up when Nancy tries to access the Financial folder?

   _____

   _____

3. Log off and log back on as **Adam**. Verify Adam can access the Medical folder but not the Financial folder.

4. Log off and log back on as **Linda**. Verify Linda can access the Financial folder but not the Medical folder.

5. Log off and log back on as **Carlos**. Verify Carlos can access the Financial folder but not the Medical folder.

PART 4: TEST YOUR SECURITY SETTINGS ON THE NETWORK FOR EACH USER ON COMPUTER2

NTFS permissions and share permissions both control access over the network, and the most restrictive permission setting applies. Best practice is to give full access using share permissions and restrictive access using NTFS permissions. Do the following to set share permissions so that all network users are given full control of both folders:

1. Log on to Computer1 as an administrator. Open the Properties dialog box for the Medical folder, and click the **Sharing** tab. In Windows 8, click **Advanced Sharing**. Check **Share this folder**, and then click **Permissions**. If necessary, add the Everyone group. Select **Everyone**, and check **Allow** next to **Full Control**. Click **Apply**, and then click **OK**. Click **Apply** again, and then click **OK**. In Windows 7, click **Share**. In the drop-down list, select **Everyone** and click **Add**. In the Name column, click **Everyone**, and, in the Permission Level column, select **Read/Write**. Click **Share**. Close the Properties dialog box.

2. In the same way, set share permissions for the Financial folder.

Even though share permissions allow full access, the NTFS permissions set earlier in this lab will limit access. Do the following to test your security settings for network users:

1. On Computer2, log on as an administrator.

2. Create user accounts for Lucas, Nancy, Adam, Linda, and Carlos. Make the password for each account the name of the user.

> **Notes** If Computer2 uses a Windows 8 or Windows 7 Home edition, you must use the PC settings page or Control Panel to create user accounts.

3. Log off and log back on to Computer2 as **Lucas**. Verify Lucas can access both the Medical and Financial folders on Computer1. If you have a problem accessing the folders, go back and check your work, making sure all settings are correct. If you still have a problem, try logging off and logging back on. If that doesn't work, try restarting both computers.

4. Log off and log back on to Computer2 as **Nancy**. Verify Nancy can access the Medical share but not the Financial share on Computer1. What text appears in the Network Error box when Nancy tries to access the Financial share?

_____

_____

5. Log off and log back on to Computer2 as **Adam**. Verify Adam can access the Medical share but not the Financial share on Computer1.

6. Log off and log back on to Computer2 as **Linda**. Verify Linda can access the Financial share but not the Medical share on Computer1.

7. Log off and log back on to Computer2 as **Carlos**. Verify Carlos can access the Financial share but not the Medical share on Computer1.

REVIEW QUESTIONS

1. Why is it necessary that Computer1 run Windows 8 or Windows 7 Professional or higher edition to implement the security used in this lab?

_____

_____

2. When viewing the permissions assigned to a folder, why might these permissions be grayed out so that you cannot change them?

_____

_____

3. When assigning permissions to a folder, why might you allow full permissions to the Administrators group?

_____

4. What is the purpose of turning on the *Use user accounts and passwords to connect to other computers* setting in the Advanced sharing settings window?

_____

_____

LAB 9.6 WORK WITH OFFLINE FILES

OBJECTIVES

The goal of this lab is to learn to work with offline files. After completing this lab, you will be able to:

◢ Enable offline files in Windows

◢ Make network files available offline

◢ Sync offline files with the network

MATERIALS REQUIRED

This lab requires the following:

◢ Two or more Windows 8 or Windows 7 computers networked together. At least one computer must use Windows 8 or Windows 7 Professional or higher.

◢ Internet access

> **Notes** It is recommended that you complete the first lab in this chapter, "Map a Network Drive and Use Wake-on-LAN," before tackling this lab.

LAB PREPARATION

Before the lab begins, the instructor or lab assistant needs to do the following:

◢ Verify Windows starts with no errors

◢ Verify Internet access is available

◢ Set up a simple network with two or more computers

ACTIVITY BACKGROUND

Sometimes, you need access to network files when the network is not available. Maybe you're traveling and you can't find a wireless connection or maybe the server is being updated and it's temporarily unavailable. Windows allows you to work with offline files and then sync up the changes with the network files later. In this lab, you set up some network files so they can be changed offline.

ESTIMATED COMPLETION TIME: 45 MINUTES

 Activity

In this lab, Computer1 is serving up a folder that is used by Computer2. Computer2 will use offline files to use the folder even when it is not connected to Computer1. Offline files is a feature of Windows 8 Professional or Enterprise editions or Windows 7 Professional, Ultimate, or Enterprise editions. Therefore, Computer2 must be using one of these editions.

1. Begin with two networked Windows computers and test your network connection. What method or utility did you use?

   _____

2. Computer1 will be your server. Using Computer1, create a folder named **Offline Files** in the root of drive C:. Share this folder with the Everyone group. (If you need help sharing the folder, see the first lab in this chapter, titled "Map a Network Drive and Use Wake-on-LAN.") In the folder, create a small text document. What is the exact name and path of your shared folder and file?

   _____

3. Computer2 must be using Windows 8/7 Professional or higher. Log on to Computer2, and create a mapped network drive to the shared folder. If you need help with this step, see the first lab in this chapter, titled "Map a Network Drive and Use Wake-on-LAN."

4. Still using Computer2, open the text file to test your connection.

5. Open the **Computer** window, right-click the drive you just mapped, and select **Always available offline** in the shortcut menu.

6. To open the Sync Center, in Windows 8, on the Start screen type **Sync Center**, and select it from the search results. In Windows 7, click **Start**, type **Sync Center** in the Search box, and then press **Enter**. In the left pane of the Sync Center, click **View sync partnerships**, if it is not already selected. The window reports progress syncing the files (see Figure 9-5). Note any messages or conflicts here:

_____

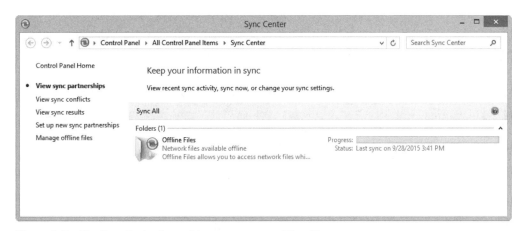

Figure 9-5   The Sync Center is used to manage your offline files

You can work with offline files by following these steps:

1. Temporarily remove Computer2 from the network by unplugging the network cable or disabling the network adapter. Windows will automatically enable offline files whenever the network is not available.

2. Open File Explorer/Windows Explorer, and open the offline version of the shared text file.

3. Make a small change to this file. What change did you make?

_____

4. In the Sync Center, click **Manage offline files**. The Offline Files dialog box opens. Answer the following questions:

◢ What objects are listed when you click **View your offline files**?

_____

_____

◢ How can you change the amount of space available for storing offline files on your computer?

_____

_____

◢ How can offline files help you when you are experiencing a slow network connection?

_____

_____

5. Now reconnect Computer2 with the network.

6. Windows updates offline files automatically, but not continuously. To make sure the offline file is updated, go to the Sync Center, right-click **Offline Files,** and then click **Sync Offline Files.**

7. After the sync finishes, go to Computer1, and, if necessary, log on. Open the shared file. Did the file update with offline changes made from Computer2?

_____

CHALLENGE ACTIVITY (ADDITIONAL 20 MINUTES)

Suppose you are working with offline files while disconnected from the network and you make a change to the file on your local computer while another change is made to the same file stored on the host computer. What happens when you reconnect to the network and sync your offline files? Which change is kept and which change is lost? Set up this scenario, and describe what happens:

_____

_____

_____

REVIEW QUESTIONS

1. What are some reasons you might choose to set up offline files?

_____

_____

_____

_____

2. How is working with offline files different from simply making a second copy of the files you need to access?

_____

3. Why might encrypting your offline files be necessary? Describe at least one situation when encrypting your offline files might be appropriate:

_____

_____

_____

4. Why might you choose to work with offline files even if the network is available?

_____

_____

Security Strategies

Labs included in this chapter:

- **Lab 10.1:** Monitor Security Events
- **Lab 10.2:** Audit Access to Private Folders
- **Lab 10.3:** Use Encryption
- **Lab 10.4:** Deal with a Rootkit
- **Lab 10.5:** Secure a Workstation
- **Lab 10.6:** Protect Against Malware in Windows 8
- **Lab 10.7:** Download and Use Microsoft Security Essentials
  in Windows 7

LAB 10.1 MONITOR SECURITY EVENTS

OBJECTIVES

The goal of this lab is to use Event Viewer to monitor security events such as failed attempts to log on to the system or changes to files and folders. Multiple failed attempts at logging on to a system can indicate a potential hacker, and sometimes audit reports can help identify unauthorized use of a file or folder. After completing this lab, you will be able to:

▲ Use the Local Security Policy tool in Control Panel to set policies to monitor failed logon attempts and changes to files and folders

▲ Use Event Viewer to monitor the events of failed logons and changes to files and folders

MATERIALS REQUIRED

This lab requires the following:

▲ Windows 8 operating system, Professional or Enterprise edition or Windows 7 operating system, Professional, Ultimate, or Enterprise edition

▲ An account with administrator privileges

LAB PREPARATION

Before the lab begins, the instructor or lab assistant needs to do the following:

▲ Verify Windows starts with no errors

▲ Verify each student has access to a user account with administrator privileges

ACTIVITY BACKGROUND

As part of its efforts to manage the security of a computer or network, your organization might ask you to report incidents of suspicious events such as failed attempts to log on (indicating a potential hacker) or unauthorized changes to certain files. For example, suppose an employee is suspected of stealing from the company; you might be called on to monitor any changes to the bookkeeping files to which this employee has access but would not normally change.

You can track auditing events by setting policies using the Local Security Policy tool, and then using Event Viewer to monitor the logged events.

The Local Security Policy tool is one of the Administrative tools available in Control Panel. The tool creates security policies that apply only to the local computer. If you needed to set other policies, you would need to use Group Policy, which covers a wider range of policies than does the Local Security Policy tool.

ESTIMATED COMPLETION TIME: 30 MINUTES

 Activity

Repeated failures at logging on to a system might indicate someone is trying to guess a password and gain unauthorized access to a user account. Follow these steps to use Local Security Policy to monitor failures when someone is attempting to log on to the system:

1. Log on as an administrator, and create a new standard user account called **Newuser**. Create a password for this new user account. What is that password?

2. Using Control Panel, open **Administrative Tools**. Double-click **Local Security Policy**. The Local Security Policy window opens.

3. Expand the **Local Policies** group, and select **Audit Policy**. How many policies appear in the right pane for the Audit Policy group?

_____

4. Double-click **Audit account logon events**. The Audit account logon events Properties dialog box opens. Check the **Failure** check box, as shown in Figure 10-1, and then click **OK**. Do the same for the **Audit logon events policy**.

Figure 10-1   Local Security Policy set to audit failed logon events

5. Examine the other Audit Policy policies. Which one would you use to monitor when a password is changed? Close the Local Security Policy window.

_____

6. To see the logged audit events, open **Event Viewer** from the Administrative Tools window. In the left pane, click **Windows Logs**, and then click **Security**. How many events are logged in this group of events? Does Event Viewer currently list any logon failures?

_____

7. Log off, and attempt to log on to the Newuser account using an incorrect password.

8. Now log back on using an administrator account.

9. Open Event Viewer and again click **Security**, as shown in Figure 10-2. What is the date and time that Windows recorded for the failed logon attempt?

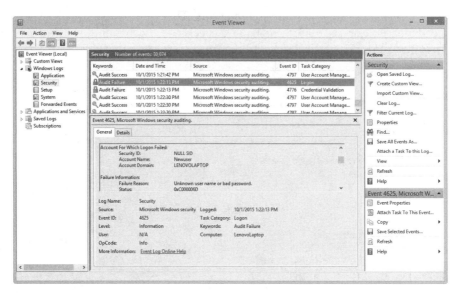

Figure 10-2   Event Viewer displays the failed logon event

Follow these steps to monitor changes to files and folders:

1. Open the Local Security Policy window, and locate the Audit Policy policies, as you did in Steps 2 and 3 earlier in this lab. Double-click **Audit object access**. The Audit object access Properties dialog box opens. Click the **Explain** tab, and answer the following questions:

   ◢ What is a SACL?

   ◢ Which dialog box do you use to set a SACL for a file system object?

2. On the Local Security Setting tab, check the **Success** and **Failure** check boxes, and then click **OK**.

3. Close the Local Security Policy window.

4. Now let's set Windows to audit activity in the Public folder. To do so, in File Explorer/Windows Explorer, open the **Properties** dialog box of the C:\Users\Public folder, and then click the **Security** tab.

5. Click **Advanced**, select the **Auditing** tab, and then click **Continue**.

6. The Advanced Security Settings for Public dialog box opens. You can now add users or groups that you want to monitor.

7. Click **Add**. In Windows 8, click **Select a principal**. Click **Advanced**, click **Find Now**, select **Newuser**, and then click **OK**.

8. Click **OK** to close the Select User or Group window.

9. In Windows 8, change the Type to **All**, and check **Full Control**. Click **OK** to close the Auditing Entry for Public dialog box. In Windows 7, check the **Full control** check boxes in the Successful and Failed columns, and click **OK** to close the Auditing Entry for Public dialog box. Click **OK** to close the Advanced Security Settings for Public dialog box. If error dialog boxes appear, click **Continue** to close each box.

10. Close all windows, and log off the system.

11. Log on as **Newuser**, and open the C:\Users\Public folder. While you're there, use Notepad to create a short text file and save it to this location. What did you name your text file?

_____

12. Log off as Newuser, and log back on using your administrator account.

13. Open **Event Viewer**. In the left pane, select **Event Viewer (Local)**. In the Summary of Administrative Events section, double-click **Audit Success** to open that group of events. Double-click the first event in the group named **Microsoft Windows security auditing**. Maximize the window so you can easily view information about each event.

14. Explore the recent events in this section until you find the ones that are associated with Newuser's activity in the C:\Users\Public folder. You might need to search other Microsoft Windows security auditing events to find the relevant events. About how many events were created?

_____

15. List one event that is related to the creation of the new text file:

_____

16. Close all open windows.

REVIEW QUESTIONS

1. How can you use the Local Security Policy to determine if someone has tried to hack into a user account?

_____

_____

2. When securing a system, why is it important to audit failed attempts to access files?

_____

_____

3. Which policy would you use to monitor when a user changes her password?

_____

4. In this lab, you monitor the activity of a single user. What would be a more efficient way to monitor the activities of a collection of users?

_____

5. Why does accessing one file create multiple events?

_____

_____

10

LAB 10.2 AUDIT ACCESS TO PRIVATE FOLDERS

OBJECTIVES

The goal of this lab is to learn how to set up folder auditing so that you can determine if unauthorized users attempt to access a private folder. After completing this lab, you will be able to:

▲ Use a local security policy to require a password for all user accounts

▲ Configure Windows to log attempts to access a private folder

▲ View the event log for folder access attempts

MATERIALS REQUIRED

This lab requires the following:

▲ Windows 8 or Windows 7 operating system, Professional or higher edition

▲ An account with administrator privileges

LAB PREPARATION

Before the lab begins, the instructor or lab assistant needs to do the following:

▲ Verify Windows starts with no errors

▲ Verify each student has access to a user account with administrator privileges

ACTIVITY BACKGROUND

Although auditing of file and folder access is usually not necessary for home computers with only a few trusted users, it can be useful in a networked environment with many users where all users are not trusted with complete access to all resources. You can set up Windows to audit activity on a file or folder so that whenever the file or folder is accessed, this activity is recorded in a log. Each user has a user profile in the C:\Users folder, and a standard user should not be able to access the folders that belong to another user. In this lab, you set up a user profile for a user, configure Windows to audit the folder, attempt to access the folder, and verify the access attempt was logged.

> **ESTIMATED COMPLETION TIME: 30 MINUTES**

 Activity

PART 1: SET A LOCAL SECURITY POLICY TO REQUIRE PASSWORDS FOR USER ACCOUNTS

In the first part of the lab, you set a local security policy to require a password on all accounts. To see the effect of the policy, you create one standard user before you set the security policy in order to verify a password is not required for the account. Then, you create another user after you set the policy and verify a password is now required. Recall that the Local Group Policy Editor is only available in the Professional or Enterprise editions of Windows 8 or the Professional, Ultimate, and Enterprise editions of Windows 7, and can be run only by an administrator. Do the following to create a standard user account:

1. Log on to the computer as an administrator.

2. Using the Computer Management window, create a standard user named **User1**, without a password.

3. Log off and log back on as **User1**. Note that you are not prompted for a password. When a user first logs on, his user profile namespace is created in the C:\Users folder. These folders are private and can be accessed only by the owner of the folder and administrators.

Do the following to set the local security policy:

1. Log off and log back on as an administrator. To start Group Policy in Windows 8, on the Start screen, type **gpedit.msc** and select it from the search results. In Windows 7, click **Start**, type **gpedit.msc** in the Search box, and then press **Enter**. The Local Group Policy Editor console opens.

2. In the left pane, expand **Computer Configuration, Windows Settings, Security Settings,** and **Account Policies,** and then click **Password Policy**.

3. Double-click **Minimum password length** in the right pane. When the Minimum password length Properties window opens, click the **Explain** tab, and read the information about password length.

4. Click the **Local Security Setting** tab, enter a non zero value in the text box, and then click **OK**. Close the Local Group Policy Editor console.

Any new user accounts created will now need a password. Existing user accounts will not be affected until their passwords are created or changed. To verify this, you'll create another user account, and then log on with that account. Follow these steps:

1. Using the Computer Management window, create a standard user named **User2**, without a password. An error message appears saying the minimum password requirement was not met. Add the password, and create the user. Log off the computer.

2. Log on as **User2**.

PART 2: ATTEMPT TO ACCESS A PRIVATE FOLDER

To verify the folders that belong to User1 are not accessible to other users, attempt to access the folders while you are logged on as User2. Follow these steps:

1. In the address bar of File Explorer/Windows Explorer, type **C:\Users\User2** to navigate to the folders that belong to this user. A user has full access to his own private folders.

2. In the address bar of File Explorer/Windows Explorer, type **C:\Users\User1**. A message informs you that you don't have access to the folder. Click **Continue**, and note that you must supply an administrator password to open the folder. Click **No**, and log off the computer.

PART 3: AUDIT FOLDER ACCESS

In this part of the lab, you configure Windows to audit access attempts on the private folders that belong to another user. First, you enable auditing in Group Policy, and then you configure auditing options on a specific folder in the folder's Properties window. Follow these steps:

1. Log on to the computer as an administrator. Use **gpedit.msc** to open the Local Group Policy Editor console again.

2. In the left pane, expand **Computer Configuration, Windows Settings, Security Settings,** and **Local Policies,** and then click **Audit Policy**.

3. Double-click **Audit object access** in the right pane to open the Audit object access Properties dialog box. Note that you can audit successful attempts, failures, or both. For the purposes of this lab, you'll audit failures only. Check the **Failure** check box, and, if necessary, uncheck the **Success** check box. See Figure 10-3. Click **OK**. Close the Local Group Policy Editor console.

10

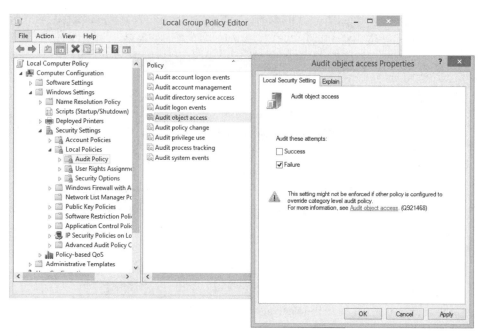

Figure 10-3   Audit failed logon attempts

Next, you edit the properties of the C:\Users\User1 folder to enable auditing for that folder. Follow these steps:

1. In File Explorer/Windows Explorer, navigate to C:\Users, and right-click the **User1** folder. If a warning dialog box opens, click **Continue** to access the User1 folder.

2. Select **Properties** in the shortcut menu, and then click the **Security** tab. Click **Advanced**, click the **Auditing** tab, and then click **Continue** to view the folder's auditing properties. The Advanced Security Settings for User1 dialog box opens.

> **Notes** Only administrator accounts are able to use the Advanced Security Settings dialog box.

3. The auditing entries box will be blank because no entries have been added yet. Click the **Add** button, and in Windows 8, click **Select a principal**, type **Everyone** in the Select User or Group dialog box, and then click **OK**.

> **Notes** To delete an auditing entry you find already listed, select it, and then click **Remove**.

4. In Windows 8, change the type to **Fail**. If necessary, click **Show advanced permissions**. Check the **Traverse folder/execute file** check box and the **List folder/read data** check box, as shown in Figure 10-4. In Windows 7, in the Auditing Entry for User1 dialog box, place check marks in the **Failed** column for Traverse folder/execute file and List folder/read data. At the bottom of the dialog box, select the option to apply these auditing settings only to objects and/or containers within this container. Click **OK** four times to close the open dialog boxes. When you click OK to apply the changes, you might receive an Error Applying Security message. Some folders will not allow this audit policy to be applied. Click **Continue** to continue applying the audit policy to other folders. You might have to address this error message several times.

5. Log off the administrator account.

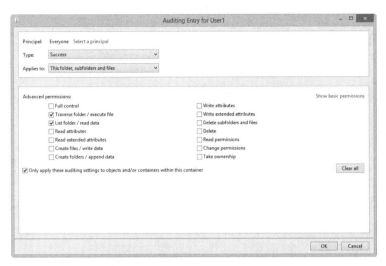

Figure 10-4 Use check marks to indicate types of access to be audited

Next, you attempt to access the User1 folder with an unauthorized account. Then, you view the event that is logged in the Event Viewer. Follow these steps:

1. Log on to the computer as User2, and, as you did before, attempt to navigate to the **C:\Users\User1** folder. You should get the same message informing you that you don't have access to the folder.

2. Log off User2, and log back on as an administrator. Open Event Viewer by typing **Eventvwr.msc** on the Start screen or in the Start search box, or in Windows 8, right-click the **Start** icon and select **Event Viewer**.

3. In the left pane, expand **Windows Logs**, and then click **Security**.

4. In the middle pane, scroll through the list of events (if necessary) and look for an event for which "Audit Failure" appears in the Keywords column and "File System" appears in the Task Category column. There might be more than one event listed.

5. Double-click the event, and read the description in the top section of the General tab of the Event Properties dialog box. (You might need to scroll or resize the window to see all the details.) Note that the account name (User2) and the object name (C:\Users\User1) are both listed, as shown in Figure 10-5.

6. Close any open windows.

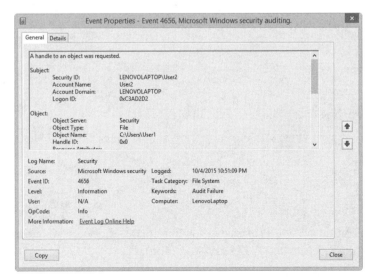

Figure 10-5 Use Event Properties to display details of an event

REVIEW QUESTIONS

1. What is the maximum number of characters that can be used in a Windows password?

    _____

2. How can you configure Windows so that passwords are not required for user accounts?

    _____

3. How can you configure a folder so that another user can view the files in the folder but not change them?

    _____

    _____

4. What group policy needs to be set to allow auditing of folder access attempts?

    _____

5. Why is it important to require passwords for all user accounts on a computer when you want to audit access to a folder?

    _____

6. What prevents a standard user from disabling auditing on a Windows computer?

    _____

LAB 10.3 USE ENCRYPTION

OBJECTIVES

The goal of this lab is to work with Windows file and folder encryption. File and folder encryption is one method you can use when you want to secure important and private data. In this lab, you learn how to encrypt a folder and how to back up your encryption key. You also learn what happens when someone tries to use an encrypted file without permission, and how to move encrypted files from one storage device to another and from one computer to another. After completing this lab, you will be able to:

◢ Encrypt a folder

◢ Save files to the encrypted folder

◢ Back up the encryption certificate key

◢ Attempt to access the encrypted files as a different user

◢ Observe what happens when you move or copy an encrypted file or folder to another computer

MATERIALS REQUIRED

This lab requires the following:

◢ Windows 8 operating system, Professional or Enterprise edition or Windows 7 operating system, Professional, Ultimate, or Enterprise edition

◢ An account with administrator privileges

LAB PREPARATION

Before the lab begins, the instructor or lab assistant needs to do the following:

⊿ Verify Windows starts with no errors

⊿ Verify each student has access to a user account with administrator privileges

ACTIVITY BACKGROUND

Despite your best efforts to set secured permissions to files and folders, unauthorized users might still gain access to sensitive files. To further decrease the possibility of this type of security breach, you can use file encryption, which prevents unauthorized users from being able to view files, even if they do manage to gain access to them. The EFS (Encrypting File System) is a Windows feature that allows a user to store information on her hard drive in an encrypted format.

You can encrypt individual files or entire folders. Encryption is the strongest protection that the operating system offers to keep your information secure. The EFS is available on hard drives that are set up as NTFS drives. In this lab, you create and encrypt a folder and its contents. Then, you test the encryption and back up the encryption certificate key. Finally, you learn how to decrypt a file and move an encrypted file to another computer.

ESTIMATED COMPLETION TIME: 30 MINUTES

 Activity

Follow these steps to prepare your system for this lab:

1. Log on as an administrator.

2. Create a new standard user account. Assign a password to the account. List below the name and password of the new account:

   _____

3. In File Explorer/Windows Explorer, open the **Documents** folder.

4. Create two folders in the Documents folder named **Normal Test** and **Encrypted Test**.

5. Create a text document in each folder. Name each document **TestFile**.

Now that you have the system prepared, let's work with the Encrypting File System. Follow these steps:

1. In the Documents folder, right-click the **Encrypted Test** folder, and select **Properties** in the shortcut menu.

2. On the General tab of the Encrypted Test Properties dialog box, click **Advanced**.

3. The Advanced Attributes dialog box appears. Check the **Encrypt contents to secure data** check box, and click **OK**.

4. Click **OK** to close the Encrypted Test Properties dialog box.

5. A Confirm Attribute Changes dialog box opens. This dialog box indicates the attribute *encrypt* has been chosen and asks how you want to apply this attribute. Select **Apply changes to this folder, subfolders and files**. Click **OK** to close the dialog box. A taskbar bubble might appear reminding you to back up your file encryption certificate and key.

10

When you start encrypting information, it is important to back up your encryption certificate. This is your key that unlocks the data. If you lose this key or the key is damaged and you didn't make a backup, the encrypted information can forever remain locked.

Follow these steps to create a backup of the encryption certificate:

1. In Windows 8, on the Start screen, type **certmgr.msc** and select **certmgr** from the search results. In Windows 7, click **Start**, enter **certmgr.msc** in the Search box, and then press **Enter**. The certmgr window opens (see the left side of Figure 10-6).

Figure 10-6   Use the certmgr window to back up encryption keys

2. In the left pane, select **Personal**, and then **Certificates**. In the right pane, select the certificate that shows **Encrypting File System** in the Intended Purposes column, as shown in Figure 10-6. If more than one certificate is listed, select them all.

3. On the menu bar, click **Action**, click **All Tasks**, and then click **Export**. The Certificate Export Wizard opens, as shown on the right side of Figure 10-6. Click **Next**.

4. Select **Yes, export the private key**, and click **Next**.

5. Select **Personal Information Exchange** for the file format, and click **Next**. The backup of the key will be saved in a PFX (.pfx) file.

6. Create a password for your key. Click **Next**. Write the password below:

_____

7. Click **Browse**. Navigate to where you want to save the file, name the file **Encryption Key Backup**, and click **Save**. What is the exact path and name of the file, including the file extension?

_____

8. To complete the process, click **Next**, click **Finish**, and then click **OK**.

Now that you have encrypted the folders and backed up the encryption key, let's investigate how an encrypted folder works. Follow these steps:

1. In File Explorer/Windows Explorer, in the Documents folder, what is the new color of the Encrypted Test folder name? What is the color of the file name in this folder?

_____

> **Notes** If the folder is not shown in a different color, you can adjust that setting. To do so, in Windows 8, on the View ribbon, click **Options** to open the Folder Options dialog box. In Windows 7, click **Organize** in the window toolbar, and then click **Folder and search options**. In the Folder Options dialog box, click the **View** tab, and check the **Show encrypted or compressed NTFS files in color** check box (see Figure 10-7). Click **OK**.

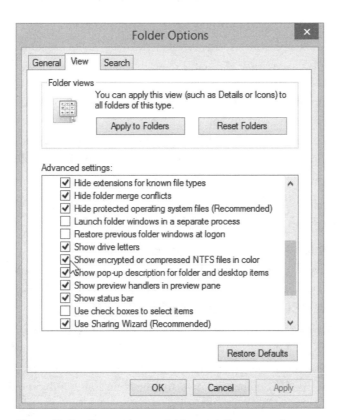

Figure 10-7 Change the way folders and files appear in File Explorer/Windows Explorer

2. Verify the file in the Encrypted Test folder is encrypted. How did you verify encryption is applied?

_____

3. Copy both the **Normal Test** folder and **Encrypted Test** folder to the root of drive C:. Are the contents of the Encrypted Test folder in the root of drive C: encrypted? How do you know?

_____

10

4. Copy the **Normal Test** folder and the **Encrypted Test** folder to a USB flash drive. Are the contents of the Encrypted Test folder on the USB flash drive encrypted? How do you know?

_____

5. Log off, and then log on using the standard user account you created earlier in this lab.

6. Open File Explorer/Windows Explorer, and locate the **Normal Test** folder in the root of drive C: Describe what happens when you double-click the file in the Normal Test folder:

_____

7. Locate the Encrypted Test folder in the root of drive C:. Describe what happens when you double-click the file in the Encrypted Test folder:

_____

8. Log off, and then log on using your administrator account.

9. Upon reaching the desktop, return to the encrypted folder in the Documents folder.

Let's assume you have moved your files to another computer that supports the Encrypted File System. When you do so, the files are still encrypted. However, you will not be able to use them unless you use your private key to access the files. You must import the private key to the new computer. Follow these steps to see how the process works:

1. To import or install your private key on a computer, you must use the Certificate Import Wizard. To launch it, double-click the **Encryption Key Backup** file you created earlier. The Certificate Import Wizard opens. Click **Next** two times.

2. Enter the password you created to the private key file, and then click **Next**. On the Certificate Store box, click **Next**. Click **Finish**. The wizard reports the import was successful. Click **OK**. Now that your private key is installed, you can use the encrypted files and folders you have moved to this computer.

There are times you may need to decrypt a folder or file to return it to unrestricted use. Follow these steps:

1. In the Documents folder, right-click the **Encrypted Test** folder that you made earlier. Click **Properties**. On the **General** tab, click **Advanced**.

2. In the Advanced Attributes dialog box, uncheck the **Encrypt contents to secure data** check box. Click **OK**. Click **OK** again.

3. To confirm the attribute change, click **OK**. Verify the file in the Encrypted Test folder is no longer encrypted. Explain how you know the file is no longer encrypted:

_____

_____

REVIEW QUESTIONS

1. Which file system must be used to enable encryption?

_____

2. What is necessary so that a USB flash drive can be used to hold encrypted files and folders?

_____

3. When you move an encrypted file from one computer to a second computer, what must you do first before you can open the encrypted file on the second computer?

_____

_____

4. What happens to encryption when you move an encrypted file to a Windows 8 or Windows 7 Home Premium computer? Explain your answer:

_____

_____

5. What is the file extension for an exported certificate backup file?

_____

6. Why is it necessary to back up or export your encryption certificate key?

_____

_____

7. (Challenge Question) Why is encryption available in the NTFS file system and not in the FAT32 file system?

_____

_____

LAB 10.4 DEAL WITH A ROOTKIT

OBJECTIVES

The goal of this lab is to identify and remove a rootkit running on your system. After completing this lab, you will be able to:

- Create a bootable device with anti-malware installed that is capable of recognizing and removing rootkits
- Use AVG Rescue CD installed on a bootable USB flash drive to scan a computer for rootkits

MATERIALS REQUIRED

This lab requires the following:

- Computer capable of booting to a USB flash drive
- An account with administrator privileges
- EICAR virus test file downloaded from *eicar.org*
- Access to the AVG Rescue CD (for USB stick) Zip file, stored on a network share
- Internet access (optional–needed to update tool before running scan)
- USB flash drive with at least 500 MB free space

10

LAB PREPARATION

Before the lab begins, the instructor or lab assistant needs to do the following:

◢ Download the AVG Rescue CD (for USB stick) Zip file from *avg.com/us-en/download. prd-arl*, and store it on a network share for student access

◢ Verify each student or team has a USB flash drive with at least 500 MB free space

◢ Download the EICAR virus test file from *eicar.org/85-0-Download.html*, and store it on drive C: on each student computer. You probably need to disable the anti-malware software on each computer so that it does not automatically remove the file.

◢ Verify Windows starts with no errors

◢ Verify Internet access is available (optional)

◢ Verify each student has access to a user account with administrator privileges

ACTIVITY BACKGROUND

A rootkit is a type of malware that uses sophisticated methods to hide itself on the system. Rootkits can prevent Windows components, such as Windows Explorer, Task Manager, or the registry editor, from displaying the rootkit processes. This stealthy behavior makes it difficult for anti-malware software to detect a rootkit. When you have already tried other methods, such as anti-malware software, to clean your system, and you still believe your system might be infected, you can try using antirootkit software.

The best way to detect a rootkit is to scan the hard drive when Windows is not loaded. In addition, a system might be so badly infected that anti-malware software will not install or run. For both situations, you can create a bootable device that contains anti-malware software and use it to scan the system. This method does not require you to boot into Windows or install anti-malware software in Windows. In this lab, you create a bootable AVG Rescue CD (for USB stick), boot to the USB flash drive, and use it to run a scan to detect and remove malware.

The AVG Rescue CD (for USB stick) Zip file has been stored on a network share. Ask your instructor for the location of this file, and record the location here:

_____

ESTIMATED COMPLETION TIME: 75 MINUTES

 Activity

Websites change often. The directions in this lab might need adjusting for changes that AVG makes to its website at *avg.com*.

PART 1: CREATE AND BOOT FROM THE AVG RESCUE USB FLASH DRIVE

Follow these steps to create a bootable USB flash drive that contains the AVG Rescue CD (for USB stick) software:

1. Log on as an administrator.

2. Plug in your USB flash drive. What drive letter did Windows assign to the drive?

3. Open your browser, and go to **avg.com/us-en/avg-rescue-cd#content**. Click **System Requirements**. How much RAM and hard disk space is required for this installation?

4. Click the **Free Download** button. What are the types of files available for download?

5. In the real world, you would download the Rescue CD Zip file from the AVG website. To save you time, however, in this lab, the file has been stored on a network share. Copy the Rescue CD (for USB stick) Zip file from the share to your desktop. What is the name of the Zip file?

6. Right-click the Zip file, and select **Extract All** in the shortcut menu. The default extract location is your desktop. Allow this default. Click **Extract**. The extracted folder should now open in a window on your desktop.

7. Double-click the **setup.exe** file. If a SmartScreen error or the UAC dialog box opens, click **Run anyway** or **Yes** to continue. Select the drive letter of the USB flash drive, and then click **Install**. When the installation is complete, the Success dialog box opens. What message appears in the dialog box? Click **OK**.

You are now ready to boot from the USB flash drive, which loads the Linux operating system. You can then use the anti-malware software on the flash drive to scan the system. Follow these steps:

1. Shut down the system, and reboot your computer to the USB flash drive. You might need to go into the UEFI/BIOS setup to change the boot device priority order so you can boot to the USB drive. A USB device might appear in the UEFI/BIOS setup as a Removable Drive.

2. When the system boots to the USB flash drive, an initial menu appears. You can let the menu time out, or press **Enter** to select AVG Rescue CD.

3. "I agree" is selected by default. Press **Enter**. If an information dialog box appears with the message, "Internet connection is not available," highlight **OK**, and press **Enter** to continue. AVG Rescue CD mounts the Windows partitions, and the Main Menu appears (see Figure 10-8).

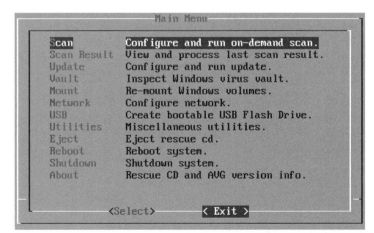

Source: AVG Rescue CD

Figure 10-8 The main menu of the AVG Rescue CD provides access to utilities and other features

10

4. In the AVG Rescue CD program, you can use the arrow keys to move through a list and the Tab key to toggle between choices of action. Alternatively, you can enter the first letter (in bold red) of any selection to highlight it. Use the arrow keys to scroll down to **Utilities**. "Select" is highlighted by default. Press **Enter** to open the Utilities Menu. Read through the list of available utilities, and answer the following questions:

◢ Which tool can be used to change a setting in the Windows registry?

_____

◢ Which tool can be used to repair a damaged Master Boot Record?

_____

◢ Which tool can be used to attempt to repair a damaged hard disk?

_____

5. If you don't have an Internet connection, skip the steps to update the virus database used by the AVG software. To skip this update, highlight **Return**, and press **Enter**. The Main Menu appears. Go to Part 2.

If you have an Internet connection, follow these steps to update the virus database used by the AVG software:

1. Select **Update** from the Main Menu. Highlight **Select**, and press **Enter**. The Update Type Menu appears (see Figure 10-9). Select **Online**. Highlight **Select**, and press **Enter**.

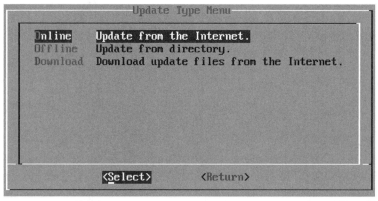

Source: AVG Rescue CD

Figure 10-9 The Update Type Menu allows you to update the virus database from the Internet

2. The Update Priority Configuration Menu appears. Leave "priority 2" selected to update the virus database. With **OK** highlighted, press **Enter**. The update should take a minute or two to run. When completed, highlight **Continue**, and press **Enter**.

PART 2: SCAN THE SYSTEM FOR MALWARE

The Main Menu is displayed. Do the following to perform the scan:

1. Use the up arrow to highlight **Scan**. With **Select** highlighted, press **Enter**. Verify **Volumes** is highlighted. With **Select** highlighted, press **Enter**.

2. The Scan Volumes Menu opens. You should see at least two volumes. One is your USB flash drive, and one is drive C: on your computer. If there are other partitions,

you might see other volumes, such as a hidden diagnostic partition or a second hard drive, on your computer. What are the types and sizes of the volumes that are shown?

_____

_____

3. You should be able to tell which volume is the drive C: partition by the size of the partition. Deselect all partitions except the drive C: partition. Then, highlight **OK**, and press **Enter**.

> **Notes** To deselect or select options, highlight an option, and then press the **Spacebar**. Notice that selected options are those with asterisks.

4. The Scan Options Menu appears. Review (do not change) the Scan Options. With the default options selected, highlight **OK**, and press **Enter**. The scan begins. The scan could take a long time to run, but it should find the EICAR_Test virus right away. After the virus is found, you can let the scan complete or cancel the scan. To cancel the scan, highlight **Cancel**, and press **Enter**.

> **Notes** To save time in this lab, you can point the scan to a specific folder where the EICAR_Test virus is located on drive C:, or you can copy the EICAR_Test virus to your USB flash drive and then search the flash drive.

5. After the scan is completed or is canceled, the results screen appears. It should show at least one infection found. Highlight **Continue**, and press **Enter**. The next page lists all rootkits, malware, and viruses found, and it presents options to deal with them all at once or individually. Verify the EICAR_Test virus is selected (an asterisk appears beside it). Highlight **Action**, and press **Enter**.

6. The Action Menu appears. What are the choices listed for actions?

_____

7. Suppose the EICAR_Test file is a dangerous file you don't want on your system. To delete it, arrow down to **Delete**, highlight **Select**, and then press **Enter**. To confirm the deletion, highlight **OK**, and press **Enter**. The Scan Type Menu appears in case you want to scan other volumes or directories. We are finished, so right-arrow to **Return**, and press **Enter**. Right-arrow to **Exit**, and press **Enter**. Press **Enter** to verify you want to quit. If an Info window appears, highlight **OK**, and press **Enter**. This will take you to the Linux command prompt.

8. Press **Ctrl+Alt+Delete** to reboot your system. You might need to go back into the UEFI/BIOS setup to fix your boot settings so that you can start the system from the computer's hard drive.

9. Verify the EICAR_Test virus file is no longer on your drive C:.

10. Close any open windows.

REVIEW QUESTIONS

1. How are rootkits different from other forms of malware?

_____

10

_____

_____

2. Why does running anti-malware software from another operating system (such as a Rescue CD/USB stick) do a better job than running the anti-malware software from Windows?

_____

_____

3. Which operating system does the AVG Rescue CD software use?

_____

_____

4. Why are kernel-mode rootkits more dangerous than user-mode ones?

_____

_____

5. Why should all other applications be closed before scanning for rootkits?

_____

_____

LAB 10.5 SECURE A WORKSTATION

OBJECTIVES

The goal of this lab is to learn how to secure a Windows 8 or Windows 7 workstation. After completing this lab, you will be able to:

◢ Require all users press Ctrl+Alt+Del to log on

◢ Require a password after the computer goes to sleep or screen saver mode

◢ Set a Local Security Policy

MATERIALS REQUIRED

This lab requires the following:

◢ A computer running Windows 8 or Windows 7 operating system, Professional or higher edition

◢ An account with administrator privileges

LAB PREPARATION

Before the lab begins, the instructor or lab assistant needs to do the following:

◢ Verify Windows starts with no errors

◢ Verify each student has access to a user account with administrator privileges

ACTIVITY BACKGROUND

Securing a workstation is one of the most important tasks you can perform when setting up security for an organization or individual. Windows provides some default security settings; however, these default settings are often exploited by malicious programs, thieves, and hackers. A few simple tweaks to your computer's security policy greatly improves the security of your system.

ESTIMATED COMPLETION TIME: 45 MINUTES

 Activity

Follow these steps to require that a user press Ctrl+Alt+Del to log on:

1. In Windows 8, on the Start screen, type **netplwiz**, and select it from the search results. In Windows 7, click **Start**, and in the Search box, type **netplwiz**, and press **Enter**. The User Accounts dialog box opens. Write down the user names displayed in the User Accounts dialog box:

   _____

   _____

2. Select the **Advanced** tab, and under "Secure sign-in" or "Secure logon," check the **Require users to press Ctrl+Alt+Delete** check box.

3. Apply the changes. Restart the computer to confirm the change has taken effect.

Follow these steps to secure the computer using a screen saver and sleep mode:

1. Open **Control Panel**. Select **Power Options**, and select **Require a password on wakeup** or **Require a password when the computer wakes**.

2. Under "Password protection on wakeup," make sure **Require a password (recommended)** is selected. If you need to change this setting, you might need to first click **Change settings that are currently unavailable**.

3. Save your changes, and close all windows.

4. In Windows 8, from the Start screen, type **Screen Saver**, and select **Change screen saver** from the search results. In Windows 7, click **Start**, and in the Search box, type **Screen Saver**, and press **Enter**. The Screen Saver Settings dialog box opens.

5. Select a screen saver from the drop-down menu to activate the screen saver function.

6. Check the **On Resume, display logon screen** check box. Apply your changes, and close all windows.

Follow these steps to require that all users have a password:

1. In Windows 8, from the Start screen, type **gpedit.msc**, and select it from the search results. In Windows 7, click **Start**, and in the Search box, type **gpedit.msc**, and press **Enter**. The Local Group Policy Editor console opens.

2. Navigate to **Computer Configuration, Windows Settings, Security Settings, Account Policies**, and, finally, **Password Policy** group.

3. Change the Minimum password length policy to a value higher than zero. How many characters did you require?

   _____

10

Follow these steps to secure the computer using UEFI/BIOS settings:

1. Restart the computer, and access the UEFI/BIOS setup. To access the UEFI/BIOS setup, you need to press a key or combination of keys at the beginning of the boot. Look for a message to tell you which key(s) to press (for example, F2, Del, or F12).

2. After you are in the UEFI/BIOS setup utility, find the screen to change the security settings.

3. Enter a value for the password that must be entered in order to boot up the computer. This password might be called the power-on password, system password, boot password, or another name. Write down the name for this password given on your UEFI/BIOS setup screen and the password you assigned:

_____

4. Enter a value for the password that must be entered in order to make changes to the UEFI/BIOS settings. This password might be called the admin password, the supervisor password, or another name. Answer the following questions:

   ▲ What is the name for the admin password as described on your UEFI/BIOS setup screen and what is the password you assigned to it?

   _____

   ▲ Does your UEFI/BIOS setup support encrypting the hard drive? If so, describe the feature in UEFI/BIOS setup:

   _____

   _____

   ▲ What other passwords does your UEFI/BIOS setup offer that can be used to secure the computer? Name and describe each password:

   _____

   _____

   _____

5. Save your changes, and restart the computer.

Do the following to test the security settings you created in this lab and record the results of your test:

1. When the computer starts up, what is the message that appears asking you for the power-on password?

   _____

2. Were you required to press Ctrl+Alt+Del before you could see the Windows logon screen?

   _____

3. After you reach the Windows desktop, put the computer in sleep mode. Were you required to enter your Windows password before you could wake up the computer?

   _____

4. Use the Computer Management window to create a new user account with no password. Then, log off and log back on using the new user account. At what point in this

process did you receive a message that required you to create a password for the user account?

_____

5. Did any of the security measures you implemented in this lab fail during this testing process? If so, what was the cause of the problem?

_____

REVIEW QUESTIONS

1. Why is it preferable to require the Ctrl+Alt+Del key combination for logon?

_____

_____

2. Why would you want to require a password to log on after the screen saver activates or the computer comes back on from sleep mode?

_____

_____

3. How many characters should the minimum password length be for best security practice?

_____

4. What does setting the admin password (sometimes called the supervisor password) in UEFI/BIOS accomplish?

_____

5. Why would you want a power-on password?

_____

_____

_____

6. Should you rely only on the Windows password to protect your sensitive data stored on the hard drive? Explain your answer:

_____

_____

_____

_____

_____

_____

10

LAB 10.6 PROTECT AGAINST MALWARE IN WINDOWS 8

OBJECTIVES

The goal of this lab is to verify your computer is clean of malicious programs using Windows Defender or free malware removal software. After completing this lab, you will be able to:

⊿ Make sure Windows Defender is turned on

⊿ Check for and install the latest Windows Defender updates

⊿ Scan for spyware or other malicious software infecting your computer

MATERIALS REQUIRED

This lab requires the following:

⊿ Windows 8 operating system

⊿ Internet access

LAB PREPARATION

Before the lab begins, the instructor or lab assistant needs to do the following:

⊿ Verify Windows starts with no errors

⊿ Verify Internet access is available

⊿ Perform a backup of important files if necessary

ACTIVITY BACKGROUND

Malware removal software is one of the largest growing technology sectors today, as new malicious programs continually flood the Internet. Malware removal software is useful because malware hides from the user and is difficult to detect. As a user surfs the web, malware can be downloaded and installed without the user's knowledge or consent.

Microsoft Windows offers Windows Defender to protect a system against spyware, viruses, and other malware. Once you turn on Windows Defender, it will run automatically to scan for malware or other unwanted programs. Definitions need to be updated daily to keep up with new malware.

ESTIMATED COMPLETION TIME: 15 MINUTES

 Activity

Windows Defender will not run if other anti-malware software is running on your system. Follow these steps to turn off other anti-malware software, and then explore how Windows Defender works:

1. To find out if anti-malware software other than Windows Defender is running on your computer, go to the **Windows desktop**, click the **Action Center** flag in the taskbar, and then click **Open Action Center**. The Action Center opens.

2. Click the **Security** title to expand the Security section. If you find in the Security section that anti-malware software other than Windows Defender is running, turn off this anti-malware program. Close the Action Center.

3. To open the Windows Defender window, go to the **Start** screen, and type **defender**. Click the **Windows Defender** tile. The Windows Defender window opens (see Figure 10-10). In the figure, Windows Defender shows the computer is potentially unprotected.

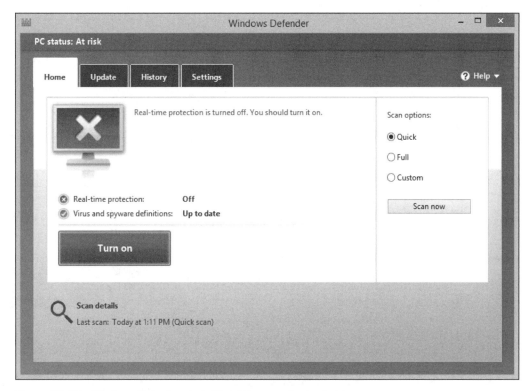

Figure 10-10 Windows Defender alerts that this computer is at risk

4. If your Real-time protection is off, click the **Turn on** button.

5. Click the **Update** tab, and then click **Update** to update your definitions.

After the virus and spyware definitions have finished updating, you are able to scan your computer with the most recent defenses against malware that Windows Defender offers. To scan your computer, follow these steps:

1. Return to the **Home** tab. With **Quick** selected as the scan option in the right pane, click the **Scan now** button.

2. After the scan is completed, you can see results from the scan. If any malicious software is found, complete the action requested by Windows Defender to remove the threat.

3. Repeat the scan, and remove any newly detected threats.

4. Keep repeating the scan until no threats are detected.

To change scan settings and delete quarantined items, follow these steps:

1. To change the scan settings, click the **Settings** tab. Explore the different setting groups in the left pane, and then click the **Advanced** group.

2. Select the boxes you want Windows Defender to use in future scans. If you made any changes, click the **Save changes** button.

3. To remove quarantined items from your computer, click the **History** tab. If necessary, with **Quarantined items** selected, click the **View details** button.

4. Select the items to delete, and click **Remove**, or to delete all quarantined items, click **Remove all**.

10

REVIEW QUESTIONS

1. Why is it important to use a malware removal program, such as Windows Defender, rather than just being careful while surfing the web?

_____

_____

_____

2. Why is it important to update virus and spyware definitions on malware removal programs, and how often should they be updated?

_____

_____

3. Why would you want to quarantine malware, and how do you delete quarantined malware from your system? Why could this be important?

_____

_____

_____

_____

_____

4. What are the options available in the Windows Defender settings? Why is the Real-time protection option important?

_____

_____

_____

_____

LAB 10.7 DOWNLOAD AND USE MICROSOFT SECURITY ESSENTIALS IN WINDOWS 7

OBJECTIVES

The goal of this lab is to learn how to use Microsoft Security Essentials to protect a computer from malware such as viruses, spyware, rootkits, and worms. After completing this lab, you will be able to:

◢ Download and install Microsoft Security Essentials

◢ Configure and use Microsoft Security Essentials

◢ Use the EICAR anti-malware test file to confirm anti-malware protection is active

MATERIALS REQUIRED

This lab requires the following:

◢ Windows 7 operating system

◢ An account with administrator privileges

◢ Internet access

LAB PREPARATION

Before the lab begins, the instructor or lab assistant needs to do the following:

◢ Verify Windows starts with no errors

◢ Verify Internet access is available

◢ Verify each student has access to a user account with administrator privileges

ACTIVITY BACKGROUND

As an IT support technician, you need to make certain that every computer you support has anti-malware software installed and that it is configured to receive automatic updates and run in the background. Many free and paid-by-subscription anti-malware software products are available and can be downloaded from the Internet. Among the free products, Microsoft Security Essentials is well rated and does a good job of protecting a system against malware. In this lab, you learn to download the software, install it, configure it, and make sure it is running in the background to protect a system against malware.

ESTIMATED COMPLETION TIME: 20 MINUTES

 Activity

> **Notes** Websites change from time to time, so you might need to adjust the following steps to accommodate changes to the Microsoft site.

Follow these steps to download and install Microsoft Security Essentials:

1. Log on to Windows using an account with administrator privileges.

2. Using your browser, navigate to **windows.microsoft.com/mse**.

3. Click **Free download**.

4. Internet Explorer asks if you want to run or save mseinstall.exe. Select **Save**, and Internet Explorer will automatically save the file to the Downloads folder in the current user's home directory. When the download is complete, click **View downloads**.

5. In the View Downloads window, click **Downloads** beside the file name you just downloaded.

   ◢ What is the path and file name (including file extension) of the downloaded file? What is the size of the file?

6. Close your browser.

7. To execute the downloaded file, double-click the file you just downloaded to your Downloads folder. If necessary, respond to the UAC dialog box.

8. The Microsoft Security Essentials window appears. Click **Next**.

10

9. On the next screen, click **I accept** to agree to the license agreement.

10. On the next screen, choose whether or not you would like to participate in the Microsoft Customer Experience Improvement Program, and then click **Next**.

11. When the "If no firewall is turned on, turn on Windows Firewall (Recommended)" option appears, leave this box checked, and click **Next**.

12. On the next screen, click **Install**.

13. On the next screen, uncheck the **Scan my computer for potential threats after getting the latest updates** check box. Click **Finish**.

14. The Microsoft Security Essentials window opens with the Update tab active and the update process already running. This process installs the latest virus and spyware definitions, and then scans your computer for malware. Wait for the entire process to complete, which might take several minutes.

15. If necessary, click the **Home** tab. On the Home tab, look for the large green check mark, which indicates that the software is configured to automatically scan for malware and that the software is up to date (see Figure 10-11).

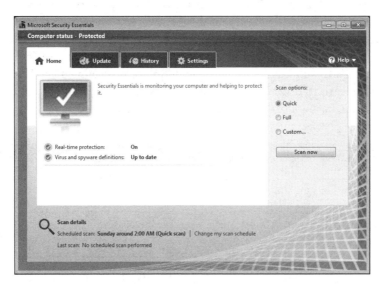

Figure 10-11   Microsoft Security Essentials is up to date with the latest virus and spyware definitions

16. Click the **History** tab. List below any suspicious items the scan recorded:

_____

_____

_____

17. Click the **Settings** tab. Answer the following questions:
    ◢ On what day of the week and time of day is a scan scheduled?

_____

    ◢ Is the software configured to check for the latest updates before running a scan?

_____

18. Click **Real-time protection**. What is the purpose of having real-time protection enabled?

_____

_____

19. List the steps to configure the software to scan removable drives:

_____

_____

_____

20. Close the Microsoft Security Essentials window.

21. To clean up your computer, delete the downloaded file in your Downloads folder. Which file did you delete?

_____

The EICAR anti-malware test file can be used to confirm your anti-malware software is working. Follow these steps to find out more:

1. Open Internet Explorer and navigate to **eicar.org/86-0-Intended-use.html**.

2. After reading the instructions for the use of the test file, scroll down the page and copy the ASCII string to your Windows Clipboard.

3. Open Notepad. Paste the string into Notepad, and save the file. What happens when you save the file?

_____

4. Open the Microsoft Security Essentials window, and click the **History** tab. Note any changes from when you viewed the list in Step 16 earlier in this lab:

_____

_____

REVIEW QUESTIONS

1. Why does EICAR release the anti-malware test string?

_____

_____

2. What is the name of the executable program file for Microsoft Security Essentials (not the downloaded file)?

_____

3. Why does Microsoft Security Essentials prompt you to activate Windows Firewall if a firewall is not active?

_____

4. Which tab on the Microsoft Security Essentials window do you use to find out the Virus definitions version and the Spyware definitions version?

_____

10

Virtualization, Linux, and Mac OS X

Labs included in this chapter:

- **Lab 11.1:** Use Oracle VirtualBox to Install and Explore Virtual Machines (VMs)

- **Lab 11.2:** Investigate Operating Systems–Mac OS

- **Lab 11.3:** Investigate Linux and Create a Bootable Ubuntu Flash Drive

- **Lab 11.4:** Compare Operating Systems

- **Lab 11.5:** Use TeamViewer to Remotely Access Another Computer

- **Lab 11.6:** Set Up a VPN

LAB 11.1 USE ORACLE VIRTUALBOX TO INSTALL AND EXPLORE VIRTUAL MACHINES (VMs)

OBJECTIVES

The goal of this lab is to become familiar with the different types of virtual machines currently available, to explore the different features and specifications needed to run these programs, and to explore their use in an enterprise environment. After completing this lab, you will be able to:

- Install and configure Oracle VirtualBox
- Understand the features of VMware
- Install an operating system from an ISO (.iso) file
- Contrast virtual machine features and capabilities

MATERIALS REQUIRED

This lab requires the following:

- A computer running Windows 8 or Windows 7
- A minimum of 2.0 GHz CPU power is advised
- A minimum of 4 GB of RAM is advised
- A minimum of 20 GB of available hard disk drive space
- Internet access

> **Notes** Virtual machine software and virtual machines tend to require heavy system resources. Don't forget that whatever memory you assign to a VM will not be available to the host operating system while the VM is open.

LAB PREPARATION

Before the lab begins, the instructor or lab assistant needs to do the following:

- Verify Windows starts with no errors
- Verify Internet access is available
- Create an ISO (.iso) file of an operating system of your choice, and make this file available to students. Make note of the location for both 32-bit and 64-bit editions, if necessary.
- Because of the time it takes to download the VirtualBox software, it is recommended that prior to the lab, the file be downloaded and then made available to students.

ACTIVITY BACKGROUND

Virtual machines are programs that can be installed on operating systems. In this lab, you explore and contrast different types of virtual machines and then install an operating system in a virtual machine using Oracle VirtualBox.

ESTIMATED COMPLETION TIME: 120 MINUTES

 Activity

PART 1: INSTALL AND USE VIRTUALBOX

Oracle VM VirtualBox is a powerful virtualization product. To learn more about it, follow these steps:

1. Open your favorite browser, and go to **virtualbox.org**. Explore the site and familiarize yourself with the available options.

2. Your instructor might have already downloaded the VirtualBox software for your use. If so, locate and execute the downloaded file, and then skip to Step 6. If not, in the left pane of the website, click **Downloads**.

3. Select **VirtualBox 5.0.6 for Windows hosts x86/amd64** or a newer version if available, as shown in Figure 11-1.

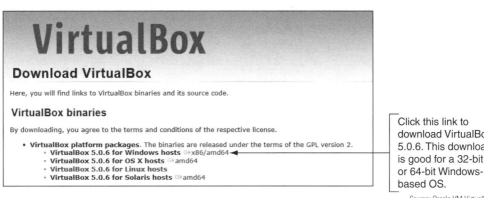

Source: Oracle VM VirtualBox.

Figure 11-1 Oracle VirtualBox download options

4. Click **Save** when prompted. By default, the file will be downloaded to your Downloads folder.

   ◢ What is the name of the downloaded file and the exact path to the file?

   _____

   ◢ About how many minutes did the file take to download?

   _____

5. Navigate to the Downloads folder, and double-click the file to launch it and install VirtualBox.

6. The Setup dialog box opens. Click **Next**.

7. The Custom Setup options dialog box opens. Leave the default values intact, and click **Next**.

8. The Custom Setup options for shortcuts dialog box opens. Accept the default values, and click **Next** to place a shortcut in the quick launch area of your taskbar and on the desktop.

9. The virtual network interface now needs to be installed. VirtualBox will reset your Internet connection to conduct this installation. Click **Yes** to allow the system to proceed with the network connection installation and reset.

11

10. Click **Install** to allow the wizard to begin the installation. If the UAC dialog box appears, click **Yes**.

11. If Windows Security warning dialog boxes appear, click **Install** for each box. The installation may take several minutes.

12. When done, click **Finish**. VirtualBox launches.

VirtualBox is now ready to create virtual machines. To create a virtual machine using VirtualBox, follow these steps:

1. If VirtualBox is not already open, in Windows 8, from the Start screen, click the **Apps button**. In Windows 7, click **Start**, and then click **All Programs**. Find and open the **Oracle VM VirtualBox** app.

2. To create a new virtual machine, on the toolbar click **New**, as shown in Figure 11-2.

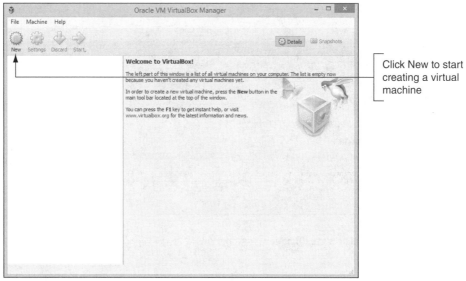

Source: Oracle VM VirtualBox.

Figure 11-2   The Oracle VirtualBox program is ready to create a virtual machine

3. The Create Virtual Machine Wizard opens.

4. Enter the name of the edition of Windows you are installing, such as Windows 8 Professional or Windows 7 Professional. Under Type, Operating System, select **Microsoft Windows**. Under Version, select the version of Windows you are installing (for example, **Windows 8**) and the type of operating system (**32-bit** or **64-bit**). Click **Next**.

5. Select the amount of memory to allocate to your virtual machine based on minimum recommended requirements for the operating system you will install. How much memory did you allocate for your virtual machine? Click **Next**.

6. In the Hard disk box, make sure **Create a virtual hard disk now** is selected, and then click **Create**.

7. For the type of file used to hold your virtual disk, select **VHD** (**Virtual Hard Disk**), and then click **Next**.

8. For the physical hard disk storage details option, select **Dynamically allocated**. Click **Next**.

9. For the size of the virtual disk, select **20 GB**. Click **Next**.

10. Review the summary of the configuration, and click **Create** in the File location and size box. The new virtual machine is now listed in the Oracle VM VirtualBox Manager window.

With the Oracle VM VirtualBox Manager window still open, use the VM help feature to answer the following questions:

◢ How many network cards can VirtualBox virtualize?

_____

◢ Which hardware can be emulated by VirtualBox?

_____

_____

◢ Several aspects of a virtual machine configuration are subject to security considerations. List three of them:

_____

_____

_____

11. Close all open windows.

PART 2: INSTALL AN OPERATING SYSTEM FROM AN ISO FILE

Your instructor has created an ISO file containing an operating system. Ask your instructor for the location of this file. Write down the location of the file here:

_____

To install an operating system from the ISO file to your VirtualBox virtual machine, follow these steps:

1. Open the **Oracle VM VirtualBox** application.

2. Select the virtual machine that you previously created for the operating system you intend to install.

3. On the toolbar, click **Settings**. The Settings dialog box opens. Select the name of the virtual machine you created earlier.

4. On the left pane of the settings windows, click **Storage**.

5. In the Storage Tree area, click the **CD** icon, and then, to the right of Optical Drive in the Attributes area, click the **CD** icon. Click **Choose Virtual Optical Disk File**, as shown in Figure 11-3. The Please choose a virtual optical disk file dialog box opens.

11

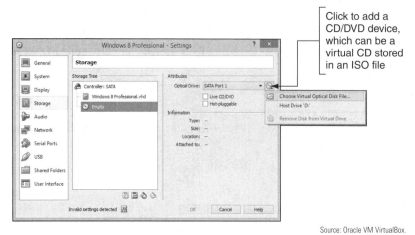

Click to add a CD/DVD device, which can be a virtual CD stored in an ISO file

Source: Oracle VM VirtualBox.

Figure 11-3 Storage Tree options allow you to mount an ISO image as a virtual CD in the virtual machine

6. Browse to the location of the ISO file that was made available by your instructor. Click the file to select it, and then click **Open**. The VM operating system – Settings dialog box opens.

7. In the VM operating system – Settings dialog box, click **OK**. You are returned to the Oracle VM VirtualBox Manager window.

8. On the toolbar, click **Start**. Your virtual machine starts up in its own VirtualBox VM window.

   ◢ If an Information dialog box appears over this window, write down important information it provides about using the virtual machine:

   _____

   _____

   ◢ When you click inside the virtual machine, your keystrokes and mouse actions are captured by the virtual machine. What key do you press to leave the virtual machine?

   _____

   _____

9. Close any Information dialog boxes that appear. The installation of the operating system begins. Figure 11-4 shows Windows 8 installed in the VirtualBox window.

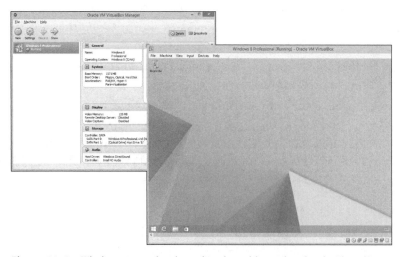

Figure 11-4 Windows 8 running in a virtual machine using Oracle VirtualBox

Answer the following questions:

◢ When using virtual machine software and virtual machines, what is the host operating system? The guest operating system?

_____

_____

◢ Can Oracle VirtualBox be used to clone images? If so, list the steps here:

_____

_____

_____

◢ How many different operating systems can Oracle VirtualBox support? List them here:

_____

_____

10. Using the Shut down menu in your Windows installation in the virtual machine, shut down the virtual machine. Close the VirtualBox Manager window.

PART 3: EXPLORE VMWARE

Another popular and powerful virtualization program is VMware. To learn more about it, follow these steps:

1. Open your favorite browser, and go to **vmware.com**.

2. Using the options on the website, answer the following questions:

◢ What are three features of VMware Player?

_____

_____

_____

◢ What are three features of VMware vSphere Hypervisor?

_____

_____

_____

◢ What is the purpose of VMware Fusion 8?

_____

_____

3. Close all open windows.

11

REVIEW QUESTIONS

1. What is the purpose of a virtual machine?

   _____

   _____

2. What is the purpose of a hypervisor?

   _____

   _____

   _____

3. What are the network requirements for virtual machines?

   _____

   _____

4. What are three advantages of using virtual machines?

   _____

   _____

   _____

5. Other than Oracle, what other company makes virtualization software?

   _____

LAB 11.2 INVESTIGATE OPERATING SYSTEMS—MAC OS

OBJECTIVES

The goal of this lab is to become familiar with the various Apple operating systems and the hardware they support. After completing this lab, you will be able to:

◢ Describe the various Apple operating systems, hardware, and applications

◢ Research Apple technology on the Apple website *(apple.com)*

MATERIALS REQUIRED

This lab requires the following:

◢ Internet access

LAB PREPARATION

Before the lab begins, the instructor or lab assistant needs to do the following:

◢ Verify Internet access is available

ACTIVITY BACKGROUND

Mac operating systems are designed to be used only on Apple Mac computers. Many developers (Apple included) have created applications for Apple products, including applications for the Mac laptop, the iPad, the iPhone, and Apple's other mobile devices. The Apple website *(apple.com)* is the best source of information about its products. In this lab, you investigate different Apple operating systems, hardware, and applications for both computers and mobile devices.

ESTIMATED COMPLETION TIME: 30 MINUTES

 Activity

1. Open your browser and go to **apple.com**. Explore the site, and when you are done, return to the main page. Use the links on the site to answer the questions in this lab (see Figure 11-5).

Source: Apple, Inc.

Figure 11-5 Line of Apple Mac products

2. What is the latest version of the Mac operating system available for a new iMac?

_____

3. What is the cost of upgrading a Mac operating system to the latest version?

_____

Compare the iPhone, iMac, Mac mini, MacBook Pro, and MacBook Air systems available for sale on the Apple website, and answer these questions:

1. What are the speeds or frequencies of the processors in each product?

_____

_____

_____

2. How much does the fastest 27-inch iMac cost?

_____

_____

3. What software comes bundled with an iMac?

_____

_____

4. What is a MacBook?

_____

_____

11

5. How much does the most expensive MacBook Pro cost?

_____

6. What features are included with the least expensive MacBook?

_____

7. Describe the features of an Apple Mighty Mouse:

_____

8. What is the function of an Airport Extreme Base Station?

_____

9. What operating systems are available for Apple mobile devices?

_____

10. What is the latest operating system available for the iPhone?

_____

11. Describe the iCloud service:

_____

_____

12. Describe the purpose of the FaceTime feature for iPhone and iPad:

_____

_____

13. What is the purpose of QuickTime software?

_____

_____

REVIEW QUESTIONS

1. What is one advantage of using an Apple computer instead of a Windows computer?

_____

_____

_____

2. What is one disadvantage of using an Apple computer instead of a Windows computer?

_____

_____

3. Can a Mac OS run on a Windows computer? Explain:

_____

_____

4. Describe the advantages of an iPad:

_____

_____

LAB 11.3 INVESTIGATE LINUX AND CREATE A BOOTABLE UBUNTU FLASH DRIVE

OBJECTIVES

The goal of this lab is to find information about Linux operating systems and use a distribution of Linux to create a bootable USB flash drive. After completing this lab, you will be able to:

◢ Create a bootable Ubuntu flash drive

◢ Explore the different distributions of Linux

◢ Compare Linux to other operating systems

MATERIALS REQUIRED

This lab requires the following:

◢ Internet access

◢ A USB flash drive (thumb drive)

◢ A computer capable of booting from a USB flash drive

LAB PREPARATION

Before the lab begins, the instructor or lab assistant needs to do the following:

◢ Verify Internet access is available

◢ Inform students they will need a flash drive with at least 2 GB capacity for this lab

ACTIVITY BACKGROUND

Linux—a scaled-down version of the UNIX operating system that is provided in basic form, free of charge—allows open access to its programming code. Linux can be used as both a server platform and a desktop platform; additionally, Linux is a portable operating system, meaning that it can be installed on any hardware platform. Ubuntu is one of various Linux distributions.

Imagine the power of having a bootable Linux flash drive that gives you the ability to boot into any computer to perform troubleshooting steps. By the end of this lab, you will have that ability in your hands, using the Ubuntu distribution.

ESTIMATED COMPLETION TIME: 60 MINUTES

11

 Activity

1. Open a browser and go to **ubuntu.com**. Spend a few minutes exploring the site on your own.

2. Click the **Download** tab.

3. Click **Ubuntu Desktop** in the middle of the page.

4. Using the download options in the "Choose your flavour" drop-down menu (see Figure 11-6), choose the bit size you will be working with. If you are not sure which bit size to use, select **32-bit**.

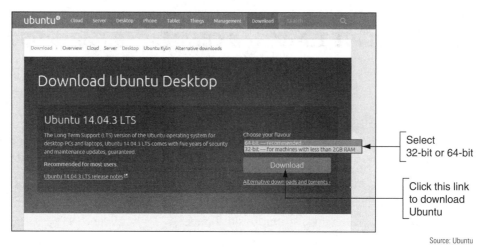

Source: Ubuntu

Figure 11-6 Ubuntu download options

5. Click the **Download** link.

6. On the next page, scroll to the bottom of the page, and then click the **Not now, take me to the download** link. The file automatically begins downloading.

7. Click the **Save** arrow, and then click **Save as**. Save the file to your desktop. Answer the following questions:

◢ What is the size of the downloaded file?

_____

◢ What is the name of the downloaded file?

_____

◢ Depending on the speed of your Internet connection, the download may take a while. How long did the file take to download?

_____

◢ What is the file extension of the downloaded file?

_____

The next step is to download a program called Universal USB Installer. This program is used to make the USB flash drive bootable. We are using the *pendrivelinux.com* website to download the program. Be careful navigating through this website because it contains an excessive number of advertisements. To download the Universal USB Installer program, follow these steps:

1. Open a browser and go to **pendrivelinux.com**. (Websites change often. If this link does not work, perform a Google search for "Universal USB Installer.")

2. On the *pendrivelinux.com* site, click **Universal USB Installer – Easy as 1 2 3**, as shown in Figure 11-7.

Source: www.pendrivelinux.com

Figure 11-7 Link to USB Installer page

3. Scroll down the page to find the download button for the USB Installer application, located near the middle of the page. At the time of this writing, the button name is DOWNLOAD UUI. Click the **DOWNLOAD UUI** button to download the application. See Figure 11-8.

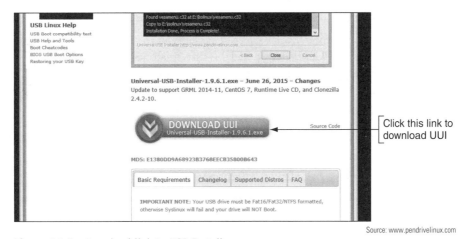

Source: www.pendrivelinux.com

Figure 11-8 Download link to USB Installer program

4. Choose to **Run** the executable file after downloading. If necessary, click **Yes** in the UAC dialog box.

5. If prompted, click **I Agree** to accept the end-user license agreement.

6. The setup dialog box appears. Complete the following (as shown in Figure 11-9):

11

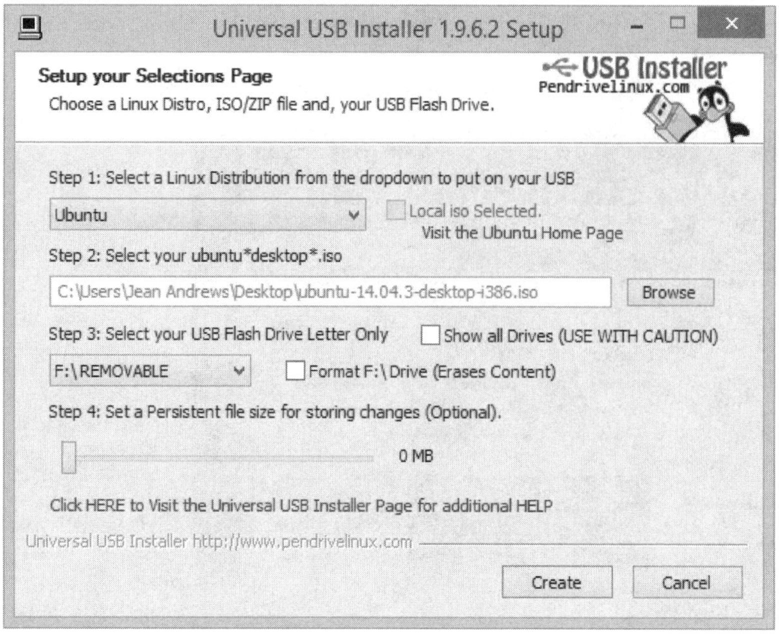

Figure 11-9 Universal USB Installer setup options

a. In the drop-down menu for Step 1, select the distribution of Linux you downloaded.

b. In the Step 2 section, browse to the location of the Ubuntu downloaded file on your desktop. The file has an .iso file extension.

c. Plug your flash drive into a USB port. (Keep in mind that ALL the data on the flash drive will be deleted.)

d. Select your USB drive letter. (Make sure this selection is correct.)

e. Check the **Format F:\ Drive (Erases Content)** check box, indicating you want to format the drive using the FAT32 file system. This option might be different for you after you have selected the USB drive letter.

7. Click **Create**.

8. Confirm your options.

9. When the process completes, click **Close**.

USB Installer will now format and configure your bootable flash drive. The process may take a few minutes to complete. After the process completes, it is time to test your Linux bootable flash drive. To test the drive, follow these steps:

1. Boot into the UEFI/BIOS setup on your computer. (To boot into UEFI/BIOS setup, press a key or key combination at startup. Near the beginning of the boot, look for a message such as "Press Del for setup" or "Press F10 to configure setup.")

2. Using the UEFI/BIOS setup utility, ensure the boot sequence is adjusted to boot from USB first.

3. Exit UEFI/BIOS setup, saving any changes you made, and shut the computer completely off.

4. Plug the USB Linux bootable flash drive into a USB port.

5. Start the computer. Your computer should boot into the Linux operating system. Your desktop should look similar to Figure 11-10.

Source: Ubuntu

Figure 11-10 Typical Linux Ubuntu desktop

6. After Ubuntu boots up, open a browser and make sure you have connectivity to the Internet.

You have just created one of the most powerful tools you can have in your arsenal of software tools. Use it wisely. Ubuntu is not the only distribution of Linux. To learn about other distributions, open a browser and go to *linuxmint.com*. Answer the following questions:

◢ How does Linux Mint compare with Ubuntu?

_____

_____

◢ Linux Mint offers free tutorials. Examine a few, and describe how detailed they are:

_____

_____

_____

◢ What is DuckDuckGo?

_____

_____

◢ What other Linux distributions are popular?

_____

◢ Who is credited with creating Linux?

_____

11

REVIEW QUESTIONS

1. What are some of the "costs" associated with installing a "free" operating system such as Linux?

_____

_____

_____

2. Why might a company not want to use Linux on its desktop computers?

_____

_____

3. What is one advantage of using Linux rather than a Windows operating system on a desktop?

_____

_____

4. Based on what you learned from the Linux Mint website, how do you think companies that provide Linux make most of their profit?

_____

_____

LAB 11.4 COMPARE OPERATING SYSTEMS

OBJECTIVES

The goal of this lab is to investigate the history of computer operating systems and learn why many of today's operating systems share similar features. After completing this lab, you will be able to:

◢ Better understand the relationships among operating systems

MATERIALS REQUIRED

This lab requires the following:

◢ Internet access

LAB PREPARATION

Before the lab begins, the instructor or lab assistant needs to do the following:

◢ Verify Internet access is available

ACTIVITY BACKGROUND

Modern operating systems, such as Windows, Linux, and Mac OS, have many similar features because they share a common history. Some of them have a direct or indirect connection with earlier operating systems. Figure 11-11 shows some highlights of this history. The arrows indicate a direct or indirect influence from an earlier operating system.

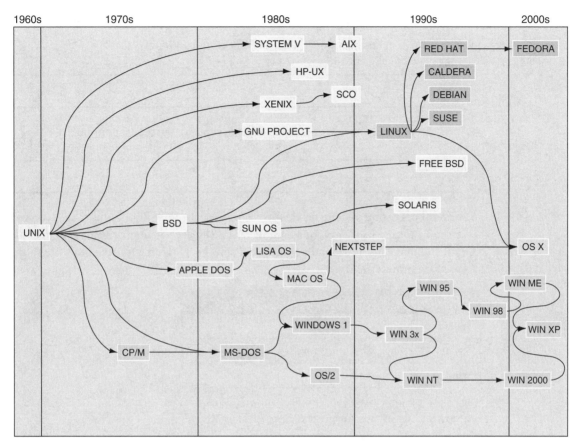

Figure 11-11 Operating system timeline

ESTIMATED COMPLETION TIME: 30 MINUTES

 Activity

Using your favorite search engine, answer the following questions:

1. Search for the "history of operating systems." List the URLs of three sites that you think do a good job of explaining this history:

_____

_____

_____

2. What are two similarities and two differences between the original Mac OS and Windows?

_____

_____

_____

11

3. How is OS/2 loosely connected to Windows 7?

_____

_____

4. What is the relationship of QDOS to CP/M and MS-DOS?

_____

_____

5. List three mobile device operating systems that are currently popular:

_____

_____

6. Several operating systems have appeared since the year 2000, and they have evolved from Fedora, Mac OS X, or Windows XP. Research new operating systems, and enter your findings in the second column of Table 11-1. (Don't forget about operating systems used on mobile devices.)

Year 2000 OSs	Present Operating System
Fedora	
Mac OS X	
Windows XP	

Table 11-1 Fill in the right column with present operating systems that have evolved from year 2000 operating systems

REVIEW QUESTIONS

Using a search engine, research operating system timelines; then, based on the OS timelines that you find, answer the following questions:

1. Why do you think Linux and UNIX share more commands than Windows 8 and UNIX?

_____

_____

2. Which line of operating systems has recently become more similar to UNIX?

_____

3. Which line of operating systems split into two lines, only to merge again later?

_____

4. Why do you think most versions of Linux and Windows use the cd command to change directories?

_____

LAB 11.5 USE TEAMVIEWER TO REMOTELY ACCESS ANOTHER COMPUTER

OBJECTIVES

The goal of this lab is to explore one method by which computers can be remotely accessed and controlled across an Internet connection. As an IT support technician, you can use TeamViewer when you are called on to support a client's computer remotely. The client can easily give you access to his or her computer if you both have Internet access. TeamViewer is also useful when you are working on a team project and you and your team members need to share information and collaborate about the project from remote locations. After completing this lab, you will be able to:

- Download and install TeamViewer
- Use TeamViewer to share desktops with other users over the Internet
- Use TeamViewer to remotely control other computers over the Internet
- Move files between computers over the Internet

MATERIALS REQUIRED

This lab requires the following:

- Two computers using Windows 8 or Windows 7 (for best results, the two computers should be sitting side by side)
- An account with administrator privileges
- Internet access on both computers
- Workgroup of two students

LAB PREPARATION

Before the lab begins, the instructor or lab assistant needs to do the following:

- Verify Windows starts with no errors
- Verify each student has access to a user account with administrator privileges
- Verify Internet access is available

ACTIVITY BACKGROUND

TeamViewer is remote control software that is free to noncommercial users. It can be used for such things as tech support, remote maintenance, online presentations and training, team meetings, or simple application and file access. TeamViewer uses 1024-bit key exchange and 256-bit session encryption, thereby providing reasonable security for most situations.

After you have connected to a target computer using TeamViewer, you can take complete control over the computer. For example, an IT support technician tells the story of a client calling to say she lost almost 400 valuable data files on her computer and desperately asking for help to recover them. The technician connected to her computer over the Internet using TeamViewer. He then used this connection to download and install the Recuva software, which you previously learned to use. The technician was able to use the Recuva software to recover 98 percent of her missing files. He became her hero that evening! (True story.)

11

In this lab, you and your partner each download and install the free full version of TeamViewer onto your computers. Then, together you remotely access one computer from the other over the Internet, and explore the settings and capabilities of the software. For best results, the two computers should be side by side, so that you can easily see what happens on each computer after each action is performed. Note that this lab can also be completed by one person using two computers. Each partner should answer all of the questions in his or her own lab manual.

ESTIMATED COMPLETION TIME: 45 MINUTES

 Activity

In this lab, you work with a partner and two computers. The host computer will use TeamViewer to access the target computer. Designate one partner as the host partner using the host computer, and the other partner as the target partner using the target computer.

◢ Who is the host partner?

_____

◢ Who is the target partner?

_____

   Note that later in the lab, the host and target roles are reversed and Parts 2–4 are repeated so that each partner has the opportunity to do all the steps in this lab.

PART 1: DOWNLOAD AND INSTALL TEAMVIEWER

Both partners follow these steps to download and install TeamViewer on their computers:

1. Log on to your computer with a user account that has administrator privileges.
2. Using your browser, go to **teamviewer.com**.

   ◢ Besides the free version of TeamViewer, what other versions are available?

   _____

   _____

   _____

   ◢ What is the current version number of the free version available for download?

   _____

3. To download the free versions of TeamViewer, click the **Download** button. Save the downloaded file to your Downloads folder.
4. What is the name of the file that was downloaded?

   _____

5. Double-click the executable file that downloaded to begin the installation. If a Security Warning dialog box appears, click **Run**. Make sure **Basic installation** is selected, select **Personal/Non-commercial use**, and then click **Accept – finish**. If necessary, click **Yes** to respond to the UAC dialog box.
6. You will see the progress bar as TeamViewer is installed in the default program folder. If necessary, review the TeamViewer welcome dialog box, and then click **Close** at the

bottom. TeamViewer opens on your desktop (see Figure 11-12). Minimize any browser windows that are blocking the TeamViewer window. What is the ID number and password displayed in TeamViewer?

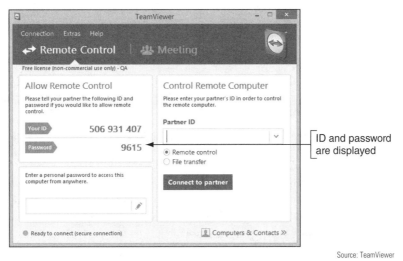

Source: TeamViewer

Figure 11-12 TeamViewer displays the ID and password needed for someone to connect to your computer

PART 2: REMOTELY ACCESS TARGET COMPUTER

The host partner uses the host computer to establish access to the target computer. If you are the host partner, follow these steps as the target partner observes:

1. On the host computer, in the Partner ID box in the TeamViewer window, type the ID generated by TeamViewer on the target computer. Click **Connect to partner**. The TeamViewer Authentication dialog box appears. Let's take a few minutes to explore the advanced settings before logging on to the target system. Click **Advanced** in the lower-left corner.

2. Full Access is selected by default. Click **Access control** to open the Access Control Details dialog box. These are the specific settings that can be allowed or denied by choosing one of the three default configurations or by choosing the Custom settings. Notice that with Full Access all of the settings are allowed. Review each of these settings, and then click **Close** to close the Access Control Details dialog box.

3. Click the **Full Access** button. What are the other three choices that appear in the drop-down menu?

4. Select **Confirm all**, and then click **Access control** again. How have the settings changed?

5. Click **Close** to close the Access Control Details dialog box. Click **Confirm all**, and then select **Custom settings**. Click **Access control** again. Notice that each setting now has a customizable drop-down menu for configuring each setting individually. What are the three choices for configuring each setting in the drop-down menu (all settings have the same three choices)?

11

6. Click **Cancel** to close the Access Control Details dialog box. Using the drop-down menu, change Custom settings back to **Full Access**. Type the TeamViewer password of the target computer, and then click **Log On**.

◢ What happened on the target computer to indicate the session is live?

_____

◢ What happened on the host computer?

_____

Now we will switch the action to the target computer. It is the host partner's turn to observe as the target partner proceeds to Part 3.

PART 3: EXPLORE TEAMVIEWER TARGET CAPABILITIES

If you are the target partner, perform the following steps on the target computer as the host partner observes:

1. On the target computer, notice the session control box in the lower-right corner of the screen (see Figure 11-13). Do *not* click the X; if you do, TeamViewer will close all sessions and disconnect you from the host.

Source: TeamViewer

Figure 11-13 Use the session control box to access tools for TeamViewer

2. Hover the mouse over each icon on the toolbar of the session control box, and list below what each of these five tools does:

_____

_____

_____

_____

_____

3. Click each of the five tool icons one at a time to see what happens. Type a sentence into the chat section, and click **Send**. What happened on the host?

_____

4. Create a text document on your desktop, and use the File Transfer feature to move the file to the host computer. After the document is moved, the host user can right-click the document and download it to any folder on his or her computer (don't do that now).

5. Create a Rich Text document on your desktop, and leave it there. The host user will retrieve it later in this lab. Write down the name of the file:

_____

6. In the Session list section, hover the mouse over the blue arrow icon on the right. What is the purpose of this icon?

_____

7. Sometimes you might want to stop a host user from remotely controlling your computer. To do so, click the **blue arrow**. Then tell the host user to try to do something (like open the Start menu) on your computer from within the TeamViewer host window. Nothing will happen because you have denied the host computer remote control.

_____

Now we will switch the action back to the host computer. It is the target partner's turn to observe again as the host partner proceeds to Part 4.

PART 4: EXPLORE TEAMVIEWER HOST CAPABILITIES

It is possible for a host user to deny a local user of the target computer from using that target computer. To find out how the host can control the target computer, the host partner performs the following steps as the target partner observes:

1. When your target partner gave you access to the target computer earlier in the lab, you had full access, which means you could have locked your target partner out from controlling his or her own computer. Using the host computer, you can lock your partner out now. On the host computer, click the **Actions** menu, and then select **Disable remote input**. Now tell your target partner to try to do something on the target computer. Nothing will happen. Now neither of you can do anything on the target computer.

2. To return control of the target computer to both users, on the host computer, uncheck **Disable remote input**. Ask your partner to uncross the **blue arrow** on the target computer. Each partner should now have access to the target computer.

3. Remember that Rich Text document your partner created on the desktop of the target computer? Rather than asking your partner to move it to the File box so that you can download it, you can just drag and drop it to your desktop. Do that now. Isn't that cool? What pops up when the file transfers?

_____

4. Click the **X** on the pop-up boxes to close them on each computer. Take a few minutes to review each of the options under each of the five menu items on the toolbar (see Figure 11-14).

11

Source: TeamViewer

Figure 11-14 The menu bar displays tools available for TeamViewer

◢ What are the choices under the "View – Quality" setting?

_____

_____

◢ What are the choices under the "Actions – Remote reboot" setting? Warning: Do not click any of them!

_____

5. Click the **Actions** menu, and select **Switch sides with partner**. Whoa! What happened? Now you are the target and your partner is the host.

6. To make your computer the host again, in the Session list section of your session control box, click the small monitor icon, which is on the right, beside the blue arrow. You are now the host again.

7. Now switch roles with your partner and repeat this lab beginning with Part 2.

CHALLENGE ACTIVITY (ADDITIONAL 10 MINUTES)

Using the Extras tab in TeamViewer, set up a meeting and invite a group of three or four users. One user is the host and starts the meeting. The other users then join the meeting. If your computers have webcams, you can use them to see and hear each other during the meeting.

REVIEW QUESTIONS

1. Does TeamViewer have to be running on both the host and the target computer in order to establish a session?

_____

2. What does the host user require from the target user in order to establish a connection?

_____

3. In what general ways can a target user limit the access of the host user?

   _____

   _____

4. After a TeamViewer session is opened, list four types of actions that can be performed between the two computers:

   _____

   _____

   _____

   _____

   _____

   _____

5. Do the ID and password assigned by TeamViewer remain the same after closing and relaunching TeamViewer?

   _____

6. What is a reason the host might need to change the "View – Quality" setting?

   _____

   _____

   _____

   _____

   _____

7. Do you think the "Optimize speed" setting makes the actual transfer rate faster? Explain your answer:

   _____

   _____

8. Under what circumstances might you, as the target user, want to limit the access of the host user connecting to your machine?

   _____

   _____

   _____

   _____

   _____

11

9. Under what circumstances might you, as the target user, want to give full access to the host user?

_____

_____

10. What are some useful TeamViewer host tools that a technician might need to use on the target system, and why might they be used?

_____

_____

_____

_____

_____

LAB 11.6 SET UP A VPN

OBJECTIVES

The goal of this lab is to set up a secure VPN. Technicians in the field are often called on to help a client who is traveling or working from home connect to the corporate network using a VPN. After completing this lab, you will be able to:

◢ Set up a VPN in Windows

◢ Use third-party software to securely access the Internet from a public network

MATERIALS REQUIRED

This lab requires the following:

◢ Two Windows 8 or Windows 7 operating systems

◢ An account with administrator privileges

◢ Internet access

◢ VPN server (optional)

◢ Workgroup of two students

LAB PREPARATION

Before the lab begins, the instructor or lab assistant needs to do the following:

◢ Verify Windows starts with no errors

◢ Verify each student has access to a user account with administrator privileges

◢ Verify Internet access is available

◢ Set up a VPN server and record the server's IP address (optional)

◢ Set up a user account on the VPN server, and record the user name and password (optional)

ACTIVITY BACKGROUND

A virtual private network (VPN) offers a very secure connection between two computers. It uses a process called tunneling to form a private connection that encrypts communications independently of the type of network being used. VPNs are often used when a user has to connect to a network over a nonsecure public network such as a wireless hotspot.

This lab presents three options for setting up a VPN connection. In Part 1, you set up a VPN connection between two Windows computers. In Part 2, you set up a VPN connection from a computer to a VPN server. In Part 3, you use software to set up a VPN connection using a third-party server.

> **ESTIMATED COMPLETION TIME: 60 MINUTES**

 Activity

PART 1: VPN CONNECTION USING TWO WINDOWS COMPUTERS

In this part of the lab, you create a VPN connection between two computers connected to the Internet. To do this, you must first set up one computer to host a VPN connection and then allow specific user names to access this connection. Follow these steps to set up an incoming VPN connection to your computer:

1. Log on using an account with administrator privileges.

2. Create a standard user account with a password. Name the standard account **Newuser**, and make the password **newuser**.

3. In Windows 8, right-click the Start button, and then click **Network Connections**. In Windows 7, click **Start**, type **Network and Sharing** in the Search box, and then press **Enter** to open the Network and Sharing Center. Click **Change adapter settings** in the left pane of the Network and Sharing Center.

4. Select your connection, and then press the **Alt** key to display the menu. Click **File** on the menu bar, and then click **New Incoming Connection** to open the "Allow connections to this computer" dialog box.

> **Notes** If you do not see the File button, click **Organize** in the toolbar, select **Layout**, and then click **Menu bar**. The menu bar is now displayed above the toolbar.

5. Click the **Newuser (Newuser)** check box, and then click **Next**.

6. Make sure **Through the Internet** is selected, and click **Next**.

7. Leave the networking software settings at their defaults to use the Internet Protocol Version 4 (TCP/IPv4), and click **Allow access**.

8. The final screen of this setup gives the computer name, which is used to establish the VPN connection. Write down the computer name, and give it to your partner, who will use this VPN connection to your computer. Click **Close**. Close any open windows.

Now that you have set up an incoming VPN connection and granted permission for your partner to use the account Newuser to connect to your computer through this VPN connection, you are ready for your partner to test the connection from his or her computer to yours. Then you can try to connect to your partner's computer using his or her VPN connection. You are only able to do this one at a time. Designate one partner as Partner 1 and the other partner as Partner 2.

11

◢ Who is Partner 1?

_____

_____

◢ Who is Partner 2?

_____

CREATE AN OUTGOING CONNECTION

Partner 1, follow these steps to make an outgoing VPN connection as Partner 2 observes:

1. If necessary, log on using an account with administrator privileges.

2. Open the **Network and Sharing Center** again, and click **Set up a new connection or network**.

3. Select **Connect to a workplace**, and click **Next**, as shown in Figure 11-15.

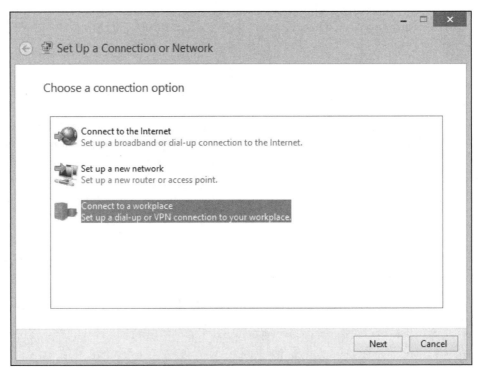

Figure 11-15 Beginning a VPN setup

4. Click **Use my Internet connection (VPN)**.

5. In the Internet address field, enter the computer name provided by your partner from Step 8 of the previous exercise. What is the name your partner gave you? In Windows 8, click **Create**. In Windows 7, click **Next**.

_____

6. Enter the account name and password for the Newuser account you created at the beginning of this lab to authenticate the VPN connection to your partner's computer. In Windows 8, click **OK**. In Windows 7, click **Connect**.

7. A message says you are connected. In Windows 8, click a blank space on the desktop to close the Networks pane. In Windows 7, click **Close**.

8. In Windows 7, a Set Network Location window appears on both computers. Click **Work network**, and then click **Close**.

9. On both machines, open the **Network and Sharing Center** again, and click **Change adapter settings** in the left pane. Notice the new connections listed on the host machine, as shown in Figure 11-16a. On the other computer, the connections are slightly different, as shown in Figure 11-16b.

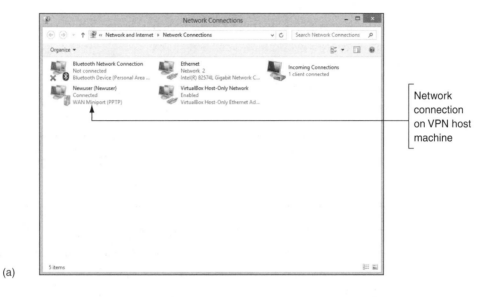

(a)

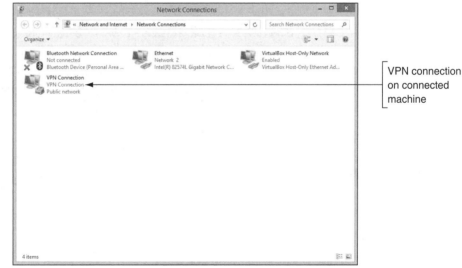

(b)

Figure 11-16 Access the VPN connection from the Network Connections window

Follow these steps to disconnect and delete this outgoing VPN connection:

1. To disconnect, click the network connection icon in the notification area of the taskbar. Click the **VPN Connection,** and then click **Disconnect**.

2. To delete the VPN connection, open the **Network and Sharing Center**.

11

3. Click **Change adapter settings** in the left pane. Right-click the **VPN Connection** icon, and select **Delete** in the shortcut menu. Click **Yes** to confirm.

Now Partner 2 makes an outgoing connection while Partner 1 observes. Partner 2 should go back to the "Create an Outgoing Connection" heading and follow the steps back to this point in the lab.

PART 2: VPN CONNECTION USING A VPN SERVER (OPTIONAL)

This part of the lab is optional. If your instructor has provided a VPN server, you can follow these steps to connect to it. If a VPN server is not available, please proceed to Part 3 of this lab. To connect to a VPN server in Windows, follow these steps:

1. Log on using an account with administrator privileges.

2. Open the **Network and Sharing Center**, and click **Set up a new connection or network**.

3. Select **Connect to a workplace**, and then click **Next**.

4. Click **Use my Internet connection (VPN)**.

5. Enter the Internet address of the VPN server provided by your instructor. What is the address you used?

_____

6. Click **Next**. Enter the user name and password provided by your instructor. What user name and password did you use?

_____

7. Click **Connect**. A message says you are connected. Click **Close**.

8. If a Set Network Location window appears, click **Work network**, and then click **Close**.

9. Disconnect and delete this VPN connection the same way you did the last VPN connection.

PART 3: VPN CONNECTION USING A THIRD-PARTY VPN SERVER

In this part of the lab, you connect a computer to a VPN server using third-party software. Several companies offer programs to secure Internet access from public wireless connections using VPNs. One such program is Hotspot Shield by AnchorFree. To set up a secure connection, follow these steps:

1. Log on using an account with administrator privileges.

2. Open Internet Explorer and go to **hotspotshield.com**.

3. Click the **Free Download** button, and follow the on-screen instructions to install Hotspot Shield. During the installation process:

   ◢ Accept the default configuration.

   ◢ In Windows 7, click **Install**, if any Windows Security windows open.

   ◢ In Windows 8, if a Networks pane opens, click **Yes** to find content on the network.

   ◢ Click **Finish**, when the install completes.

4. When the installation is complete, if necessary, launch Hotspot Shield, and wait for an automatic connection to a VPN server that is provided by AnchorFree to secure your connections.

5. Browse several websites. When Hotspot Shield is running, all your data transmitted or received to and from these websites is secured. How do you know that Hotspot Shield is running?

_____

6. When you're finished, uninstall Hotspot Shield, and close any open windows. How did you uninstall the software?

_____

REVIEW QUESTIONS

1. Will VPNs work on both wired and wireless networks?

_____

2. What process do VPNs use to form a private connection between computers?

_____

_____

3. Why might it be dangerous to do online banking transactions through a public Internet hotspot without using a VPN connection?

_____

_____

4. What type of secure connection does an online banking site usually offer its customers?

_____

_____

5. How does a VPN connection differ from using Remote Desktop? Is a Remote Desktop connection a secured connection?

_____

_____

6. Why is a VPN more secure than other forms of wireless encryption such as WPA2?

_____

_____

7. Why do you think using Hotspot Shield for secured connections slows down response time when surfing the web?

_____

_____

11

GLOSSARY

Software Key Terms

32-bit operating system Type of operating system that processes 32 bits at a time.

64-bit operating system Type of operating system that processes 64 bits at a time.

802.11 a/b/g/n/ac The collective name for the IEEE 802.11 standards for local wireless networking, which is the technical name for Wi-Fi.

A+ Certification A certification awarded by CompTIA (The Computer Technology Industry Association) that measures an IT technician's knowledge and skills.

accelerometer A type of gyroscope used in mobile devices to sense the physical position of the device.

acceptable use policy (AUP) A document that explains to users what they can and cannot do on the corporate network or with company data, and the penalties for violations.

access control list (ACL) A record or list of the resources (for example, a printer, folder, or file) that a user, device, or program has access to on a corporate network, server, or workstation.

Action bar On an Android device, an area at the bottom of the screen that can contain up to five custom software buttons, called Home touch buttons. The three default buttons are back, home, and overview.

Action Center A tool in Windows 8/7 that lists errors and issues that need attention.

Active Directory A Windows server directory database and service that is used in managing a domain to allow for a single point of administration for all shared resources on a network, including files, peripheral devices, databases, websites, users, and services.

active partition For Master Boot Record (MBR) hard drives, the primary partition on the drive that boots the OS. Windows calls the active partition the system partition.

active recovery image In Windows 8, the custom refresh image of the Windows volume that will be used when a refresh of the Windows installation is performed. *Also see* custom refresh image.

ActiveX control A small app or add-on that can be downloaded from a website along with a webpage and is executed by a browser to enhance the webpage.

adapter address *See* MAC (Media Access Control) address.

address reservation When a DHCP server assigns a static IP address to a DHCP client. For example, a network printer might require a static IP address so that computers on the network can find the printer.

administrative share The folders that are shared by default on a network domain that administrator accounts can access.

Administrative Tools A group of tools accessed through the Control Panel that you can use to manage the local computer or other computers on the network.

administrator account In Windows, a user account that grants to the administrator(s) rights and privileges to all hardware and software resources, such as the right to add, delete, and change accounts and to change hardware configurations. *Compare with* standard account.

Administrators group A type of user group. When a user account is assigned to this group, the account is granted rights that are assigned to an administrator account.

Advanced Boot Options menu   A Windows 7/Vista menu that appears when you press F8 when Windows starts. The menu can be used to troubleshoot problems when loading Windows.

Aero user interface   The Windows 7/Vista 3D user interface that gives a glassy appearance. *Also called* Aero glass.

AES (Advanced Encryption Standard)   An encryption standard used by WPA2 and is currently the strongest encryption standard used by Wi-Fi.

AFP (Apple Filing Protocol)   An outdated file access protocol used by early editions of the Mac operating system by Apple and is one protocol in the suite of AppleTalk networking protocols.

AirDrop   A feature of iOS whereby iPhones and iPads can transfer files between nearby devices. The devices use Bluetooth to detect nearby devices and Wi-Fi to establish connectivity and transfer files.

air filter mask   A mask that filters the dust and other contaminants from the air for breathing safety. *Also called* air-purifying respirator.

airplane mode   A setting within a mobile device that disables the cellular, Wi-Fi, and Bluetooth antennas so the device cannot transmit signals.

alternate IP address   When configuring TCP/IP in Windows, the static IP address that Windows uses if it cannot lease an IP address from a DHCP server.

alternating current (AC)   Current that cycles back and forth rather than traveling in only one direction. In the United States, the AC voltage from a standard wall outlet is normally between 110 and 115 V. In Europe, the standard AC voltage from a wall outlet is 220 V.

amp (A)   A measure of electrical current.

Android   An operating system used on mobile devices that is based on the Linux OS and supported by Google.

anonymous users   User accounts that have not been authenticated on a remote computer.

ANSI (American National Standards Institute)   A nonprofit organization dedicated to creating trade and communications standards.

answer file   A text file (.bat) that contains information that Windows requires in order to do an unattended installation.

anti-malware software   Utility software that can prevent infection, scan a system, and detect and remove all types of general malware, including viruses, spyware, worms, and rootkits.

antistatic bag   Static shielding bags that new computer components are shipped in.

antistatic wrist strap   *See* ESD strap.

antivirus software   Utility software that can prevent infection, scan a system, and detect and remove viruses.

anycast address   Using TCP/IP version 6, a type of IP address used by routers and identifies multiple destinations. Packets are delivered to the closest destination.

APK (Android Application Package)   The format used by Android apps for distributing the app in a package of files wrapped into one file with an .apk file extension.

App Store   The app on an Apple device (iPad, iPhone, or iPod touch) that can be used to download content from the iTunes Store website (*itunes.apple.com*).

Apple ID   A user account that uses a valid email address and password and is associated with a credit card number that allows you to download iOS updates and patches, apps, and multimedia content.

Apple menu   In OS X, the menu that appears when the user clicks the Apple icon in the upper-left corner of the screen.

AppleTalk   An outdated suite of networking protocols used by early editions of the Apple Mac OS, and has been replaced by the TCP/IP suite of protocols.

application virtualization   Using this virtualization, a virtual environment is created in memory for an application to virtually install itself.

Application Virtualization (App-V)   Software by Microsoft used for application virtualization.

Apps Drawer An Android app that lists and manages all apps installed on the device. By default, this app's icon is in the Favorites tray on an Android screen.

apt-get A Linux and OS X command to install and remove software packages and install OS updates.

ATAPI (Advanced Technology Attachment Packet Interface) An interface standard, part of the IDE/ATA standards, that allows tape drives, optical drives, and other drives to be treated like an IDE hard drive by the system.

ATA Secure Erase Standards developed by the American National Standards Institute (ANSI) that dictate how to securely erase data from solid-state devices such as a USB flash drive or SSD drive in order to protect personal privacy.

Authenticated Users group All user accounts that have been authenticated to access the system except the Guest account. *Compare with* anonymous users.

authentication server A server responsible for authenticating users or computers to the network so they can access network resources.

Automatic Private IP Address (APIPA) In TCP/IP Version 4, IP address in the address range 169.254.x.y, used by a computer when it cannot successfully lease an IP address from a DHCP server.

Backup and Restore The Windows 7/Vista utility used to create and update scheduled backups of user data and the system image.

Backup Operators group A type of Windows user account group. When a user account belongs to this group, it can back up and restore any files on the system regardless of its having access to these files.

Bash shell The default shell used by the terminal for many distributions of Linux.

basic disk The term Windows uses that applies to a hard drive when the drive is a stand-alone drive in the system. *Compare with* dynamic disk.

batch file A text file containing a series of OS commands. Autoexec.bat is a batch file.

bcdedit A Windows command used to manually edit the BCD (Boot Configuration Data).

beamforming A technique supported by IEEE 802.11ac Wi-Fi standard that can detect the location of connected devices and increase signal strength in that direction.

Berg power connector A type of power connector used by a power cord to provide power to a floppy disk drive.

best-effort protocol *See* connectionless protocol.

biometric authentication To authenticate to a network, computer, or other computing device by means of biometric data, such as a fingerprint or retinal data. Touch ID on an iPhone or face lock on an Android device can perform biometric authentication.

biometric device An input device that inputs biological data about a person; the data can identify a person's fingerprints, handprints, face, voice, eyes, and handwriting.

BIOS (basic input/output system) Firmware that can control much of a computer's input/output functions, such as communication with the keyboard and the monitor. *Compare with* UEFI.

BitLocker Drive Encryption A utility in Windows 8/7/Vista that is used to lock down a hard drive by encrypting the entire Windows volume and any other volume on the drive.

BitLocker To Go A Windows utility that can encrypt data on a USB flash drive and restrict access by requiring a password.

blue screen error *See* blue screen of death (BSOD).

blue screen of death (BSOD) A Windows error that occurs in kernel mode, is displayed against a blue screen, and causes the system to halt. The error might be caused by problems with devices, device drivers, or a corrupted Windows installation. Also called a stop error.

Bluetooth PIN code A code that may be required to complete the Bluetooth connection in a pairing process.

Boot Camp A utility in OS X that allows you to install and run Windows on a Mac computer.

Boot Configuration Data (BCD) store A small Windows database structured the same as a registry file and contains configuration information about how Windows is started. The BCD file replaces the Boot.ini file used in Windows 2000/XP.

G

boot loader menu A startup menu that gives the user the choice of which operating system to load, such as Windows 8 or Windows 7, when both are installed on the same system, creating a dual boot.

boot partition The hard drive partition where the Windows OS is stored. The system partition and the boot partition may be different partitions.

booting The process of starting up a computer and loading an operating system.

BootMgr In Windows 8/7/Vista, the boot manager program responsible for loading Windows.

bootrec A Windows command used to repair the BCD (Boot Configuration Data) and boot sectors.

bootsect A Windows command used to repair a dual-boot system.

botnet A network of zombies or robots.

brownout Temporary reductions in voltage, which can sometimes cause data loss. *Also called* sags.

brute force attack A method to hack or discover a password by trying every single combination of characters.

BYOD (Bring Your Own Device) A corporate policy that allows employees or students to connect their own devices to the corporate network.

call tracking software A system that tracks the dates, times, and transactions of help-desk or on-site IT support calls, including the problem presented, the issues addressed, who did what, and when and how each call was resolved.

Category view Default view in Windows Control Panel that presents utilities grouped by category. *Compare with* Classic view.

cd (change directory) The Windows command to change the current default directory.

CDFS (Compact Disc File System) The 32-bit file system for CD discs and some CD-R and CD-RW discs. *Also see* Universal Disk Format (UDF).

CDMA (Code Division Multiple Access) A protocol standard used by cellular WANs and cell phones for transmitting digital data over cellular networks.

cellular network analyzer Software and hardware that can monitor cellular networks for signal strength of cell towers, wireless access points (WAPs), and repeaters, which can help technicians better position antennas in a distributed antenna system (DAS).

chmod A Linux and OS X command to change modes (or permissions) for a file or directory.

chown A Linux and OS X command to change the owner of a file or directory.

CPU *See* central processing unit (CPU).

Certificate of Authenticity A sticker that contains the Windows product key.

certificate of destruction Digital or paper documentation, which assures that data has been destroyed beyond recovery.

Certification Authority (CA) An organization, such as VeriSign, that assigns digital certificates or digital signatures to individuals or organizations.

chain of custody Documentation that tracks evidence used in an investigation and includes exactly what, when, and from whom the evidence was collected, the condition of the evidence, and how the evidence was secured while in possession of a responsible party.

channel A specific radio frequency within a broader frequency.

charm A shortcut that appears in the charms bar.

charms bar A menu that appears on the right side of any Windows 8 screen when you move your pointer to a right corner.

child directory *See* subdirectory.

chkdsk (check disk) A Windows command to verify the hard drive does not have bad sectors that can corrupt the file system.

chkdsk /r A Windows command to check the hard drive for errors and repair the file system.

CIDR notation A shorthand notation (pronounced "*cider notation*") for expressing an IPv4 address and subnet mask with the IP address followed by a / slash and the number of bits in the IP address that identifies the network. For example, 15.50.35.10/20.

CIFS (Common Internet File System) A file access protocol and the cross-platform version of SMB used between Windows, Linux, Mac OS, and other operating systems. *Also called* SMB2.

Class C fire extinguisher A fire extinguisher rated to put out electrical fires.

Classic view View in Windows Control Panel that presents utilities in small or large icons and are not grouped. *Compare with* Category view.

clean boot A process of starting Windows with a basic set of drivers and startup programs that can be useful when software does not install properly.

clean install Used to overwrite the existing operating system and applications when installing Windows on a hard drive.

client/server Two computers communicating using a local network or the Internet. One computer (the client) makes requests to the other computer (the server), which answers the request.

client-side desktop virtualization Using this virtualization, software installed on a desktop or laptop manages virtual machines used by the local user.

client-side virtualization Using this virtualization, a personal computer provides multiple virtual environments for applications.

clone In Linux and OS X, an image of the entire partition on which the OS is installed.

closed source Software owned by a vendor that requires a commercial license to install and use the software. *Also called* vendor-specific or commercial license software.

cloud computing A service where server-side virtualization is delegated to a third-party service, and the Internet is used to connect server and client machines.

cluster On a magnetic hard drive, one or more sectors that constitute the smallest unit of space on the drive for storing data (also referred to as a file allocation unit). Files are written to a drive as groups of whole clusters.

cold boot *See* hard boot.

commercial license As applied to software, the rights to use the software, which have been assigned to the user by the software vendor.

community cloud Online resources and services that are shared between multiple organizations, but not available publicly.

compatibility mode A group of settings that can be applied to older drivers or applications that might cause them to work using a newer version of Windows than the one the programs were designed to use.

Complete PC Backup A Vista utility that can make a backup of the entire volume on which Vista is installed and can also back up other volumes. *Compare with* system image.

Component Services (COM+) A Microsoft Management Console snap-in that can be used to register components used by installed applications.

compressed (zipped) folder A folder with a .zip extension that contains compressed files. When files are put in the folder, they are compressed. When files are moved to a regular folder, the files are decompressed.

computer infestation *See* malicious software.

Computer Management A Windows console (compmgmt.msc) that contains several administrative tools used by support technicians to manage the local computer or other computers on the network.

computer name *See* host name.

connectionless protocol A TCP/IP protocol such as UDP that works at the OSI Transport layer and does not guarantee delivery by first connecting and checking where data is received. It might be used for broadcasting, such as streaming video or sound over the web, where guaranteed delivery is not as important as fast transmission. *Also called* a best-effort protocol. *Also see* UDP (User Datagram Protocol).

connection-oriented protocol In networking, a TCP/IP protocol that confirms a good connection has been made before transmitting data to the other end, verifies data was received, and resends it if it is not. An example of a connection-oriented protocol is TCP.

G

console   A window that consolidates several Windows administrative tools.

Control Panel   A window containing several small Windows utility programs called applets that are used to manage hardware, software, users, and the system.

copy   The Windows command to copy a single file, group of files, or folder and its contents.

copyright   The right to copy the work that belongs to the creators of the works or others to whom the creator transfers this right.

custom installation   In the Windows setup program, the option used to overwrite the existing operating system and applications, producing a clean installation of the OS. The main advantage is that problems with the old OS are not carried forward.

custom refresh image   In Windows 8, an image of the entire Windows volume including the Windows installation. The image can be applied during a Windows 8 refresh operation.

Dashboard   In OS X, a screen that contains widgets, such as a calendar, a calculator, a clock, and a weather report.

data loss prevention (DLP)   Methods that protect corporate data from being exposed or stolen; for example, software that filters employee email to verify privacy laws are not accidentally or intentionally being violated.

data source   A resource on a network that includes a database and the drivers required to interface between a remote computer and the data.

Data Sources   A tool in the Administrative Tools group of Control Panel that is used to allow data files to be connected to applications they normally would not use.

Date and Time applet   Accessed through Control Panel, used to set the date and time in Windows.

dd   A Linux and OS X command to copy and convert files, directories, partitions, and entire DVDs or hard drives. You must be logged in as a superuser to use the command.

default gateway   The gateway a computer on a network uses to access another network unless it knows to specifically use another gateway for quicker access to that network.

default program   A program associated with a file extension that is used to open the file.

defrag   The Windows command that examines a magnetic hard drive for fragmented files and rewrites these files to the drive in contiguous clusters.

defragment   A drive maintenance procedure that rearranges fragments or parts of files on a magnetic hard drive so each file is stored on the drive in contiguous clusters.

defragmentation tool   A utility or command to rewrite a file to a disk in one contiguous chain of clusters, thus speeding up data retrieval.

degausser   A machine that exposes a magnetic storage device such as a hard drive or tape drive to a strong magnetic field to completely erase the data on the storage device.

del   The Windows command to delete a file or group of files. *Also called* the erase command.

deployment strategy   A procedure to install Windows, device drivers, and applications on a computer, and can include the process to transfer user settings, application settings, and user data files from an old installation to the new installation.

Destination Network Address Translation (DNAT)   When a firewall using network address translation (NAT) allows uninitated communication to a computer behind the firewall through a port that is normally closed. *Also see* port forwarding.

device driver   Small program stored on the hard drive and installed in Windows that tell Windows how to communicate with a specific hardware device such as a printer, network, port on the motherboard, or scanner.

Device Manager   Primary Windows tool (devmgmt.msc) for managing hardware.

DHCP (Dynamic Host Configuration Protocol)   A protocol used by a server to assign a dynamic IP address to a computer when it first attempts to initiate a connection to the network and requests an IP address.

DHCP client   A computer or other device (such as a network printer) that requests an IP address from a DHCP server.

DHCPv6 server   A DHCP server that serves up IPv6 addresses.

dictionary attack   A method to discover or crack a password by trying words in a dictionary.

digital certificate   A code used to authenticate the source of a file or document or to identify and authenticate a person or organization sending data over a network. The code is assigned by a certificate authority such as VeriSign and includes a public key for encryption. Also called digital ID or digital signature.

digital rights management (DRM)   Software and hardware security limitations meant to protect digital content and prevent piracy.

dir   The Windows command to list files and directories.

direct current (DC)   Current that travels in only one direction (the type of electricity provided by batteries). Computer power supplies transform AC to low DC.

DirectX   A Microsoft software development tool that software developers can use to write multimedia applications such as games, video-editing software, and computer-aided design software.

disc image   *See* ISO image.

Disk Cleanup   A Windows utility to delete temporary files to free up space on a drive.

disk cloning   *See* drive imaging.

disk imaging   *See* drive imaging.

diskpart   A Windows command to manage hard drives, partitions, and volumes.

distribution server   A file server holding Windows setup files used to install Windows on computers networked to the server.

distribution share   The collective files in the installation that include Windows, device drivers, and applications. The package of files is served up by a distribution server.

DMG file   In Mac OS X, a disk image file similar to WIM or ISO files in Windows.

DMZ (demilitarized zone)   Refers to removing firewall protection from a computer or network within an organization of protected computers and networks.

DNS (Domain Name System or Domain Name Service)   A distributed pool of information (called the name space) that keeps track of assigned host names and domain names and their corresponding IP addresses. DNS also refers to the system that allows a host to locate information in the pool and the protocol the system uses.

DNS client   When Windows queries the DNS server for a name resolution, which means to find an IP address for a computer when the fully qualified domain name is known.

DNS server   A Doman Name Service server that uses a DNS protocol to find an IP address for a computer when the fully qualified domain name is known. An Internet Service Provider is responsible for providing access to one or more DNS servers as part of the service it provides for Internet access.

dock   (1) For an Android device, the area at the bottom of the Android screen where up to four apps can be pinned. (2) For a Mac computer, a bar that appears by default at the bottom of the screen and contains program icons and shortcuts to files and folders.

domain   In Windows, a logical group of networked computers, such as those on a college campus, that share a centralized directory database of user account information and security for the entire domain.

domain account   *See* global account.

domain name   A name that identifies a network and appears before the period in a website address such as *microsoft.com*. A fully qualified domain name is sometimes loosely called a domain name. *Also see* fully qualified domain name.

drive imaging   Making an exact image of a hard drive, including partition information, boot sectors, operating system installation, and application software to replicate the hard drive on another system or recover from a hard drive crash. *Also called* disk cloning or disk imaging.

G

dual boot The ability to boot using either of two different OSs, such as Windows 8 and Windows 7. *Also called* multiboot.

dumb terminal *See* zero client.

dump In Linux, a collection of data that is copied to a backup media.

dxdiag.exe A Windows command used to display information about hardware and diagnose problems with DirectX.

dynamic disk A way to partition one or more hard drives so that the drives can work together to store data in order to increase space for data or to provide fault tolerance or improved performance. *Also see* RAID. *Compare with* basic disk.

dynamic IP address An IP address assigned by a DHCP server for the current session only, and is leased when the computer first connects to a network. When the session is terminated, the IP address is returned to the list of available addresses. *Compare with* static IP address.

dynamic volume A volume type used with dynamic disks by which you can create a single volume that uses space on multiple hard drives.

EFI System Partition (ESP) For a GPT hard drive, the bootable partition used to boot the OS and contains the boot manager program for the OS.

electrostatic discharge (ESD) Another name for static electricity, which can damage chips and destroy motherboards, even though it might not be felt or seen with the naked eye.

elevated command prompt window A Windows command prompt window that allows commands that require administrator privileges.

email filtering To search incoming or outgoing email messages for matches kept in databases, searching for known scams and spammers to protect against social engineering.

email hoax An email message that is trying to tempt you to give out personal information or trying to scam you.

emergency notifications Government alerts, such as AMBER alerts, that are sent to mobile devices in an emergency.

emulator A virtual machine that emulates hardware, such as the hardware buttons on a smart phone.

Encrypted File System (EFS) A way to use a key to encode a file or folder on an NTFS volume to protect sensitive data. Because it is an integrated system service, EFS is transparent to users and applications.

End User License Agreement (EULA) A digital or printed statement of your rights to use or copy software, which you agree to when the software is installed.

enterprise license A license to use software that allows an organization to install multiple instances of the software. *Also called* site license.

entry control roster A list of people allowed into a restricted area and a log of any approved visitors that is used and maintained by security guards.

erase *See* del.

escalate Assigning a problem to someone higher in the support chain of an organization. This action is normally recorded in call tracking software.

ESD mat A mat that dissipates electrostatic discharge (ESD) and is commonly used by technicians who repair and assemble computers at their workbenches or in an assembly line. *Also called* ground mat.

ESD strap A strap you wear around your wrist that is attached to the computer case, ground mat, or another ground so that electrostatic discharge (ESD) is discharged from your body before you touch sensitive components inside a computer. *Also called* antistatic wrist strap *or* ground bracelet.

Event Viewer A Windows tool (eventvwr. msc) useful for troubleshooting problems with Windows, applications, and hardware. It displays logs of significant events such as a hardware or network failure, OS failure, OS error messages, a device or service that has failed to start, or General Protection Faults.

Everyone group In Windows, the Authenticated Users group as well as the Guest account. When you share a file or folder on the network, Windows, by default, gives access to the Everyone group.

executive services   In Windows, a group of components running in kernel mode that interfaces between the subsystems in user mode and the HAL (hardware abstraction layer).

expand   The Windows command that extracts files from compressed distribution files, which are often used to distribute files for software installation.

expert system   Software that uses a database of known facts and rules to simulate a human expert's reasoning and decision-making processes.

ext3   The Linux file system that was the first to support journaling, which is a technique that tracks and stores changes to the hard drive and helps prevent file system corruption.

ext4   The current Linux file system, which replaced the ext3 file system. Stands for "fourth extended file system."

extended partition   On an MBR hard drive, the only partition on the drive that can contain more than one logical drive. In Windows, a hard drive can have only a single extended partition. *Compare with* primary partition.

factory default   To restore a mobile device or other computer to its state at the time of purchase. The operating system is reinstalled and all user data and settings are lost.

Fast Startup   A Windows 8 feature to speed up startup by performing a partial hibernation at shutdown. At shutdown, Windows saves the drivers and kernel state in the Windows hibernate file, hiberfil.sys, and then reads from this file on the next cold boot.

FAT (file allocation table)   A table on a hard drive, USB flash drive, or floppy disk used by the FAT file system that tracks the clusters used to contain a file.

fat client   *See* thick client.

Favorites tray   On Android devices, the area above the Action bar that contains up to seven apps or groups of apps. These apps stay put as you move from home screen to home screen.

file allocation unit   *See* cluster.

file association   The association between a data file and an application to open the file that is determined by the file extension.

file attributes   The properties assigned to a file. Examples of file attributes are read-only and hidden status.

File Explorer   The Windows 8 utility used to view and manage files and folders.

file extension   A portion of the name of a file that indicates how the file is organized or formatted, the type of content in the file, and what program uses the file. In command lines, the file extension follows the filename and is separated from it by a period, for example, Msd.exe, where exe is the file extension.

File History   In Windows 8, the utility that can schedule and maintain backups of data. It can also create a system image for backward compatibility with Windows 7.

file name   The first part of the name assigned to a file, which does not include the file extension. In DOS, the file name can be no more than eight characters long and is followed by the file extension. In Windows, a file name can be up to 255 characters.

file server   A computer dedicated to storing and serving up data files and folders.

file system   The overall structure that an OS uses to name, store, and organize files on a disk. Examples of file systems are NTFS and FAT32. Windows is always installed on a volume that uses the NTFS file system.

Finder   An app embedded in Mac OS X that functions similar to File Explorer in Windows; use it to find and access files and applications in OS X.

firewall   Hardware and/or software that blocks unwanted traffic initiated from the Internet into a private network and can restrict Internet access for local computers behind the firewall.

fixboot   A Windows 7/Vista command that repairs the boot sector of the system partition.

fixmbr   A Windows 7/Vista command to repair the MBR (Master Boot Record).

floppy disk drive (FDD)   A drive that can hold either a 5½ inch or 3¼ inch floppy disk. *Also called* floppy drive.

G

folder *See* subdirectory.

Folder Options applet Accessed through the Control Panel, manages how files and folders are displayed in File Explorer or Windows Explorer.

force stop To abruptly end an app without allowing the app to go through its close process.

force quit In OS X, to abruptly end an app without allowing the app to go through its close process.

format The Windows command to prepare a hard drive volume, logical drive, or USB flash drive for use by placing tracks and sectors on its surface to store information (for example, format d:). This process erases all data on the device.

formatting *See* format.

fragmented file A file that has been written to different portions of the disk so that it is not in contiguous clusters.

FTP (File Transfer Protocol) A TCP/IP protocol and application that uses the Internet to transfer files between two computers.

FTP server A server using the FTP or Secure FTP protocol that downloads or uploads files to remote computers.

full duplex Communication that happens in two directions at the same time.

fully qualified domain name (FQDN) Identifies a computer and the network to which it belongs and includes the computer name and domain name. For example, *jsmith.amazon. com*. Sometimes loosely referred to as a domain name.

gadget A mini-app that appears on the Windows 7 desktop or Vista sidebar.

gateway Any device or computer that network traffic can use to leave one network and go to a different network.

geotracking A mobile device routinely reports its position to Apple, Google, or Microsoft at least twice a day, which makes it possible for these companies to track your device's whereabouts.

gestures In OS X, finger movements on the trackpad of a Mac laptop.

global account An account is used at the domain level, created by an administrator, and stored in the SAM (security accounts manager) database on a Windows domain controller. *Also called* domain account *or* network ID. *Compare with* local account.

global address *See* global unicast address.

global unicast address In TCP/IP Version 6, an IP address that can be routed on the Internet. *Also called* global address.

Globally Unique Identifier Partition Table (GUID or GPT) A partitioning system installed on a hard drive that can support 128 partitions and is recommended for drives larger than 2 TB.

Gmail An email service provided by Google at *mail.google.com*.

Google account A user account, which is a valid email address, that is registered on the Google Play website (*play.google.com*) and is used to download content to an Android device.

Google Play The official source for Android apps, also called the Android marketplace, at *play.google.com*.

gpresult The Windows command to find out group policies that are currently applied to a system for the computer or user.

gpupdate The Windows command to refresh local group policies as well as group policies set in Active Directory on a Windows domain.

GPS (Global Positioning System) A receiver that uses the system of 24 or more satellites orbiting the earth. The receiver locates four or more of these satellites, and from these four locations, calculates its own position in a process called triangulation.

graphical user interface (GUI) An interface that uses graphics as compared to a command-driven interface.

grayware A program that is potentially harmful or potentially unwanted.

grep A Linux and OS X command to search for and display a specific pattern of characters in a file or in multiple files.

ground bracelet *See* ESD strap.

ground mat *See* ESD mat.

Group Policy A console (gpedit.msc) available only in Windows professional and business editions that is used to control what users can do and how the system can be used.

GRUB (GRand Unified Bootloader) The current Linux boot loader, which can handle dual boots with another OS installed on the system.

GSM (Global System for Mobile Communications) An open standard for cellular networks and cell phones that uses digital communication of data and is accepted and used worldwide.

Guests group A type of user group in Windows. User accounts that belong to this group have limited rights to the system and are given a temporary profile that is deleted after the user logs off.

gyroscope A device that contains a disc that is free to move and can respond to gravity as the device is moved.

HAL (hardware abstraction layer) The low-level part of Windows, written specifically for each CPU technology, so that only the HAL must change when platform components change.

half duplex Communication between two devices whereby transmission takes place in only one direction at a time.

Handoff A technique of devices and computers made by Apple that lets you start a task on one device, such as an iPad, then pick up that task on another device, such as a Mac desktop or laptop.

hard boot Restart the computer by turning off the power or by pressing the Reset button. *Also called* a cold boot.

hard-link migration A method used by USMT (User State Migration Tool) that does not copy user files and settings when the source computer and destination computer are the same.

hard reset (1) For Android devices, a factory reset, which erases all data and settings and restores the device to its original factory default state. (2) For iOS devices, a forced restart similar to a full shutdown followed by a full clean boot of the device.

hardware address *See* MAC (Media Access Control) address.

hardware RAID One of two ways to implement RAID. Hardware RAID is more reliable and better performing than software RAID, and is implemented using UEFI/BIOS on the motherboard or a RAID controller card.

hardware-assisted virtualization (HAV) A feature of a processor whereby it can provide enhanced support for hypervisor software to run virtual machines on a system. The feature must be enabled in UEFI/BIOS setup.

help The Windows command to get help about another command.

hibernation A power-saving state that saves all work to the hard drive and powers down the system.

hidden share A folder whose folder name ends with a $ symbol. When you share the folder, it does not appear in the File Explorer or Windows Explorer window of remote computers on the network.

high-level formatting A process performed by the Windows Format program (for example, FORMAT C:/S), the Windows installation program, or the Disk Management utility. The process creates the boot record, file system, and root directory on a hard drive volume or logical drive, a floppy disk, or USB flash drive. Also called formatting, OS formatting, or operating system formatting. *Compare with* low-level formatting.

high-touch using a standard image A strategy to install Windows that uses a standard image for the installation. A technician must perform the installation on the local computer. *Also see* standard image.

high-touch with retail media A strategy to install Windows where all the work is done by a technician sitting at the computer using Windows setup files. The technician also installs drivers and applications after the Windows installation is finished.

HKEY_CLASSES_ROOT (HKCR) A Windows registry key that stores information to determine which application is opened when the user double-clicks a file.

G

HKEY_CURRENT_CONFIG (HKCC) A Windows registry key that contains information about the hardware configuration that is used by the computer at startup.

HKEY_CURRENT_USER (HKCU) A Windows registry key that contains data about the current user. The key is built when a user signs in using data kept in the HKEY_USERS key and data kept in the Ntuser.dat file of the current user.

HKEY_LOCAL_MACHINE (HKLM) An important Windows registry key that contains hardware, software, and security data. The key is built using data taken from the SAM hive, the Security hive, the Software hive, and the System hive and from data collected at startup about the hardware.

HKEY_USERS (HKU) A Windows registry key that contains data about all users and is taken from the Default hive.

homegroup A type of peer-to-peer network where each computer shares files, folders, libraries, and printers with other computers in the homegroup. Access to the homegroup is secured using a homegroup password.

host name A name that identifies a computer, printer, or other device on a network, which can be used instead of the computer's IP address to address the computer on the network. The host name together with the domain name is called the fully qualified domain name. *Also called* computer name.

Hosts file A file in the C:\Windows\System32\ drivers\etc folder that contains computer names and their associated IP addresses on the local network. The file has no file extension.

hot-plugging Plugging in a device while the computer is turned on. The computer will sense the device and configure it without rebooting. In addition, the device can be unplugged without an OS error. *Also called* hot-swapping.

hotspot A small area that offers connectivity to a wireless network, such as a Wi-Fi network.

hot-swappable The ability to plug or unplug devices without first powering down the system. USB devices are hot-swappable.

HTTP (Hypertext Transfer Protocol) The TCP/IP protocol used for the World Wide Web and used by web browsers and web servers to communicate.

HTTPS (HTTP secure) The HTTP protocol working with a security protocol such as Secure Sockets Layer (SSL) or Transport Layer Security (TLS), which is better than SSL, to create a secured socket that includes data encryption.

hybrid cloud A combination of public, private, and community clouds used by the same organization. For example, a company might store data in a private cloud, but use a public cloud email service.

hypervisor Software that creates and manages virtual machines on a server or on a local computer. *Also called* virtual machine manager (VMM).

IaaS (Infrastructure as a Service) A cloud computing service that provides only the hardware, which can include servers, storage devices, and networks.

iCloud A website by Apple (*www.icloud.com*) used to sync content on Apple devices in order to provide a backup of the content.

iCloud Backup A feature of an iPhone, iPad, or iPod touch whereby the device's content is backed up to the cloud at *icloud.com*.

iCloud Drive Storage space at *icloud.com* that can be synced with files stored on any Apple mobile device or any personal computer, including an OS X or Windows computer.

IDE (Intergrated Drive Electronics or Integrated Device Electronics) A hard drive whose disk controller is integrated into the drive, eliminating the need for a controller cable and thus increasing speed, as well as reducing price.

IEEE 802.11ac The latest Wi-Fi standard that supports up to 7 Gbps (actual speeds are currently about 1300 Mbps) and uses 5.0 GHz radio frequency and beamforming.

IEEE 802.11n A Wi-Fi standard that supports up to 600 Mbps and uses 5.0 GHz or 2.4 GHz radio frequency and supports MIMO.

ifconfig (interface configuration) A Linux and OS X command similar to the Windows ipconfig command that displays details about network interfaces and can enable and disable an interface. When affecting the interface, the command requires root privileges.

image deployment Installing a standard image on a computer.

IMAP4 (Internet Message Access Protocol, version 4) A protocol used by an email server and client that allows the client to manage email stored on the server without downloading the email. *Compare with* POP3.

IMEI (International Mobile Equipment Identity) A unique number that identifies a mobile phone or tablet device worldwide. The number can usually be found imprinted on the device or reported in the About menu of the OS.

IMSI (International Mobile Subscriber Identity) A unique number that identifies a cellular subscription for a device or subscriber, along with its home country and mobile network. Some carriers store the number on a SIM card installed in the device.

inherited permissions Permissions assigned by Windows that are attained from a parent object.

initialization files Text files that keep hardware and software configuration information, user preferences, and application settings and are used by the OS when first loaded and when needed by hardware, applications, and users.

in-place upgrade A Windows installation that is launched from the Windows desktop. The installation carries forward user settings and installed applications from the old OS to the new one. A Windows OS is already in place before the installation begins.

interface In TCP/IP Version 6, a node's attachment to a link. The attachment can be a physical attachment (for example, when using a network adapter) or a logical attachment (for example, when using a tunneling protocol). Each interface is assigned an IP address.

interface ID In TCP/IP Version 6, the last 64 bits or 4 blocks of an IP address that identify the interface.

Internet Options A dialog box used to manage Internet Explorer settings.

Internet Protocol version 4 (IPv4) A group of TCP/IP standards that uses IP addresses that have 32 bits.

Internet Protocol version 6 (IPv6) A group of TCP/IP standards that uses IP addresses that have 128 bits.

intranet Any private network that uses TCP/IP protocols. A large enterprise might support an intranet that is made up of several local networks.

intrusion detection system (IDS) Software that can run on a UTM (Unified Threat Management) appliance, router, server, or workstation to monitor all network traffic and create alerts when suspicious activity happens.

intrusion prevention system (IPS) Software that can run on a UTM (Unified Threat Management) appliance, router, server, or workstation to monitor all network traffic, create alerts, and prevent the threatening traffic from burrowing into the system.

inverter An electrical device that converts DC to AC.

iOS The operating system owned and developed by Apple and used for their various mobile devices.

iPad A handheld tablet developed by Apple.

IP address A 32-bit or 128-bit address used to uniquely identify a device or interface on a network that uses TCP/IP protocols. Generally, the first numbers identify the network; the last numbers identify a host. An example of a 32-bit IP address is 206.96.103.114. An example of a 128-bit IP address is 2001:0000:B80::D3:9C5A:CC.

ipconfig (IP configuration) A Windows command that displays TCP/IP configuration information and can refresh TCP/IP assignments to a connection including its IP address.

iPhone A smart phone developed by Apple.

iPod touch A multimedia recorder and player developed by Apple.

ISATAP In TCP/IP Version 6, a tunneling protocol that has been developed for IPv6 packets to travel over an IPv4 network and stands for Intra-Site Automatic Tunnel Addressing Protocol.

G

ISO file *See* ISO image.

ISO image A file format that has an .iso file extension and holds an image of all the data, including the file system that is stored on an optical disc. ISO stands for International Organization for Standardization. *Also called* disc image.

iTunes Store The Apple website at *itunes.apple .com* where apps, music, TV shows, movies, books, podcasts, and iTunes U content can be purchased and downloaded to Apple devices.

iTunes U Content at the iTunes Store website (*itunes.apple.com*) that contains lectures and even complete courses from many schools, colleges, and universities.

iwconfig A Linux and OS X command similar to ifconfig, but applies only to wireless networks. Use it to display information about a wireless interface and configure a wireless adapter.

jailbreaking A process to break through the restrictions that only allow apps to an iOS device to be downloaded from the iTunes Store at *itunes.apple.com*. Gives the user root or administrator privileges to the operating system and the entire file system and complete access to all commands and features. Note that jailbreaking voids any manufacturer warranty on the device, violates the End User License Agreement (EULA) with Apple, and might violate BYOD (Bring Your Own Device) policies in an enterprise environment.

joule A measure of work or energy. One joule of energy produces one watt of power for one second.

kernel The portion of an OS that is responsible for interacting with the hardware.

kernel mode A Windows "privileged" processing mode that has access to hardware components.

kernel panic A Linux or OS X error from which it cannot recover, similar to a blue screen of death in Windows.

Keychain In OS X, a built-in password manager utility.

key fob A device, such as a type of smart card, that can fit conveniently on a key chain.

keylogger A type of spyware that tracks your keystrokes, including passwords, chat room sessions, email messages, documents, online purchases, and anything else you type on your computer. Text is logged to a text file and transmitted over the Internet without your knowledge.

Last Known Good Configuration In Windows 7/Vista, registry settings and device drivers that were in effect when the computer last booted successfully. These settings are saved and can be restored during the startup process to recover from errors during the last boot. Windows 8 does not save the Last Known Good Configuration.

launcher The Android graphical user interface (GUI) that includes multiple home screens, and supports windows, panes, and 3D graphics.

Launchpad In OS X, the screen that shows all apps installed on the computer, similar to the Windows 8 Start screen.

library In Windows 7, a collection of one or more folders that can be stored on different local drives or on the network.

Lightweight Directory Access Protocol (LDAP) A protocol used by various client applications when the application needs to query a database.

LILO (LInux boot LOader) The outdated Linux boot loader that could handle a dual boot and has been replaced by GRUB.

link (local link) In TCP/IP version 6, a local area network or wide area network bounded by routers. *Also called* local link.

link-local address *See* link-local unicast address.

link-local unicast address In TCP/IP Version 6, an IP address used for communicating among nodes in the same link and is not allowed on the Internet. *Also called* local address *and* link-local address.

Linux An OS based on Unix that was created by Linus Torvalds of Finland. Basic versions of this OS are open source, and all the underlying programming instructions are freely distributed.

lite-touch, high-volume deployment   A strategy that uses a deployment server on the network to serve up a Windows installation after a technician starts the process at the local computer.

live CD   In Linux, a CD, DVD, or flash drive that can boot up a live version of Linux, complete with Internet access and all the tools you normally have available in a hard drive installation of Linux, but without installing the OS on the hard drive.

live sign in   Sign in to Windows 8 using a Microsoft account.

live tiles   On the Windows 8 Start screen, some apps use live tiles, which offer continuous real-time updates.

loadstate   A command used by the User State Migration Tool (USMT) to copy user settings and data temporarily stored at a safe location to a new computer. *Also see* scanstate.

local account   A Windows user account that applies only to the local computer and cannot be used to access resources from other computers on the network. *Compare with* global account.

local area network (LAN)   A network bound by routers or other gateway devices.

local link   *See* link.

Local Security Policy   A Windows Administrative Tools snap-in in Control Panel that can manage the group of policies in the Local Computer Policy, Computer Configuration, Windows Settings, Security Settings group of Group Policy.

local share   Folders on a computer that are shared with others on the network by using a folder's Properties box. Local shares are used with a workgroup and not with a domain.

local snapshot   In OS X, the temporary backups that Time Machine creates when the Mac is not connected to the backup media. When the media is later available, local snapshots are copied to the media.

Local Users and Groups   For business and professional editions of Windows, a Windows

utility console (lusrmgr.msc) that can be used to manage user accounts and user groups.

location data   Data that a device can routinely report to a website, which can be used to locate the device on a map.

location independence   A function of cloud computing whereby customers generally are not aware of where the physical devices providing cloud services are located geographically.

logical drive   On an MBR hard drive, a portion or all of a hard drive extended partition that is treated by the operating system as though it were a physical drive or volume. Each logical drive is assigned a drive letter, such as drive F, and contains a file system. *Compare with* volume.

logical topology   The logical way computers connect on a network.

login item   In OS X, programs that are automatically launched after a user logs in. Login items are managed in the Users & Groups utility in System Preferences.

LoJack   A technology by Absolute Software used to track the whereabouts of a laptop computer and, if the computer is stolen, lock down access to the computer or erase data on it. The technology is embedded in the UEFI/BIOS of many laptops.

Long Term Evolution (LTE)   The latest standard used to transmit both voice and digital data over cellular networks and is expected to eventually replace CDMA and GSM.

loopback address   An IP address that indicates your own computer and is used to test TCP/IP configuration on the computer.

low-level formatting   A process (usually performed at the factory) that electronically creates the hard drive tracks and sectors, and tests for bad spots on the disk surface. *Compare with* high-level formatting.

LPT (Line Printer Terminal)   Assignments of system resources that are made to a parallel port and that are used to manage a print job. Two possible LPT configurations are referred to as LPT1: and LPT2:.

G

MAC (Media Access Control) address A 48-bit (6-byte) hardware address unique to each network interface card (NIC) or onboard network controller that is assigned by the manufacturer at the factory and embedded on the device. The address is often printed on the adapter as hexadecimal numbers. An example is 00 00 0C 08 2F 35. *Also called* a physical address, an adapter address, or a hardware address.

MAC address filtering A technique used by a router or wireless access point to allow access to a private network to only certain computers or devices identified by their MAC addresses.

malicious software Any unwanted program that is transmitted to a computer without the user's knowledge and that is designed to do varying degrees of damage to data and software. Types of infestations include viruses, Trojan horses, worms, adware, spyware, keyloggers, browser hijackers, dialers, and downloaders. *Also called* malware, infestation, or computer infestation.

malware *See* malicious software.

malware definition Information about malware that allows anti-malware software to detect and define malware. *Also called* a malware signature.

malware encyclopedia Lists of malware, including symptoms and solutions, often maintained by manufacturers of anti-malware and made available on their websites.

malware signature *See* malware definition.

man-in-the-middle attack An attack that pretends to be a legitimate website, network, FTP site, or person in a chat session in order to obtain private information.

mantrap A physical security technique of using two doors on either end of a small entryway where the first door must close before the second door can open. A separate form of identification might be required for each door, such as a badge for the first door and a fingerprint scan for the second door. In addition, a security guard might monitor people as they come and go.

mapping The client computer creates and saves a shortcut, called a network drive, to a folder or drive shared by a remote computer on the network. The network drive has a drive letter associated with it, which points to the network share.

Master Boot Record (MBR) On an MBR hard drive, the first sector on the drive, which contains the partition table and a program BIOS uses to boot an OS from the drive.

master file table (MFT) The database used by the NTFS file system to track the contents of a volume or logical drive.

Material Safety Data Sheet (MSDS) A document that explains how to properly handle substances such as chemical solvents; it includes information such as physical data, toxicity, health effects, first aid, storage, disposal, and spill procedures.

md (make directory) The Windows command to create a directory.

measured service When a cloud computing vendor offers services that are metered for billing purposes or to ensure transparency between vendors and customers.

Memory Diagnostics A Windows 8/7/Vista utility (mdsched.exe) used to test memory.

Metro User Interface (Metro UI) *See* modern interface.

Microsoft account For Windows 8 and above, an email address and password that allows access to several types of online accounts including Microsoft OneDrive, Facebook, LinkedIn, Twitter, Skype, Outlook, and others.

Microsoft Assessment and Planning (MAP) Toolkit Software that can be used by a system administrator from a network location to query hundreds of computers in a single scan to determine if a computer qualifies for a Windows upgrade.

Microsoft Exchange A server application that can handle email, contacts, and calendars and is a popular application used by large corporations for employee email, contacts, and calendars.

Microsoft Management Console (MMC) A Windows utility to build customized consoles. These consoles can be saved to a file with an .msc file extension.

Microsoft Store The official source for Windows apps at *microsoftstore.com*.

MIMO *See* multiple input/multiple output (MIMO).

Miracast A wireless display-mirroring technology that requires a Miracast-capable screen or dongle in order to mirror a smart phone's display to a TV, a wireless monitor, or a wireless projector.

Mission Control In OS X, a utility and screen that gives an overview of all open windows and thumbnails of the Dashboard and desktops.

mobile payment service An app that allows you to use your smart phone or other mobile device to pay for merchandise or services at a retail checkout counter.

modern interface An interface that presents the Start screen to the user. *Also called* Windows 8 interface, *formerly called* Metro User Interface *or* Metro UI.

mount point A folder that is used as a shortcut to space on another volume, which effectively increases the size of the folder to the size of the other volume. *Also see* mounted drive.

mounted drive A volume that can be accessed by way of a folder on another volume so that the folder has more available space. *Also see* mount point.

mstsc (Microsoft Terminal Services Client) A Windows command that allows you to start Remote Desktop Connection to remote in to your host computer using Remote Desktop.

multiboot *See* dual boot.

multicast address In TCP/IP version 6, an IP address used when packets are delivered to a group of nodes on a network.

multicasting In TCP/IP version 6, one host sends messages to multiple hosts, such as when the host transmits a video conference over the Internet.

multifactor authentication (MFA) To use more than one method to authenticate access to a computer, network, or other resource.

multimonitor taskbar The Windows 8 option to extend the desktop taskbar across multiple monitors. Use the taskbar properties box to adjust the taskbar.

multiple desktops A feature of Mission Control in OS X, where several desktop screens, each with its own collection of open windows, are available to the user.

multiple input/multiple output (MIMO) A feature of the IEEE 802.11n/ac standards for wireless networking whereby two or more antennas are used at both ends of transmissions to improve performance.

multiple monitor misalignment When the display is staggered across multiple monitors, making the display difficult to read. Fix the problem by adjusting the display in the Windows Screen Resolution window.

multiple monitor orientation When the display does not accurately represent the relative positions of multiple monitors. Use the Windows Screen Resolution window to move the display for each monitor so they are oriented correctly.

multitouch A touch screen on a computer or mobile device that can handle a two-finger pinch.

mutual authentication To authenticate in both directions at the same time, as both entities confirm the identity of the other.

name resolution The process of associating a character-based name with an IP address.

NAT (Network Address Translation) A technique that substitutes the public IP address of the router for the private IP address of computer on a private network when these computers need to communicate on the Internet. *See also* Destination Network Address Translation (DNAT).

native resolution The actual (and fixed) number of pixels built into an LCD monitor. For the clearest display, always set the resolution to the native resolution.

navigation pane In File Explorer, Windows Explorer, or the Computer window, pane on the left side of the window where devices, drives, and folders are listed. Double-click an item to drill down into the item.

neighbors In TCP/IP version 6, two or more nodes on the same link.

G

NetBIOS A legacy suite of protocols used by Windows before TCP/IP.

NetBIOS over TCP/IP A feature of Server Message Block (SMB) protocols that allows legacy NetBIOS applications to communicate on a TCP/IP network.

NetBoot A technology that allows a Mac to boot from the network and then install OS X on the machine from a clone DMG file stored on the server.

network adapter *See* network interface card (NIC).

Network and Sharing Center The primary Windows 8/7/Vista utility used to manage network connections.

Network Attached Storage (NAS) A device that provides multiple bays for hard drives and an Ethernet port to connect to the network. The device is likely to support RAID.

network drive map Mounting a drive to a computer, such as drive E:, that is actually hard drive space on another host computer on the network.

Network File System (NFS) A Windows component that is a distributed file system used to manage shared files on a network.

network ID *See* global account.

network interface card (NIC) An expansion card that plugs into a computer's motherboard and provides a port on the back of the card to connect a computer to a network. *Also called* a network adapter.

Network Places Wizard *See* User Accounts.

network share One computer (the client) on the network appears to have a hard drive, such as drive E:, that is actually hard drive space on another host computer (the server). *Also see* mapping.

next-generation firewall (NGFW) A firewall that combines firewall software with anti-malware software and other software that protects resources on a network.

node Any device that connects to the network, such as a computer, printer, or router.

non-compliant system A system that violates security best practices, such as out-of-date anti-

malware software or no anti-malware software installed.

nonvolatile RAM (NVRAM) Flash memory on the motherboard that UEFI firmware uses to store device drivers and information about Secure Boot. Contents of NVRAM are not lost when the system is powered down.

Notepad A Windows text editing program.

notification area An area to the right of the taskbar that holds the icons for running services; these services include the volume control and network connectivity. *Also called* the system tray *or* systray.

notifications Alerts and related information about apps and social media sent to mobile devices.

NTFS permissions A method to share a folder or file over a network and can apply to local users and network users. The folder or file must be on an NTFS volume. *Compare with* share permissions.

octet In TCP/IP version 4, each of the four numbers that are separated by periods and make up a 32-bit IP address. One octet is 8 bits.

Offline Files A utility that allows users to work with files in the folder when the computer is not connected to the corporate network. When the computer is later connected, Windows syncs up the offline files and folders with those on the network.

ohm (Ω) The standard unit of measurement for electrical resistance. Resistors are rated in ohms.

onboard NIC A network port embedded on the motherboard.

on-demand A service that is available to users at any time. On-demand cloud computing means the service is always available.

OneDrive Microsoft cloud service that allows users with a Microsoft account to store, sync, and share files with other people and devices.

Open Database Connectivity (ODBC) A technology that allows a client computer to create a data source so that the client can interface with a database stored on a remote (host) computer on the network. *Also see* data source.

open source Source code for an operating system or other software whereby the source code is available for free and anyone can modify and redistribute the source code.

operating system (OS) Software that controls a computer. An OS controls how system resources are used and provides a user interface, a way of managing hardware and software, and ways to work with files.

Original Equipment Manufacturer (OEM) license A software license that only manufacturers or builders of personal computers can purchase to be installed only on a computer intended for sale.

OS X The latest version of the proprietary operating system only available for Macintosh computers by Apple Inc. (*apple.com*). OS X was originally based on Unix.

OSI Model A model for understanding and developing computer-to-computer communication, it divides networking functions among seven layers: Physical, Data Link, Network, Transport, Session, Presentation, and Application.

PaaS (Platform as a Service) A cloud computing service that provides the hardware and the operating system and is responsible for updating and maintaining both.

packet A message sent over a network as a unit that contains the data and information at the beginning that identifies the type of data, where it came from, and where it's going. *Also called* data packet or datagram.

pagefile.sys The Windows swap file that is used to hold the virtual memory that is used to enhance physical memory installed in a system.

pairing The process of two Bluetooth devices establishing connectivity.

parallel ATA (PATA) An older IDE cabling method that uses a 40-pin flat or round data cable or an 80-conductor cable and a 40-pin IDE connector. *Also see* serial ATA.

partition A division of a hard drive that can hold a volume. MBR drives can support up to four partitions on one hard drive. In Windows, GPT drives can have up to 128 partitions.

partition table A table that contains information about each partition on the drive. For MBR drives, the partition table is contained in the Master Boot Record. For GPT drives, the partition table is stored in the GPT header and a backup of the table is stored at the end of the drive.

patch A minor update to software that corrects an error, adds a feature, or addresses security issues. *Also called* an update. *Compare with* service pack.

path A drive and list of directories pointing to a file such as C:\Windows\System32.

PC Card A card that uses a PC Card slot on a laptop, and provides a port for peripheral devices or adds memory to the laptop. A PC Card is about the size of a credit card, but thicker.

PCL (Printer Control Language) A printer language developed by Hewlett-Packard that communicates to a printer how to print a page.

peer-to-peer (P2P) As applied to networking, a network of computers that are all equals, or peers. Each computer has the same amount of authority, and each can act as a server to the other computers.

Performance Monitor A Microsoft Management Console snap-in that can track activity by hardware and software to measure performance.

permission propagation When Windows passes permissions from parent objects to child objects.

permissions Varying degrees of access assigned to a folder or file and given to a user account or user group. Access can include full control, write, delete, or read-only.

personal license A license to use software that gives the right to install one instance of the software.

phishing Sending an email message with the intent of getting the user to reveal private information that can be used for identify theft. *Also see* spear phishing *and* spoofing.

physical address *See* MAC (Media Access Control) address.

physical topology The physical arrangement of connections between computers.

pinning To make a frequently used application more accessible, add its icon to the taskbar on the desktop.

platform The hardware, operating system, runtime libraries, and modules on which an application runs.

POP or POP3 (Post Office Protocol, version 3) The protocol that an email server and client use when the client requests the downloading of email messages. The most recent version is POP version 3. *Compare with* IMAP4.

port (1) As applied to services running on a computer, a number assigned to a process on a computer so that the process can be found by TCP/IP. *Also called* a port address *or* port number. (2) A physical connector, usually at the back of a computer, that allows a cable from a peripheral device, such as a printer, mouse, or modem, to be attached.

port address *See* port.

port filtering To open or close certain ports so they can or cannot be used. A firewall uses port filtering to protect a network from unwanted communication.

port forwarding A technique that allows a computer on the Internet to reach a computer on a private network using a certain port when the private network is protected by NAT and a firewall that controls the use of ports. *Also called* port mapping.

port mapping *See* port forwarding.

port number *See* port.

port triggering When a firewall opens a port because a computer behind the firewall initiates communication on another port.

POST (power-on self test) A self-diagnostic program used to perform a simple test of the CPU, RAM, and various I/O devices. The POST is performed by startup UEFI/BIOS when the computer is first turned on.

PostScript A printer language developed by Adobe Systems that tells a printer how to print a page.

Power Options applet Accessed through the Control Panel, manages power settings to conserve power.

Power Users group A type of user account group. Accounts assigned to this group can read from and write to parts of the system other than their own user profile folders, install applications, and perform limited administrative tasks.

Preboot eXecution Environment (PXE) Programming contained in the UEFI/BIOS code on the motherboard used to start up the computer and search for a server on the network to provide a bootable operating system. *Also called* Pre-Execution Environment (PXE).

presentation virtualization Using this virtualization, a remote application running on a server is controlled by a local computer.

primary partition A hard disk partition that can be designated as the active partition. An MBR drive can have up to three primary partitions. In Windows, a GPT drive can have up to 128 primary patitions. *Compare with* extended partition.

principle of least privilege An approach where computer users are classified and the rights assigned are the minimum rights required to do their job.

Print Management A utility located in the Administrative Tools group in Windows 8/7/Vista professional and business editions that allows you to monitor and manage printer queues for all printers on the network.

print server Hardware or software that manages the print jobs sent to one or more printers on a network.

print spooler A queue for print jobs.

privacy filter A device that fits over a monitor screen to prevent other people from viewing the monitor from a wide angle.

private cloud Services on the Internet that an organization provides on its own servers or established virtually for a single organization's private use.

private IP address In TCP/IP version 4, an IP address that is used on a private network that is isolated from the Internet.

PRL (Preferred Roaming List) A list of preferred service providers or radio frequencies your carrier wants a mobile device to use and is stored on a Removable User Identify Module (R-UIM) card installed in the device.

process A program that is running under the authority of the shell, together with the system resources assigned to it.

product activation The process that Microsoft uses to prevent software piracy. For example, once Windows 8 is activated for a particular computer, it cannot be legally installed on another computer.

Product Release Instructions (PRI) Information published by the manufacturer of an operating system that describes what to expect from a published update to the OS.

Programs and Features A window within Control Panel that lists the programs installed on a computer, where you can uninstall, change, or repair programs.

protocol A set of rules and standards that two entities use for communication. For example, TCP/IP is a suite or group of protocols that define many types of communication on a TCP/IP network.

proxy server A computer that intercepts requests that a client (for example, a browser) makes of a server (for example, a web server) and can serve up the request from a cache it maintains to improve performance or can filter requests to secure a large network.

public cloud Cloud computing services provided over the Internet to the general public. Google or Yahoo! email services are examples of public cloud deployment.

public IP address In TCP/IP version 4, an IP address available to the Internet.

pull automation A Windows installation that requires the local user to start the process. *Compare with* push automation.

push automation An installation where a server automatically pushes the installation to a computer when a user is not likely to be sitting at the computer. *Compare with* pull automation.

Quality of Service (QoS) A feature used by Windows and network hardware devices to improve network performance for an application that is not getting the best network performance. VoIP (Voice over IP) requires a high QoS.

quarantined computer A computer that is suspected of infection and is not allowed to use the network, is put on a different network dedicated to quarantined computers, or is allowed to access only certain network resources.

quick format A format procedure, used to format a hard drive volume or other drive, that doesn't scan the volume or drive for bad sectors; use it only when a drive has been previously formatted and is in healthy condition.

Quick Launch menu The menu that appears when the Windows Start button is right-clicked.

radio frequency (RF) The frequency of waves generated by a radio signal, which are electro-magnetic frequencies above audio and below light. For example, Wi-Fi 802.11n transmits using a radio frequency of 5 GHz and 2.4 GHz.

RAID (redundant array of inexpensive disks or redundant array of independent disks) Several methods of configuring multiple hard drives to store data to increase logical volume size and improve performance, or to ensure that if one hard drive fails, the data is still available from another hard drive.

RAID 0 Using space from two or more physical disks to increase the disk space available for a single volume. Performance improves because data is written evenly across all disks. Windows calls RAID 0 a striped volume. *Also called* striping *or* striped volume.

ransomware Malware that holds your computer system hostage with encryption techniques until you pay money or a time period expires when the encrypted content is destroyed.

rapid elasticity A cloud computing service that is cabable of scaling up or down as a customer's need level changes.

G

raw data   Data sent to a printer without any formatting or processing.

rd (remove directory)   The Windows command to delete a directory (folder) or group of directories (folders).

ReadyBoost   A Windows utility that uses a flash drive or secure digital (SD) memory card to boost hard drive performance.

ReadyDrive   The Windows 7/Vista technology that supports a hybrid hard drive.

recover   The Windows command that can recover a file when part of the file is corrupted.

recovery drive   A Windows 8 bootable USB flash drive that can be used to recover the system when startup fails and can be created using the Recovery applet in Control Panel.

recovery image   A backup of the Windows volume.

recovery partition   A partition on a hard drive that contains a recovery utility and installation files.

Recovery System   In OS X, a lean operating system that boots from a hidden volume on the OS X startup disk and is used to troubleshoot OS X when startup errors occur.

rectifier   An electrical device that converts AC to DC. A computer power supply contains a rectifier.

Recycle Bin   In Windows, location on the hard drive where deleted files are stored.

refresh   A Windows 8 technique to recover from a corrupted Windows installation and can recover using a custom refresh image, a recovery partition, or the Windows setup DVD. Depending on the health of the system, user settings, data, and Windows 8 apps might be restored from backup near the end of the refresh operation.

refresh rate   As applied to monitors, the number of times in one second the monitor can fill the screen with lines from top to bottom. *Also called* vertical scan rate.

registry   A database that Windows uses to store hardware and software configuration information, user preferences, and setup information.

Registry Editor   The Windows utility (regedit.exe) used to edit the Windows registry.

Regsvr32   A utility that is used to register component services used by an installed application.

Reliability and Performance Monitor   A Vista utility (perfmon.msc) that collects, records, and displays events, called Data Collector Sets, that can help track the performance and reliability of Windows.

Reliability Monitor   A Windows 8/7 utility that provides information about problems and errors that happen over time.

Remote Admin share   Gives an administrator access to the Windows folder on a remote computer in a Windows domain.

remote application   An application that is installed and executed on a server and is presented to a user working at a client computer.

Remote Assistance   A Windows tool that allows a technician to remote in to a user's computer while the user remains signed, retains control of the session, and can see the screen. This is helpful when a technician is troubleshooting problems on a computer.

remote backup application   A cloud backup service on the Internet that backs up data to the cloud and is often used for laptops, tablets, and smart phones.

Remote Desktop Connection (RDC)   A Windows tool that gives a user access to a Windows desktop from anywhere on the Internet.

Remote Desktop Protocol (RDP)   The Windows protocol used by Remote Desktop and Remote Assistance utilities to connect to and control a remote computer.

Remote Disc   A feature of OS X that gives other computers on the network access to the Mac's optical drive.

remote network installation   An automated installation where no user intervention is required.

remote wipe   Remotely erases all contacts, email, photos, and other data from a device to protect your privacy.

ren (rename) The Windows command to rename a file or group of files.

repair installation A reinstallation of Windows using the recovery utilty and installation files stored on the recovery partition.

reset Restore a Window 8 installation to factory state or to the state after a clean install of Windows. The hard drive is formatted and all user data and settings are lost.

resiliency In Windows 8 Storage Spaces, the term refers to the degree the configuration can resist or recover from drive failure.

Resilient File System (ReFS) A file system that offers excellent fault tolerance and compatibility with virtualization and data redundancy in a RAID system.

resolution The number of pixels on a monitor screen that are addressable by software (example: 1024 × 768 pixels).

Resource Monitor A Windows tool that monitors the performance of the processor, memory, hard drive, and network.

resource pooling Cloud computing services to multiple customers that are hosted on shared physical resources and dynamically allocated to meet customer demand.

restore point A snapshot of the Windows system, usually made before installation of new hardware or applications. Restore points are created by the System Protection utility.

retinal scanning As part of the authentication process, some systems use biometric data by scanning the blood vessels on the back of the eye and is considered the most reliable of all biometric data scanning.

RFID badge A badge worn by an employee and is used to gain entrance into a locked area of a building. A Radio Frequency Identification token transmits authentication to the system when the token gets in range of a query device.

RJ-45 A port that looks like a large phone jack and is used by twisted-pair cable to connect to a wired network adapter or other hardware device. RJ stands for registered jack. *Also called* Ethernet port.

robocopy (robust file copy) A Windows command that is similar to and more powerful than the xcopy command, used to copy files and folders.

root account In Linux and OS X, the account that gives the user access to all the functions of the OS; the principal user account.

root certificate The original digitate certificate issued by a Certification Authority.

root directory The main directory, at the top of the top-down hierarchical structure of subdirectories, created when a hard drive or disk is first formatted. In Linux, it's indicated by a forward slash. In DOS and Windows, it's indicated by a backward slash.

rooting The process of obtaining root or administrator privileges to an Android device which then gives you complete access to the entire file system and all commands and features. Note that rooting may void any manufacturer warranty on the device and might violate BYOD (Bring Your Own Device) policies in an enterprise environment.

rootkit A type of malicious software that loads itself before the OS boot is complete and can hijack internal Windows components so that it masks information Windows provides to user-mode utilities such as File Explorer or Task Manager.

router A device that manages traffic between two or more networks and can help find the best path for traffic to get from one network to another.

RSA tokens A type of smart card that contains authentication information.

S/MIME (Secure/Multipurpose Internet Mail Extensions) A protocol that encrypts an outgoing email message and includes a digital signature and is more secure than SMTP, which does not use encryption.

S1 state On the UEFI/BIOS power screen, one of the five S states used by ACPI power-saving mode to indicate different levels of power-savings functions. In the S1 state, the hard drive and monitor are turned off and everything else runs normally.

G

S2 state On the UEFI/BIOS power screen, one of the five S states used by ACPI power-saving mode to indicate different levels of power-savings functions. In S2 state, the hard drive and monitor are turned off and everything else runs normally. In addition, the processor is also turned off.

S3 state On the UEFI/BIOS power screen, one of the five S states used by ACPI power-saving mode to indicate different levels of power-savings functions. In S3 state, everything is shut down except RAM and enough of the system to respond to a wake-up. S3 is sleep mode.

S4 state On the UEFI/BIOS power screen, one of the five S states used by ACPI power-saving mode to indicate different levels of power-savings functions. In S4 state, everything in RAM is copied to a file on the hard drive and the system is shut down. When the system is turned on, the file is used to restore the system to its state before shut down. S4 is hibernation.

S5 state On the UEFI/BIOS power screen, one of the five S states used by ACPI power-saving mode to indicate different levels of power-savings functions. S5 state is the power off state after a normal shutdown.

SaaS (Software as a Service) A cloud computing service whereby the service is responsible for the hardware, the operating systems, and the applications installed.

Safe Mode The technique of launching Windows with a minimum configuration, eliminating third-party software and reducing Windows startup to only essential processes. The technique can sometimes launch Windows when a normal Windows startup is corrupted.

safety googles Eye googles worn while working in an unsafe environment such as a factory where fragments, chips, or other particles might injure eyes.

sag *See* brownout.

SCSI (Small Computer System Interface) An interface between a host adapter and the CPU that can daisy chain as many as 7 or 15 devices on a single bus.

scanstate A command used by the User State Migration Tool (USMT) to copy user settings

and data from an old computer to a safe location such as a server or removable media. *Also see* loadstate.

screen orientation The layout or orientation of the screen that is either portrait or landscape.

screen resolution The number of dots or pixels on the monitor screen expressed as two numbers such as 1680 x 1050.

Screen Sharing In OS X, a utility to remotely view and control a Mac and is similar to Remote Assistance in Windows.

SDK (Software Development Kit) A group of tools that developers use to write apps. For example, Android Studio is a free SDK that is released as open source.

secondary click In OS X, right-click the mouse or tap the bottom-right corner of the trackpad on a Mac laptop.

secondary logon Using administrator privileges to perform an operation when you are not logged on with an account that has these privileges.

sector On a hard disk drive or SSD, the smallest unit of bytes addressable by the operating system and UEFI/BIOS. On hard disk drives, one sector usually equals 512 bytes; SSD drives might use larger sectors.

Secure Boot A UEFI feature that prevents a system from booting up with drivers or an OS that are not digitally signed and trusted by the motherboard or computer manufacturer.

Secure FTP (SFTP) A TCP/IP protocol used to transfer files from an FTP server to an FTP client using encryption.

Secure Shell (SSH) A protocol that is used to pass login information to a remote computer and control that computer over a network using encryption.

Security Center A center in Vista where you can confirm Windows Firewall, Windows Update, anti-malware settings, including that of Windows Defender, and other security settings.

security token A smart card or other device that is one factor in multifactor authentication or can serve as a replacement for a password.

self-grounding   A method to safeguard against ESD that involves touching the computer case or power supply before touching a component in the computer case.

Server Message Block (SMB)   A protocol used by Windows to share files and printers on a network.

Service Set Identifier (SSID)   The name of a wireless access point and wireless network.

server-side virtualization   Using this virtualization, a server provides a virtual desktop or application for users on multiple client machines.

service   A program that runs in the background to support or serve Windows or an application.

service pack   A collection of several patches or updates that is installed as a single update to an OS or application.

Services console   A console used by Windows to stop, start, and manage background services used by Windows and applications.

setup UEFI/BIOS   Used to change motherboard settings. For example, you can use it to enable or disable a device on the motherboard, change the date and time that is later passed to the OS, and select the order of boot devices for startup UEFI/BIOS to search when looking for an operating system to load.

shadow copy   A copy of open files made so that open files are included in a backup.

share permissions   A method to share a folder (not individual files) to remote users on the network, including assigning varying degrees of access to specific user accounts and user groups. Does not apply to local users of a computer and can be used on an NTFS or FAT volume. *Compare with* NTFS permissions.

shell   The portion of an OS that relates to the user and to applications.

shell prompt   In Linux and OS X, the command prompt in the terminal.

Short Message Service (SMS)   A technology that allows users to send a test message using a cell phone.

shoulder surfing   As you work, other people secretly peek at your monitor screen to gain valuable information.

shutdown   The Windows command to shut down the local computer or a remote computer.

sidebar   Located on the right side of the Vista desktop and displays Vista gadgets.

side-by-side apps   In Windows 8, an application or page can be snapped to the left or right side of the screen so a second page can share the screen.

SIM (Subscriber Identity Module) card   A small flash memory card that contains all the information a device needs to connect to a GSM or LTE cellular network, including a password and other authentication information needed to access the network, encryption standards used, and the services that a subscription includes.

Simple Network Management Protocol (SNMP)   A TCP/IP protocol used to monitor network traffic.

simple volume   A type of volume used on a single hard drive. *Compare with* dynamic volume.

single sign-on (SSO)   An account that accesses multiple, independent resources, systems, or applications after signing in one time to one account. An example is a Microsoft account.

site license   A license that allows a company to install multiple copies of software, or to allow multiple employees to execute the software from a file server. *Also called* enterprise license.

slack   Wasted space on a hard drive caused by not using all available space at the end of a cluster.

sleep mode   A power-saving state for a computer used to save power when not using the computer. *Also see* S3 state.

sleep timer   The number of minutes of inactivity before a computer goes into a power-saving state such as sleep mode.

smart card   Any small device that contains authentication information that can be keyed into a sign-in window or read by a reader to authenticate a user on a network.

G

smart card reader A device that can read a smart card used to authenticate a person onto a network.

SMB2 *See* CIFS (Common Internet File System).

SMTP (Simple Mail Transfer Protocol) A TCP/IP protocol used by email clients to send email messages to an email server and on to the recipient's email server. *Also see* POP and IMAP.

SMTP AUTH (SMTP Authentication) An improved version of SMTP and used to authenticate a user to an email server when the email client first tries to connect to the email server to send email. The protocol is based on the Simple Authentication and Security Layer (SASL) protocol.

snap-in A Windows utility that can be installed in a console window by Microsoft Management Console.

social engineering The practice of tricking people into giving out private information or allowing unsafe programs into the network or computer.

socket An established connection between a client and a server, such as the connection between a browser and web server.

soft boot To restart a computer without turning off the power, for example, in Windows 8, press Win+X, point to Shut down or sign out, and click Restart. *Also called* warm boot.

soft reset (1) For Android, to forcefully reboot the device (full shut down and cold boot) by pressing and holding the power button. (2) For iOS, to put the device in hibernation and not clear memory by pressing the Wake/sleep button.

Software Explorer A Vista tool used to control startup programs.

software piracy The act of making unauthorized copies of original software, which violates the Federal Copyright Act of 1976.

software RAID Using Windows to implement RAID. The setup is done using the Disk Management utility.

solid-state drive (SSD) A hard drive that has no moving parts. *Also see* solid state device (SSD).

Sound applet Accessed through the Control Panel, used to select a default speaker and microphone and adjust how Windows handles sounds.

Space In OS X, one desktop screen is called a Space. Multiple desktops or Spaces can be open and available to users.

spear phishing A form of phishing where an email message appears to come from a company you already do business with. *See also* phishing.

spoofing A phishing technique where you are tricked into clicking a link in an email message, which takes you to an official-looking website where you are asked to enter your user ID and password to enter the site. *See also* phishing.

spooling Placing print jobs in a print queue so that an application can be released from the printing process before printing is completed. Spooling is an acronym for simultaneous peripheral operations online.

Spotlight In OS X, the search app that can be configured to search the local computer, Wikipedia, iTunes, the Maps app, the web, and more.

spyware Malicious software that installs itself on your computer or mobile device to spy on you. It collects personal information about you that it transmits over the Internet to web-hosting sites that intend to use your personal data for harm.

standard account The Windows 8/7/Vista user account type that can use software and hardware and make some system changes, but cannot make changes that affect the security of the system or other users. *Compare with* administrator account.

standard image An image that includes Windows, drivers, and applications that are standard to all the computers that might use the image.

Start screen Introduced in Windows 8, the Start screen contains tiles that represent lean apps, which use few system resources and are designed for social media, social networking, and the novice end user.

startup disk   In OS X, the entire volume on which OS X is installed.

startup items   In OS X, programs that automatically launch at startup. Apple discourages the use of startup items, which are stored in two directories: /Library/StartupItems and /System/Library/StartupItems. Normally, both directories are empty.

startup UEFI/BIOS   Part of UEFI or BIOS firmware on the motherboard that is responsible for controlling the computer when it is first turned on. Startup UEFI/BIOS gives control over to the OS once the OS is loaded.

startup repair   A Windows 8/7/Vista utility that restores many of the Windows files needed for a successful boot.

static electricity   *See* electrostatic discharge (ESD).

static IP address   A permanent IP address that is manually assigned to a computer.

Storage Spaces   A Windows 8 utility that can create a storage pool using any number of internal or external backup drives. The utility is expected to replace Windows software RAID.

striping   *See* RAID 0.

strong password   A password that is not easy to guess.

su   A Linux and OS X command to open a new terminal shell for a different user account. Stands for "substitute user".

subdirectory   A directory or folder contained in another directory or folder. *Also called* a child directory *or* folder.

subnet   A group of local networks when several networks are tied together in a subsystem of the larger intranet. In TCP/IP Version 6, one or more links that have the same 16 bits in the subnet ID of the IP address. *See* subnet ID.

subnet ID   In TCP/IP Version 6, the last block (16 bits) in the 64-bit prefix of an IP address. The subnet is identified using some or all of these 16 bits.

subnet mask   In TCP/IP Version 4, 32 bits that include a series of ones followed by zeroes. For example, 11111111.11111111.11110000 .00000000, which can be written as 255.255.240.0. The 1s identify the network portion of an IP address, and the 0s identify the host portion of an IP address. The subnet mask tells Windows if a remote computer is on the same or different network.

subscription model   A method of licensing software with a paid annual subscription where the software is installed on your local computer. For example, Office 365 uses a subscription model.

sudo   A Linux and OS X command to execute another command as a superuser when logged in as a normal user with an account that has the right to use root commands. Stands for "substitute user to do the command."

superuser   Refers to a Linux or Mac OS X user who is logged in to the root account.

surge supressor   A device designed to protect against voltage spikes by blocking or grounding excessive voltage.

suspend mode   *See* sleep mode.

switch   A device used to connect nodes on a network in a star network topology. When it receives a packet, it uses its table of MAC addresses to decide where to send the packet.

system UEFI/BIOS   UEFI (Unified Extensible Firmware Interface) or BIOS (basic input/output system) firmware on the motherboard that is used to control essential devices before the OS is loaded.

System Configuration   A Windows utility (msconfig.exe) that can identify what processes are launched at startup and can temporarily disable a process from loading.

System File Checker (SFC)   A Windows utility that verifies and, if necessary, refreshes a Windows system file, replacing it with one kept in a cache of current system files.

system image   The backup of the entire Windows 8/7 volume and can also include backups of other volumes. The backup is made using the Windows 8 File History or Windows 7 Backup and Restore utility.

System Information   A Windows tool (msinfo32. exe) that provides details about a system, including installed hardware and software, the current system configuration, and currently running programs.

G

system partition The active partition of the hard drive containing the boot loader or boot manager program and the specific files required to start the Windows launch.

System Preferences In OS X, a utility to customize the OS X interface and is available on the Apple menu.

System Protection A Windows utility that automatically backs up system files and stores them in restore points on the hard drive at regular intervals and just before you install software or hardware.

system repair disc A disc you can create using Windows 7 that can be used to launch Windows RE. The disc is not available in Windows 8.

System Restore A Windows utility used to restore the system to a restore point.

system state data In Windows, files that are necessary for a successful load of the operating system.

system tray *See* notification area.

System window A window that displays brief and important information about installed hardware and software and gives access to important Windows tools needed to support the system.

systray *See* notification area.

tailgating When someone who is unauthorized follows an employee through a secured entrance to a room or building.

Task Manager A Windows utility (taskmgr. exe) that lets you view the applications and processes running on your computer as well as information about process and memory performance, network activity, and user activity.

Task Scheduler A Windows tool that can set a task or program to launch at a future time, including at startup.

taskbar A bar normally located at the bottom of the Windows desktop, displaying information about open programs and providing quick access to others.

taskkill A Windows command that uses the process PID to kill a process.

tasklist A Windows command that returns the process identifier (PID), which is a number that identifies each running process.

TCP (Transmission Control Protocol) The protocol in the TCP/IP suite of protocols that works at the OSI Transport layer and establishes a session or connection between parties and guarantees packet delivery.

TCP/IP (Transmission Control Protocol/Internet Protocol) The group or suite of protocols used for almost all networks, including the Internet. Fundamentally, TCP is responsible for error checking transmissions, and IP is responsible for routing.

technical documentation The technical reference manuals, included with software packages and hardware, that provide directions for installation, usage, and troubleshooting. The information extends beyond that given in user manuals.

Telnet A TCP/IP protocol used by the Telnet client/ server applications to allow an administrator or other user to control a computer remotely.

Teredo In TCP/IP Version 6, a tunneling protocol to transmit TCP/IPv6 packets over a TCP/IPv4 network, named after the Teredo worm that bores holes in wood. Teredo IP addresses begin with 2001, and the prefix is written as 2001::/32.

terminal In Linux and OS X, the command-line interface.

tether To connect a mobile device with a cellular connection to the Internet to a computer so that the computer can access the Internet by way of the mobile device.

thick client A regular desktop computer or laptop that is sometimes used as a client by a virtualization server. *Also called* fat client.

thin client A computer that has an operating system, but has little computing power and might only need to support a browser used to communicate with a virtualization server.

thin provisioning A technique used by Storage Spaces in Windows whereby virtual storage free space can be configured as if it has more virtual storage than the physical storage allotted to it. When the virtual storage free space is close to depletion, the administrator is prompted to install more physical storage.

third-party driver Drivers that are not included in UEFI/BIOS or Windows and must come from the manufacturer.

thread Each process that the processor is aware of; a single task that is part of a longer task or request from a program.

ticket An entry in a call-tracking system made by whoever receives a call for help and used to track and document actions taken. The ticket stays open until the issue is resolved.

Time Machine In OS X, a built-in backup utility that can be configured to automatically back up user-created data, applications, and system files onto an external hard drive attached either directly to the computer or through the local network.

TKIP (Temporal Key Integrity Protocol) A type of encryption protocol used by WPA to secure a wireless Wi-Fi network. *Also see* WPA (WiFi Protected Access).

TPM (Trusted Platform Module) A chip on a motherboard that holds an encryption key required at startup to access encrypted data on the hard drive. Windows 8/7/Vista BitLocker Encryption can use the TPM chip.

track One of many concentric circles on the surface of a hard disk drive.

transformer An electrical device that changes the ratio of current to voltage. A computer power supply is basically a transformer and a rectifier.

trip hazard Loose cables or cords in a traffic area where people can trip over them.

Trojan A type of malware that tricks you into downloading and/or opening it by substituting itself for a legitimate program.

Type 1 hypervisor Software to manage virtual machines that is installed before any operating system is installed.

Type 2 hypervisor Software to manage virtual machines that is installed as an application in an operating system.

UDF (Universal Disk Format) A file system for optical media used by all DVD discs and some CD-R and CD-RW discs. *Also see* CDFS (Compact Disc File System).

UDP (User Datagram Protocol) A connectionless TCP/IP protocol that works at the OSI Transport layer and does not require a connection to send a packet or guarantee that the packet arrives at its destination. The protocol is commonly used for broadcasting to multiple nodes on a network or the Internet. *Compare with* TCP (Transmission Control Protocol).

UEFI CSM (Compatibility Support Module) mode Legacy BIOS in UEFI firmware.

ultra-thin client *See* zero client.

unattended installation A Windows installation that is done by storing the answers to installation questions in a text file or script that Windows calls an answer file so that the answers do not have to be typed in during the installation.

Unified Threat Management (UTM) A computer, security appliance, network appliance, or Internet appliance that stands between the Internet and a private network and runs firewall, anti-malware, and other software to protect the network.

unicast address Using TCP/IP version 6, an IP address assigned to a single node on a network.

Unified Extensible Firmware Interface (UEFI) An interface between firmware on the motherboard and the operating system that improves on legacy BIOS processes for booting, handing over the boot to the OS, and loading device drivers and applications before the OS loads. UEFI also manages motherboard settings and secures the boot to ensure that no rogue operating system hijacks the system.

uninterruptible power supply (UPS) A device that raises the voltage when it drops during brownouts.

unique local address (ULA) In TCP/IP Version 6, an address used to identify a specific site within a large organization. It can work on multiple links within the same organization. The address is a hybrid between a global unicast address that works on the Internet and a link-local unicast address that works on only one link.

G

Universal Plug and Play (UPnP) An unsecure method a router can use to allow unfiltered communication between nodes on a private network. Hackers sometimes are able to exploit UPnP, so use with caution.

Upgrade Advisor *See* Upgrade Assistant.

Upgrade Assistant Software used to find out if a system can be upgraded to Windows 8.1.

upgrade path A qualifying OS required by Microsoft in order to perform an in-place upgrade.

USB 3.0 B-Male connector A USB connector used by SuperSpeed USB 3.0 devices such as printers or scanners.

User Account Control (UAC) dialog box A Windows security feature that displays a dialog box when an event requiring administrative privileges is about to happen.

User Accounts A Windows utility (netplwiz.exe) that can be used to change the way Windows sign-in works and to manage user accounts, including changing passwords and changing the group membership of an account. *Also called* Network Places Wizard.

Users group A type of Windows user account group. An account in this group is a standard user account, which does not have as many rights as an administrator account.

user mode In Windows, a mode that provides an interface between an application and the OS, and only has access to hardware resources through the code running in kernel mode.

user profile A collection of files and settings about a user account that enables the user's personal data, desktop settings, and other operating parameters to be retained from one session to another.

user profile namespace The group of folders and subfolders in the C:\Users folder that belong to a specific user account and contain the user profile.

User State Migration Tool (USMT) A Windows utility that helps you migrate user files and preferences from one computer to another to help a user make a smooth transition from one computer to another.

usmtutils A command used by the User State Migration Tool (USMT) that provides encryption options and hard-link management.

vi editor A Linux and OS X text editor that works in command mode (to enter commands) or in insert mode (to edit text).

virtual assistant A mobile device app that responds to a user's voice commands with a personable, conversational interaction to perform tasks and retrieve information. *Also called* a personal assistant.

Virtual Desktop Infrastructure (VDI) A presentation of a virtual desktop made to a client computer by a server that is serving up a virtual machine.

virtual machine (VM) Software that simulates the hardware of a physical computer, creating one or more logical machines within one physical machine.

virtual machine manager (VMM) *See* hypervisor.

virtual memory A method whereby the OS uses the hard drive as though it were RAM. *Also see* pagefile.sys.

virtual private network (VPN) A security technique that uses encrypted data packets between a private network and a computer somewhere on the Internet.

virtualization When one physical machine hosts multiple activities that are normally done on multiple machines.

virtual XP mode The term used by CompTIA for Windows XP mode. *See* Windows XP mode.

virus A program that often has an incubation period, is infectious, and is intended to cause damage. A virus program might destroy data and programs.

Voice over LTE (VoLTE) A technology used on cellular networks for LTE to support voice communication.

VoIP (Voice over Internet Protocol) A TCP/IP protocol and an application that provides voice communication over a TCP/IP network. *Also called* Internet telephone.

volume A primary partition that has been assigned a drive letter and can be formatted with a file system such as NTFS. *Compare with* logical drive.

volt (V) A measure of potential difference or electrical force in an electrical circuit. A computer ATX power supply usually provides five separate voltages: 112 V, 212 V, 15 V, 25 V, and 13.3 V.

Wake-on-LAN Configuring a computer so that it will respond to network activity when the computer is in a sleep state.

warm boot *See* soft boot.

watt (W) The unit of electricity used to measure power. A typical computer may use a power supply that provides 500W.

WEP (Wired Equivalent Privacy) An encryption protocol used to secure transmissions on a Wi-Fi wireless network; however, it is no longer considered secure because the key used for encryption is static (it doesn't change).

Wi-Fi (Wireless Fidelity) The common name for standards for a local wireless network as defined by IEEE 802.11. *Also see* 802.11 a/b/g/n/ac.

Wi-Fi analyzer Hardware and/or software that monitors a Wi-Fi network to detect devices not authorized to use the network, identify attempts to hack transmissions, or detect performance and security vulnerabilities.

Wi-Fi calling On mobile devices, voice calls that use VoIP over a Wi-Fi connection to the Internet.

Wi-Fi Protected Setup (WPS) A method to make it easier for users to connect their computers to a secured wireless network when a hard-to-remember SSID and security key are used, and is considered a security risk that should be used with caution.

wildcard An * or ? character used in a command line that represents a character or group of characters in a file name or extension.

Windows 7 Windows 7 editions include Windows 7 Starter, Windows 7 Home Basic, Windows 7 Home Premium, Windows 7 Professional, Windows 7 Enterprise, and Windows 7 Ultimate. Each edition comes at a different price with different features and capabilities.

Windows 8.1 A free update or release of the Windows 8 operating system. The edition of choice for a laptop or desktop computer used in a home or small office. This edition supports homegroups, but it doesn't support joining a domain or BitLocker Encryption.

Windows 8.1 Enterprise A Windows 8 edition that allows for volume licensing in a large, corporate environment.

Windows 8.1 Pro for Students A version of Windows 8 that includes all the same features as Windows 8 Pro, but at a lower price, available only to students, faculty, and staff at eligible institutions.

Windows 8.1 Professional (Windows 8.1 Pro) A version of Windows 8 that includes additional features at a higher price. Windows 8.1 Pro supports homegroups, joining a domain, BitLocker, Client Hyper-V, Remote Desktop, and Group Policy.

Windows Assessment and Deployment Kit (ADK) The Windows ADK for Windows 8 contains a group of tools used to deploy Windows 8 in a large organization and contains the User State Migration Tool (USMT).

Windows Automated Installation Kit (AIK) The Windows AIK for Windows 7 contains a group of tools used to deploy Windows 7 in a large organization and contains the User State Migration Tool (USMT).

Windows Boot Loader One of two programs that manage the loading of Windows 8/7/Vista. The program file (winload.exe or winload.efi) is stored in C:\ Windows\ System32, and it loads and starts essential Windows processes.

Windows Boot Manager (BootMgr) The Windows 8/7/Vista program that manages the initial startup of Windows. For a BIOS system, the program is bootmgr; for a UEFI system, the program is bootmgfw.efi. The program file is stored in the root of the system partition.

Windows Defender Anti-malware software embedded in Windows 8 that can detect, prevent, and clean up a system infected with viruses and other malware. Antispyware utility included in Windows 8/7/Vista.

G

Windows Easy Transfer A Windows tool used to transfer Windows 8/7/Vista user data and preferences to the Windows 8/7/Vista installation on another computer.

Windows Experience Index A Windows 7/Vista feature that gives a summary index designed to measure the overall performance of a system on a scale from 1.0 to 7.9.

Windows Explorer The Windows 7/Vista utility used to view and manage files and folders.

Windows Firewall A personal firewall that protects a computer from intrusion and is automatically configured when you set your network location in the Network and Sharing Center.

Windows Phone (WP) An operating system by Microsoft (*microsoft.com*) that is based on Windows and is used on various smart phones (not on tablets).

Windows Powershell A command-line interface (CLI) that processes objects, called cmdlets, which are pre-built programs built on the .NET Framework, rather than processing text in a command line.

Windows Preinstallation Environment (Windows PE) A minimum operating system used to start the Windows installation.

Windows Pro Pack An upgrade available to Windows 8 that adds the functionality of Windows 8.1 Pro to the more basic edition.

Windows Recovery Environment (Windows RE) A lean operating system installed on the Windows 8/7/Vista setup DVD and also on the Windows 8/7 volume that can be used to troubleshoot problems when Windows refuses to start.

Windows RT A Windows 8 edition that is a lighter version, designed for tablets, netbooks, and other mobile devices.

Windows Store Access to purchase and download apps that use the Windows 8 interface.

Windows Vista Windows Vista editions include Windows Vista Starter, Windows Vista Home Basic, Windows Vista Home Premium, Windows Vista Business, Windows Vista Enterprise, and Windows Vista Ultimate. Each edition comes at a different price with different features and capabilities.

Windows XP Mode A Windows XP environment installed in Windows 8/7 that can be used to support older applications.

Windows.old folder When using an unformatted hard drive for a clean installation, this folder is created to store the previous operating system settings and user profiles.

wireless access point (WAP) A wireless device that is used to create and manage a wireless network.

wireless LAN (WLAN) A type of LAN that does not use wires or cables to create connections, but instead transmits data over radio or infrared waves.

wireless locator A tool that can locate a Wi-Fi hotspot and tell you the strength of the RF signal.

wireless wide area network (WWAN) A wireless broadband network for computers and mobile devices that uses cellular towers for communication. *Also called* a cellular network.

workgroup In Windows, a logical group of computers and users in which administration, resources, and security are distributed throughout the network, without centralized management or security.

worm An infestation designed to copy itself repeatedly to memory, on drive space, or on a network, until little memory, disk space, or network bandwidth remains.

WPA (WiFi Protected Access) A data encryption method for wireless networks that use the TKIP (Temporal Key Integrity Protocol) encryption method and the encryption keys are changed at set intervals while the wireless LAN is in use. WPA is stronger than WEP.

WPA2 (WiFi Protected Access 2) A data encryption standard compliant with the IEEE802.11i standard that uses the AES (Advanced Encryption Standard) protocol. WPA2 is currently the strongest wireless encryption standard.

XaaS (Anything as a Service or Everything as a Service) An open-ended cloud computing service that can provide any combination of functions depending on a customer's exact needs.

xcopy   A Windows command more powerful than the copy command that is used to copy files and folders.

zero client   A client computer that does not have an operating system and merely provides an interface between the user and the server. *Also called* dumb terminal.

zero-day attack   When a hacker discovers and exploits a security hole in software before the developer of the software can develop and provide a protective patch to close the hole.

zero-fill utility   A hard drive utility that fills every sector on the drive with zeroes.

zero-touch, high volume deployment   An installation strategy that does not require the user to start the process. Instead a server pushes the installation to a computer when a user is not likely to be sitting at it.

zombie   A computer that has been hacked, and the hacker is using the computer to run repetitive software in the background without the knowledge of its user. *Also see* botnet.

G